Mixed Method Data Collection Strategies

Social scientists have long relied on a wide range of tools to collect information about the social world; but as individual fields have become more specialized, researchers are trained to use a narrow range of the possible data collection methods. This book draws on a broad range of available social data collection methods to formulate a new set of data collection approaches that combines elements of those existing methods. The new approaches described here are ideal for social science researchers who plan to collect new data about people, organizations, or social processes. The methods the authors present are designed to create a comprehensive empirical description of the subject being studied, with an emphasis on accumulating the information needed to understand causes and consequences with a minimum of error. In addition to providing methodological motivation and underlying principles, the book is filled with detailed instructions and concrete examples for those who wish to apply the methods to their own research.

WILLIAM G. AXINN is a sociologist, demographer, professor of sociology, and research professor at the Survey Research Center and Population Studies Center of the Institute for Social Research at the University of Michigan. He has directed the Population and Ecology Research Laboratory in Nepal for 13 years.

LISA D. PEARCE is an assistant professor of sociology at the University of North Carolina at Chapel Hill. Her research articles have appeared in such journals as the *American Sociological Review, Social Forces, Sociological Methodology*, and *Journal for the Scientific Study of Religion*.

New Perspectives on Anthropological and Social Demography

Series editors:
David I. Kertzer and Dennis P. Hogan (Brown University)

Associate editors:
Jack Caldwell, Andrew Cherlin, Tom Fricke, Frances Goldscheider, Susan Greenhalgh, and Richard Smith

Demography deals with issues of great social importance, and demographic research fuels some of the central current policy debates of our time. Yet, demographic theory has not changed much over the years, and old and sometimes inappropriate models are still being applied to new problems. Increasingly, however, demographers have become aware of the limitations of standard surveys and statistics and are moving to incorporate theoretical and methodological approaches from other disciplines, in particular anthropology. For their part, anthropologists have generally failed to take account of the advances in modern demography, but they are now beginning to take part in the central debates on questions of theory and policy in population research. A new wave of interdisciplinary research is emerging, combining the interests and approaches of demographers, anthropologists, and other social scientists. Some of the most interesting products of this new wave will be published in *New Perspectives on Anthropological and Social Demography*.

Books in this series include:

Census and Identity
  The Politics of Race, Ethnicity, and Language in National Censuses
  edited by David Kertzer and Dominique Arel
  ISBN 0 521 80823 5 HB / 0 521 00427 6 PB
Demography in the Age of the Postmodern
  Nancy E. Riley and James McCarthy
  ISBN 0 521 82626 8 HB / 0 521 53364 3 PB
Culture, Biology, and Anthropological Demography
  Eric Abella Roth
  ISBN 0 521 80905 3 HB / 0 521 00541 8 PB

Mixed Method Data Collection
Strategies

William G. Axinn
University of Michigan

Lisa D. Pearce
University of North Carolina at Chapel Hill

CAMBRIDGE
UNIVERSITY PRESS

CAMBRIDGE UNIVERSITY PRESS
Cambridge, New York, Melbourne, Madrid, Cape Town, Singapore, São Paulo

Cambridge University Press
32 Avenue of the Americas, New York, NY 10013-2473, USA

www.cambridge.org
Information on this title: www.cambridge.org/9780521855686

First published 2006

Printed in the United States of America

A catalog record for this publication is available from the British Library.

Library of Congress Cataloging in Publication Data
Axinn, William G.
Mixed method data collection strategies / William G. Axinn, Lisa D. Pearce.
     p.   cm. – (New perspectives on anthropological and social demography)
Includes bibliographical references and index.
ISBN 0-521-85568-3 (hardcover) – ISBN 0-521-67171-X (pbk.)
1. Population research.   2. Demography – Methodology.   3. Social sciences –
Research – Methodology.   I. Pearce, Lisa D. (Lisa Deanne), 1971–   II. Title
III. Series.
HB850.A95   2006
300.72′3 – dc22   2005031247

ISBN-13   978-0-521-85568-6 hardback
ISBN-10   0-521-85568-3 hardback

ISBN-13   978-0-521-67171-2 paperback
ISBN-10   0-521-67171-X paperback

Contents

Acknowledgments

Like most scholarly endeavors, this book rests on the contributions, guidance, and support of a large cast of characters. This book would not be possible were it not for the generous mentoring, collegiality, and support of many of our teachers and collaborators. We feel an immense intellectual debt to these people, having benefited greatly from the stimulation their conversations and ideas provided for this book. Here we take a few lines to thank them by name, hoping that the reflection of their contributions in this manuscript is a high compliment and that all who benefit from these ideas will honor their contributions as well. Of course, any errors, omissions, or indications of poor judgment are solely our responsibility.

William Axinn was initially put on the path toward mixed method strategies by his undergraduate mentors at Cornell University, Professors J. Mayone Stycos and Charles Hirschman. Their pioneering work in these areas and unfailing encouragement of young, impressionable minds were cornerstones of the methods described here. The other essential cornerstones were a pair of research projects at the University of Michigan: the Intergenerational Panel Study designed and conducted by Arland Thornton and his colleagues and the Tamang Family Research Project designed and conducted by Tom Fricke and his colleagues. Thornton and Fricke have been invaluable mentors and colleagues of ours. This book would not be possible without their many, many contributions. In fact, Chapter 3 is based on a journal article published jointly by Axinn, Fricke, and Thornton.[1] Many of the best ideas we have provided here developed directly from the advice and guidance of these two colleagues and friends.

Likewise, we owe much gratitude to our close, long-time collaborator Jennifer Barber. She has co-taught the University of Michigan's Summer Institute course on mixed method data collection with one or the other of us for the last four years. We are grateful for the ideas that have come out of this course. Both Barber and our many students have offered valuable advice and helped us refine our manuscript. Moreover, Barber collaborated in the design of many of the methods we describe here. In fact she is co-author, with Axinn and Dirgha Ghimire, of a paper that serves as the basis for our Chapter 5.[2] She deserves a great deal of credit for many of the ideas and methods in this book – thank you Jennifer!

Next, we owe Dirgha Ghimire great appreciation and thanks. Ghimire collaborated closely with us on every aspect of the Chitwan Valley Family Study, which is referenced heavily in this book. For more than a decade he has managed every aspect of our fieldwork operations in Nepal, and for an equally long period he has been designing, revising, and refining the methods we use. In addition to his work on the paper that forms the basis of Chapter 5, Ghimire is a co-author with us on the paper that forms the basis of Chapter 6.[3] He deserves a good deal of the credit for the ideas and approaches reported on throughout this book.

Many other colleagues have graciously assisted us in the development of this book. First and foremost are David Kertzer and Dennis Hogan, editors of the Anthropological Demography series for Cambridge University Press and themselves pioneers and advocates of mixed method strategies. Literally years of their mentoring, encouragement, and patience went into the production of this book. Their dual convictions that such a book could be done, and that we could produce it, never wavered. Next, several colleagues and friends provided careful reading and exceptionally helpful commentary on early versions of the manuscript. We would like to extend thanks for this to David Card, Robert Moffit, Susan Murphy, and Ronald Rindfuss. Their reactions and insights proved essential to the final form of the book. Finally, two anonymous reviewers for Cambridge University Press deserve significant credit for their careful reading and clear and useful suggestions for revision. Altogether, the feedback from these many sources proved essential to the refinement and completion of this book.

We have also benefited greatly from the intellectual environments in which we have been fortunate enough to work, and this book would not be the same without input from the many faculty, staff, and students of these organizations. These environments include the Population Research Institute and Department of Sociology at the Pennsylvania State University, where we first began to work together and where Pearce's dissertation and the paper that forms the basis of Chapter 4 evolved.[4] There are also the Population Studies Center, Survey Research Center, and Sociology Department at the University of Michigan, where Pearce was a postdoc and Axinn continues to be appointed. Thank you to everyone in those organizations for their many contributions to our work. Thank you also to the Carolina Population Center and Department of Sociology at the University of North Carolina at Chapel Hill where Pearce is appointed now and Axinn has been a visitor as we worked to complete this book. Pearce is especially grateful to her colleagues Christian Smith and Melinda Denton for involving her in the mixed method National Study of Youth and Religion. A great deal of what she's learned from helping to direct this study is reflected in these chapters.

Special thanks to the faculty and staff of the Institute for Social and Environmental Research and the Population and Ecology Research Laboratory in Nepal for all of their dedication and hard work in helping us implement the methods described in this book. Much credit is also due the faculty, staff, and students of the Michigan Survey Methodology Program, who provided immense stimulation for this book and a great deal of mentoring, though often unknowingly. And many thanks to the faculty, staff, and students of Michigan's Family and Demography Program, who provided a great deal of mentoring, all too knowingly. We are especially grateful to Heather Gatny for helping us manage all phases of referencing, formatting, and indexing for the manuscript.

Many of the projects on which specific examples presented in this book are based, and the authors' time to write this book, were made possible by generous grants from the National Institute of Child Health and Human Development (NICHD) of the National Institutes of Health (NIH), the Fogarty International Center of NIH, the Andrew W. Mellon Foundation, and the Lilly Endowment, Inc. Specifically, this support includes two NICHD-funded research projects, "Changing Social Contexts and Family Formation" (R01-HD32912) and "Reciprocal Relations between Population and Environment" (R01-HD33551), and two Lilly Endowment Inc.–funded projects, "The Religious Practices of American Youth" and "Continuity and Change in the Religious Lives of American Youth." Support also came from Research Infrastructure grants to the University of Michigan (R24-HD041028) and the University of North Carolina (P30HD005798-30). The book also benefited from training grants to the University of Michigan from the Fogarty International Center of NIH (D43-TW000657) and the Mellon Foundation (40200685).

Finally, we wish to acknowledge the support of our families, Jennifer and Elena and Thomas, who have been endlessly encouraging, loving, and patient through the development and refinement of this manuscript. You keep us balanced, mostly sane, and happy. We could not have done this without you!

Preface

This is a book about data collection methods for the social sciences. Our focus is on mixed method data collection. Our purpose is to provide detailed documentation of many of the most useful mixed method data collection approaches in the social sciences. We provide concrete operational examples so that those interested in using these methods have a clear starting point. We also identify several of the principles at the foundation of these methods. We hope this will stimulate the continued creation of new mixed method data collection approaches.

We do this within the context of research aimed at advancing the understanding of cause and consequence in the social world. Although data collection cannot itself resolve the questions of cause and consequence, we argue that the data collection methods described here are particularly powerful tools for advancing our understanding of cause and consequence. The methods we describe are also useful for social research that is not focused on causal questions. In fact, the mixed method approaches we describe are extremely useful for reducing measurement errors in social research no matter what the topic. We present them in the context of research on causal processes because we argue that they are particularly useful for that purpose.

This is *not* a book about survey methods, ethnographic methods, focus group methods, archival methods, quantitative methods, or qualitative methods. It is a book about data collection methods that combine elements of survey methods, unstructured interview methods, observational methods, focus group methods, and archival methods. We assume that readers already have familiarity with these methods. They form the building blocks of the mixed method approaches we describe, so readers may want to review descriptions of those methods before using this book. We provide a number of helpful references to resource materials covering those methods in Chapter 1.

Empirical social research includes research design, data collection, data coding, and data analysis. Although this book touches on each of these dimensions of the research process, our primary focus is on data collection. We also explore issues of the intersection between research design and data collection methods. The book does not provide a review of data coding or data analysis issues.

The authors have substantial data collection experience employing mixed method approaches in sociological and demographic research in Nepal and the United States. The vast majority of the specific examples used in the book come from research projects the authors direct in either Nepal or the United States. In every case, however, the examples are designed to illuminate a research strategy that can be used in many different settings to study many different topics. Our presentation specifically addresses issues involved in applying these methods to data collection in a broad range of settings and about a wide range of topics. We hope you find it a useful collection of tools for your research.

1   Motivations for Mixed Method Social Research

High-quality data collection is fundamental to the advancement of knowledge in the social sciences. Yet, advances in techniques for data analysis in the past half-century have far outpaced advances in data collection methods. This is likely to change in the coming decades, as new technologies and strategies bring the social sciences to the brink of a revolution in data collection methods. Some of the seeds of that revolution lay in mixed method data collection approaches. This book is devoted to recent innovations in mixed method strategies for collecting social science data.

The three main goals of this book are: (1) to demonstrate that by combining multiple methods it is possible to elicit important new insights into the causes and consequences of beliefs and behavior; (2) to provide concrete, operational examples of mixed method data collection techniques so that those interested in using these methods have a clear starting point; and (3) to highlight state-of-the-art developments in these data collection strategies, identifying a set of common principles that underlie them with the aim of stimulating continued methodological innovation in this area.

Mixed method data collection strategies are those that are explicitly designed to combine elements of one method, such as structured survey interviews, with elements of other methods, such as unstructured interviews, observations, or focus groups in either a sequential or a simultaneous manner (Axinn, Fricke, and Thornton 1991; Edin 1999; Fricke 1997; Kertzer 1997; Kertzer and Fricke 1997; Pearce 2002; Sieber 1973). We consider mixed method data collection to be a subset of multimethod research in which what is learned from one particular method is integrated in the application of another method.

We argue that mixed method strategies afford special opportunities to use multiple sources of information from multiple approaches to gain new insights into the social world (Axinn, Fricke, and Thornton 1991; Kertzer and Fricke 1997). Varying the data collection approach can (1) provide information from one approach that was not identified in an alternative approach; (2) reduce non-sampling error by providing redundant information from multiple sources; and (3) ensure that a potential bias coming from one particular approach is not replicated in alternative approaches (Axinn, Fricke, and Thornton 1991;

1

Edin 1998). Although every data collection approach may be characterized by some type of bias, replicating empirical evidence across approaches characterized by varying forms of bias substantially increases confidence in the empirical results (Rosenbaum 2001). Thus, mixed method strategies are extremely valuable tools for social research.

Systematic consideration of mixed method data collection strategies reveals two key themes. The first is that mixing multiple methods affords opportunities to use the strengths of some methods to counterbalance the weaknesses of other methods. Because all methods have strengths and weaknesses, combinations of multiple methods that achieve this counterbalancing aim are particularly valuable. The second theme is that mixing multiple methods is a valuable strategy for producing a comprehensive empirical record about a topic. Empirical documentation that combines redundant measurement using radically different approaches has special strengths for reducing errors, discovering new hypotheses, and testing hypotheses. Counterbalancing strengths and weaknesses and comprehensive empirical documentation will be two themes we return to again and again in our review and analysis of mixed method data collection strategies.

In this chapter, we consider three sources of fundamental background to understand and motivate mixed method data collection strategies. The first issue is the divide between "qualitative" and "quantitative" approaches to research in the social sciences. We review this divide and consider the extent to which it does or does not add a constructive dimension to the consideration of alternative data collection strategies. The second source is a brief review of various approaches to the investigation of cause and consequence in the social sciences. Consideration of the issues of causal inference in the social sciences both motivates some aspects of mixed method data collection and focuses our efforts on specific types of mixed method strategies. The third source involves consideration of the role of introspection in the social sciences and the ways that investigator introspection intersects with data collection strategies. This review of background issues points us toward a relatively small set of key principles in the design of mixed method strategies – principles closely related to the counterbalancing and comprehensiveness themes.

Qualitative vs. Quantitative Approaches: Is This Distinction Useful?

Many social scientists use the words "qualitative" and "quantitative" to divide the world of approaches to research. Unfortunately, discussions of this distinction usually do not derive from uniform definitions of these terms nor from careful analyses of the meaning of this distinction. In our view, a dichotomous, unidimensional distinction between quantitative and qualitative approaches is not particularly useful, because it ultimately refers only to whether the data were coded into numbers or into text (Bazeley 2003; Lieberson 1992).[1] Certainly, a distinction between the statistical analysis of numerically coded data and the interpretive analysis of data coded as text is useful. However, the results of both of these analytic approaches depend on investigators' insights as they go about simplifying and reducing the information at hand. We argue that other distinctions speak more directly to these insights. In fact, as we choose among approaches to research problems, making distinctions among types of research designs, data collection techniques, data coding strategies, and analytic approaches is at least as useful as considering the notion of quantitative versus qualitative approaches. Some use the words "quantitative" and "qualitative" to summarize distinctions between various dimensions of research approaches, such as large versus small samples, survey interviews versus unstructured interviews, or research aimed at hypothesis testing versus description or hypothesis generation. We argue that such dichotomies are far too simplistic. Rather, we argue that each research project or approach may vary along continua of many different dimensions in ways that cannot be summarized by a simplistic quantitative/qualitative dichotomy.

Distinctions among research designs are particularly important for telling us what types of questions a specific research project may be able to answer and what threats to validity a project may face (Campbell and Stanley 1963). Essential elements of research design involve selecting a unit of analysis and a comparative design. Research projects can be designed to compare nations, regions, communities, individuals, or time periods. Research projects that compare individuals can be designed to study the population of a country, a community, a set of communities, or some other group. Research projects can be designed as single cross-sectional studies, repeated cross-sectional studies, or longitudinal studies. And research projects can feature experimental, quasi-experimental, or non-experimental designs. Data collection methods are the focus of this book. Therefore, we confine our discussions of research design to the intersection between research design and data collection strategies. For readers seeking more information on research design, we suggest review of works offering more thorough advice on these issues (Babbie 2004; Campbell and Stanley 1963; Cook and Campbell 1979; Miller 1983).

Comparing Data Collection Methods

We discuss five specific types of data collection methods: surveys, semistructured/unstructured interviews, focus groups, observations, and historical/ archival research. Our discussion of each type is relatively limited because we have chosen to highlight the features of each method most relevant to a comparison across methods. The distinctions we emphasize include (1) whether the data come from primary or secondary sources; (2) whether people are observed or interviewed; (3) whether the interviews are structured or unstructured; and (4) whether or not the principal investigator interacts with the study population. We also discuss the extent to which the quantitative-versus-qualitative dichotomy is useful in helping us understand what can be learned from these methods. We believe each method has something unique to offer in terms of gaining insights into social scientific research problems.

Surveys   Research on survey methods has generated a particularly high volume of scholarship, and survey methodology itself has evolved into a substantial subfield of the social sciences. Numerous books and articles describe survey methods, explain the application of survey methods, discuss the shortcomings of survey methods, and investigate ongoing methodological issues related to survey methods (Babbie 2004; Biemer et al. 1991; Converse and Presser 1986; Groves and Couper 1998; Groves et al. 2004; Rossi et al. 1983; Sudman and Bradburn 1974; Tourangeau et al. 2000). Here we focus on a few characteristics of survey methods that distinguish this approach from other data collection methods.

A key feature of surveys is standardized questions. Although social scientists recognize that respondents' interpretations of questions are not standardized, many feel that question standardization is a minimum criterion for using data to test hypotheses. Comparability of the questions is the key. Many social scientists would treat comparisons based on asking respondents different questions as perhaps interesting, but not a rigorous test of a hypothesis. Substantial evidence indicates that differences in question wording result in responses that are not comparable (Cantril 1967; Rugg 1941; Sudman and Bradburn 1974; Tourangeau 1989). For purposes of standardization, survey questions are compiled in a questionnaire. The use of a questionnaire imposes a high level of structure on the survey interview, which makes it difficult to use surveys to uncover completely new hypotheses (Caldwell 1985; Sieber 1973). That is, researchers' ideas about what should be measured and how it should be measured must be concrete before a survey begins in order to produce a questionnaire. The discovery of new research questions or new approaches to measurement is limited, and to the extent that it does occur, revised measurement must await the next survey.

This level of standardization and structure allows well-trained interviewers to administer a survey as intended by the survey designer and to administer it to a very large number of respondents. Thus, survey methods can be used to take a census of a population or to interview a large representative sample of a population. This is generally considered a positive aspect of surveys, because inferences based on large, representative samples are known to be more reliable than inferences based on small or nonrepresentative samples (Kish 1965). However, the use of trained interviewers and mail or Web questionnaires in survey administration reduces or eliminates the need for the survey designer or principal investigator to have direct contact with the people being studied (Groves et al. 2004).

Changes over time in the technology of questionnaires, particularly in the form of Computer-Assisted Personal Interviewing (CAPI), have added a new dimension to the standardization of survey interviews (Baker et al. 1994; Couper 1998; Couper and Rowe 1996; Saris 1991). A key example is Audio Computer-Assisted Self-Interviewing (ACASI), in which respondents listen to computer-generated questions on headphones and key-in their own responses. Although this technology also limits the investigator's interaction with study participants, it removes interviewers from the data collection process – study participants respond directly to questions posed by the investigator via a computer.

Because surveys are often administered to large numbers of people, survey research is occasionally referred to as quantitative research. But for the purposes of this book, we argue that this reference is both misleading and counterproductive. Nothing about a survey is inherently numeric. Highly structured questionnaires can be administered to an extremely small number of people. And although surveys that feature highly structured response alternatives may be easy to code into numbers, it's the process of coding that turns data into numbers, not the survey itself (Lieberson 1992).

For example, the U.S. Intergenerational Panel Study asks respondents if they strongly agree, agree, disagree, or strongly disagree with the statement: "A young couple should not live together unless they are married." It seems fairly straightforward to code their responses as a 1, 2, 3, or 4. But interviewers also record on the questionnaires respondents' reactions outside the structured response alternatives. Examples for the question above might include "respondent asked if the couple is engaged," "respondent said it depends on the couple's age," "respondent paused for a long time before answering," or "respondent laughed at the question." If we listen to tape recordings of the interviews, even more details may become available to us. So, we ask the respondents standardized questions, and they provide us with reactions in verbal and behavioral responses. When we summarize these reactions by coding them into numbers, we may lose much of the information the respondent provided. But summarizing is a part of every data collection and analysis process, even if no numbers are used to code responses. Thus, as we examine other data collection techniques, we will argue that nothing makes surveys any more quantitative than any other technique.

Less Structured Interviewing Research literature also provides a great deal of information on less structured interviewing, which is sometimes called "unstructured," "ethnographic," "focused in-depth," or "qualitative" interviewing. This literature sometimes contrasts less structured and structured interviewing and often discusses techniques (Briggs 1986; Hammer and

Wildavsky 1993; Mishler 1986; Weiss 1994). Here we make some methodological comparisons in the context of our discussion of qualitative versus quantitative.

Some researchers consider less structured interviewing to be the opposite of survey interviewing, but the primary difference, as the name we chose implies, is the degree of structure or standardization in the questions. An unstructured or semi-structured interview can be much more flexible, allowing the respondent to change the course of the conversation and bring up new issues that the researcher had not preconceived. This flexibility is much more likely to yield new hypotheses than highly structured surveys (Sieber 1973; Weiss 1994).

Semi- or unstructured interviews are often considered too intensive and demanding to carry out with large numbers of respondents. Researchers often conclude that trained interviewers cannot administer less structured interviews as well as they themselves could, particularly because direct participation may inform the research process. Limiting interviews to those conducted by the principal investigator constrains the number of informants who can be interviewed. The main limitation is imposed by the time required to field interviews, compile notes, transcribe audio recordings, and analyze transcripts. However, note that nothing inherent in less structured interviewing makes it impossible to apply this method to large numbers of individuals or systematically selected samples of individuals, given sufficient time and energy. In fact, a number of recent research projects incorporate components featuring interviews and/or observations of hundreds of participants (Burton et al. 2002; Edin and Lein 1997; Smith and Denton 2005).

Many of the concerns that are commonly associated with survey research should also be raised with respect to less structured interviewing. For example, less structured interviews are just as vulnerable to errors that result when characteristics of the interviewer influence the respondents'/informants' answers to questions. Likewise, the principal investigator is not necessarily less likely to produce errors and omissions than properly trained interviewers. Thus, shortcomings that arise when data are generated by an interview affect less structured and survey methods alike. Literatures exist that highlight these unavoidable biases for both more structured survey data collection (e.g., Biemer et al. 1991) and less structured interviews or observations (e.g., Kleinman and Copp 1993).

We use the label "less structured interviews" for this data collection method rather than some alternatives sometimes treated as synonyms, such as "long interviews" or "in-depth interviews." Our rational for this label is that it most clearly reflects the key difference between this type and other forms of interviewing: the freedom to deviate from structure. The term "long interview" can be misleading because interviews at all points on the structure continuum can be long. In fact, some surveys are quite long, while some less structured interviews are designed to be much shorter. We also find the term "in-depth interview" misleading because highly structured survey interviews can be very rich in detail, particularly when they include a high density of questions in one area. The level of depth on a particular topic is a function of this density of questions, not a function of the type of interviewing.

On the qualitative-quantitative dimension, although less structured interviews generally produce data in the form of either notes or audio recordings, nothing prevents researchers from coding these data numerically for statistical analyses. In fact, it is quite common for researchers engaged in less structured interviewing to tally the occurrence of certain themes or characteristics among their informants (Anspach 1997; Edin and Lein 1997; Gerson 1985; Hochschild 1989). Also, as mentioned above, given sufficient time and resources, less structured interviews can be conducted with very large numbers of people.

Focus Groups   The literature on focus group methods is also substantial (e.g., Agar and MacDonald 1995; Hughes and DuMont 1993; Knodel 1993, 1995; Krueger 1994; Morgan 1997, Vaughn et al. 1996). We urge those interested in implementing focus group methods to consult those materials directly. As before, our interest is not in describing techniques but in comparing data collection methods on a few dimensions.

Focus groups are unique in that they explicitly call for respondents to interact with one another in formulating responses to interviewers' questions. A potential benefit of this approach is that informants may feel greater confidence in a group setting, which may encourage them to offer comments and discuss matters they wouldn't in a one-on-one interview. They may also corroborate or challenge the responses of other members and remind one another of certain phenomena (Knodel 1993; Morgan 1997). On the other hand, this collaborative setting may present problems for data collection. Informants may be hesitant to share ideas in front of peers that they would offer in individual interviews. For example, Helitzer et al. (1994) found that adolescent girls in Malawi are more likely to reveal information on their menstruation, sexual experiences, contraceptive use, and abortion in one-on-one interviews than in focus groups with their peers. Another potential problem is that focus group members may conspire to either avoid issues or cast them in a particular light (Godsell 2000). In these cases, this method may not be appropriate.

Otherwise, focus groups share many characteristics with less structured interviews (Merton et al. 1990). An interviewer generally asks questions, guides the conversation, and records the participants' responses. Therefore, errors resulting from the involvement of interviewers are also potential hazards in focus group methods. The unstructured nature of focus groups also allows researchers to learn new information to inform their hypotheses. Focus groups are generally considered too intensive for anything except relatively small samples, although given sufficient time and resources they can be administered to large, representative samples. Focus group results, usually in the form of long narrative texts that repeat the questions and participants' responses, can also be coded numerically and analyzed using statistical methods (Knodel et al. 1984; Morgan 1997).

Observation   Methods of observation are an important tool in the social sciences, and a substantial literature describes these methods (Atkinson and Hammersly 2003; Burgess 1982; Lofland and Lofland 1994; Spradley 1997). These methods contrast in key ways to the three discussed above.

Like focus groups and less structured interviews, observational methods have the advantage of being relatively unstructured. However, observational methods are different because they have the potential to yield unique sources of insight and introspection. Methods of observation can be further divided into different types based on the level of contact with those being studied: direct observation, unobtrusive observation, and participant observation.

Participant observation methods may be particularly important for providing researchers with the opportunity to put themselves "in the shoes" of the people they study and use introspection as a tool (Burawoy 1991). However, researchers can never fully fill these shoes. For example, when an American researcher goes to Nepal and transplants rice, he or she is unlikely to ever feel exactly like someone who does it every year and who knows that if the crop fails he or she will not eat in the coming year. The challenge for participant observers is to recognize their own inherent biases and incorporate this knowledge in their analyses (Burawoy 1991).

Some social scientists argue that any data collection that involves interviewing distorts the social reality because of interference from either the interviewers' interpretation of the respondents' answers or the respondents' own lack of knowledge about their motivations and actions. This point of view usually leads to an argument for observation as a better means of obtaining data on social phenomena. Of course, both participant observation and direct observation methods involve the presence of a researcher as well, which is also likely to influence the behavior of the people being studied. For some topics, this is very easy to imagine. For example, we are convinced that using direct observation to record couples' contraceptive use during sex might influence their behavior. In this type of situation, it seems likely that direct observation, or for that matter participant observation, would generate at least as much distortion of the social reality as interviewing. Even in situations where a researcher's presence is less obtrusive, his/her presence is likely to have some kind of influence.

The intensive nature of observational methods generally prevents them from being used to study large numbers of people. However, nothing about the method, per se, prevents this. If a researcher had sufficient time and resources she or he could observe a large number of people, a representative sample of a population, or an entire population. Observations usually generate data in the form of field notes or recordings. However, as with any other data, it is entirely possible to code these data into numbers and analyze the numbers with statistical techniques. We don't mean to suggest that it is always useful to conduct statistical analyses on data from observations, focus groups, or unstructured interviews; we just argue that it's possible.

Historical/Archival Methods   Similar to survey methods, historical or archival methods constitute a substantial subfield of the social sciences. In fact, the close association between these methods and the field of history might lead some to argue that archival methods constitute much more than a subfield. The literature on these methods includes some very useful summaries (Hall 1992; Mahoney 1999; Sewell 1996), and uses of the methods in disciplines outside of history may be of particular interest to the readers of this book (Bonnell 1980; Gould 1995; Kertzer 1995; Kertzer and Hogan 1989; Tuchman 1978), but a comprehensive examination of the literature on these methods would be an enormous task. Once again, we focus instead on comparisons to the methods described above.

For some research problems, archival methods and the use of secondary sources are the only options available. This is true of many historical research problems for which it is often impossible to interview or observe the study population because none are still living. However, written records and previous studies may provide useful information for more contemporary research problems. For example, when we study the impact of social change on contraceptive use in Nepal, the timing of major community events is critical information. For one such event, the construction of a road linking the village to major cities, we may get a more accurate date of completion from Department of Transportation records than from interviewing members of the study population.

Searching official records and other published sources has the advantage of being relatively unstructured. It is quite possible for researchers to discover something they had not thought of before the search began. However, many of the parameters we have discussed with regard to other methods are out of the researcher's control when using this method. When using documents or other secondary sources, the researcher is at the mercy of whoever recorded the information in the first place. The degree of structure involved in obtaining the information or whether interviewing was involved may be impossible to tell. Certainly, whatever was done is impossible for the researcher to change.

Data from secondary sources may be obtained in the form of either numbers or text, and, of course, archival data in the form of text can be coded into numbers. In fact, social scientists doing historical research sometimes engage in a combination of statistical analyses of archival data and interpretive analyses of archival texts (Gould 1991, 1993, 1995, 1999; Kertzer 1995; Kertzer and

Hogan 1989). Finally, it's quite possible that historical records and other archival documents pertain to large numbers of people, although the extent to which these records reflect a representative sample of people is outside of the researcher's control.

Key Distinctions Among Methods

Each of the methods described above has specific advantages making it particularly well suited to some types of research aims. Surveys are particularly useful when a high level of standardization is desirable. This may be true when the research aim involves creation of a standardized fact for a large population, such as a summary statistic (Groves et al. 2004). It is also likely to be true when the research aim involves testing hypotheses. Less highly structured data collection methods (see Figure 1.1) offer greater flexibility, so that they offer advantages

Data Collection Method	Level of Structure	Interviewer Involvement	Researcher Involvement with Study Population
Surveys	**high**	**usually**	**low**
Less Structured Interviews	**low**	**always**	**high**
Focus Groups	**low**	**always**	**medium**
Observation	**low**	**usually**	**high**
Historical/ Archival Methods	**out of researcher's control**	**out of researcher's control**	**low**

Figure 1.1. Comparison of structure, interviewer involvement, and researcher involvement among data collection methods

for uncovering new hypotheses. Less structured interviewing offers flexibility and more opportunity for new respondents to introduce new topics than survey interviews. Aside from this distinction, both methods are most appropriate when an interview is considered the appropriate process for measurement. The distinct advantage of focus groups is interaction among respondents in the framing of answers to questions. Use of this method should be reserved for research aims for which such interaction is desirable. Observational methods eliminate questions and answers from the data collection. This has the benefit of creating a great deal of flexibility and allowing those being studied to dictate exactly what can be measured. This advantage may be a disadvantage if those being studied do not act in ways that are informative of the research aims. Historical/ archival methods are aimed at understanding something in the past. In this case, the subject matter itself often eliminates the option to exercise any of the other methods, forcing researchers to resort to historical methods.

Mixed method data collection – data collection involving two or more of these types of methods – is not automatically superior to single method data collection. If one of the above methods has exactly the characteristics desired, it is likely the best alternative. Mixed method data collection is only desirable when the characteristics of more than one of the other methods is desirable either sequentially or simultaneously. Below, we argue that there are many such situations. Likewise, mixed method approaches do not necessarily produce higher-quality data. Mixed method data collection is only likely to produce high-quality data if each of the component parts is of the highest possible quality.

Our comparison of these methods also contrasts the level of interviewer involvement in the data collection (see Figure 1.1 for a summary). We have argued that interviewers are more involved in some methods than others, although the person collecting the data can influence the people being studied in every method. This means that researchers should be attentive to the potential consequences of interviewer/investigator characteristics no matter which method is used.

Our comparison also highlights differences in the potential for the investigator to interact with those being studied (see Figure 1.1). We argue that some methods afford more opportunity than others for investigators to interact with the people they are studying. This means that less structured interviewing and observations have greater advantages for generating insights into the lives of the study population than other methods. As such, these methods may be better than others for providing insights into the lives of the people we study.

Finally, in comparing these data collection methods we have argued that the distinction between qualitative and quantitative is not helpful in understanding the contrasts among them. Although we might interpret quantitative/qualitative differences as referring to the type of data that are generated, every method

Data Collection Method	Data on Large Numbers of People	Could Be Coded as Numbers	Could Be Analyzed as Text
Surveys	usual approach	X	X
Less Structured Interviews	possible	X	X
Focus Groups	possible	X	X
Observation	possible	X	X
Historical/ Archival Methods	possible	X	X

Figure 1.2. Comparing sample size and coding among data collection methods

discussed generates some data that are fundamentally qualitative but that can also be coded into numbers and analyzed using statistics (see Figure 1.2). We might also interpret quantitative/qualitative differences to refer to the size of the group being studied. Again, some methods may be easier to use on large groups than others, but with sufficient time and resources any method can be administered to a large, representative sample. The data quality may vary – that is, one set of data may have more errors and omissions than another – but this quality is just as likely to vary across different applications of the same method as it is to vary across methods. As we discuss in subsequent chapters, our work indicates that it is the level of involvement by the principal investigator that is most influential on the quality of data obtained from any of these methods.

Beyond the Qualitative/Quantitative Distinction

Once data are collected, they are coded and analyzed. As we said earlier, we believe that summarizing data, or coding and analysis, is the step most clearly linked to the distinction between quantitative and qualitative. If we code data into numbers and analyze the numbers with statistical methods, we often describe these procedures as quantitative. If we leave the data in the form of text and interpret the text, we often describe these procedures as qualitative. But we still face the task of summarizing the text when we analyze the data. In either case, the common aspect of coding and analysis is summarizing the social reality we observed.

The process of summarizing is a critical point at which a researcher's insights shape what is learned from the study. No matter which approach to coding and analysis one chooses, the researcher's insights into the study population have profound consequences for the outcome of the study (H. Becker 1996; Blumer 1969; Weiss 1968). Insights into the process involved in obtaining the data can also help the researcher understand the limits of his or her evidence (Burawoy 1991; Sieber 1973).

Having said this, however, there *are* important differences between the statistical analysis of data coded as numbers and the interpretive analysis of data coded as text, and these differences may have important consequences for the results (Bazeley 2003). Furthermore, different data collection methods lead more naturally to either statistical or interpretive analysis. Although we have argued that nearly any data can be coded as numbers, clearly statistical analysis is only sensible when we have data from a large enough group of respondents to merit its use.

Each research problem has specific goals upon which the selection of an appropriate research design and data collection method depends. However, the different strengths and weaknesses of the data collection methods we described indicate that combinations of methods may be most advantageous for a variety of goals. For example, even when the standardization of a survey is useful, combining survey methods with other less structured methods may lend the flexibility required to generate new insights into the people we study (Axinn, Fricke, and Thornton 1991). Thus, combinations of data collection methods generate advantages that no one method can offer (Sieber 1973).

How important is it to use combined approaches? One can hardly argue with the empirical record. Researchers who have used a combination of data collection methods and have been intensively involved with the data collection have made many critical contributions to theories of social behavior. This started long before the survey research industry was as large as it is today. Drake and Cayton (1993) used a variety of methods to study the organization of black communities in South Chicago. In the mid-1950s, Stycos's intensive involvement in structured and semi-structured surveys of Latin American populations helped him make important contributions to the social-demographic study of fertility behavior (Back and Stycos 1967; Stycos 1955). Also around this time, Lipset, Trow, and Coleman (1956) explained the democratic internal politics of a typographical union through combined application of observations, semi-structured interviews, and a sample survey; and Becker, Geer, Hughes, and Strauss (1961) studied medical school culture using a variety of methods.

In the 1980s and '90s, the insights from combined approaches helped Caldwell and his colleagues make contributions to the social-demographic study of fertility, marriage, and mortality that have reshaped the way social scientists think of these processes (Caldwell 1982, 1986; Caldwell, Reddy, and Caldwell 1983, 1988b). The insights generated by Massey's ethnosurvey approach have helped him to make equally important contributions to theories of migration (Massey 1987a, 1987b; Massey et al. 1987, 1998; Massey and Espinoza 1997; Massey, Goldring, and Durand 1994). Kertzer and Hogan's integrated program of anthropological, demographic, and archival research fueled their numerous contributions to the study of family and demographic change (Hogan and Kertzer 1985; Kertzer and Hogan 1989, 1991). Knodel and colleagues' mix of survey and focus group or key informant methods have shed light on important factors in the study of fertility, aging, and AIDS in Thailand (Knodel et al. 1987, 2001; Knodel and Im-em 2004). In fact, in almost any area of social demography we can find examples in which combined data collection approaches have made significant contributions. Other areas of study have benefited as well. Mercer's (1973) study of the social character of mental retardation made use of data collected from community surveys, official records, and unstructured interviews. Rank (1992) used multiple methods to study childbearing among welfare recipients.

Most recently, a set of welfare reform studies – including the New Hope project (Huston et al. 2003), the Three-City Study (Winston et al. 1999), and the Project on Devolution and Urban Change (Michalopoulos et al. 2000) – are using a mix of methods to better understand the consequences of poverty and welfare in the United States. Likewise, the National Study of Youth and Religion, through a nationally representative telephone survey and a subset of in-person, semi-structured interviews, is shedding light on the role of religion in adolescence and the transition to adulthood (Smith and Denton 2005).

Thus, we have good reason to expect much to gain in our research by a continued effort to combine data collection methods and develop hybrid methods that go beyond the quantitative/qualitative distinction. As Stanley Lieberson said in his 1991 presidential address to the American Sociological Association:

> The qualitative/quantitative distinction is itself somewhat arbitrary. . . . What we really need is an effort to integrate both these methods, to take advantage of both procedures and combine their outcomes. . . . Thinking this through would be far more useful than method bashing. If we are truthseekers, then there should not be a qualitative truth and a quantitative truth. (Lieberson 1992, p. 3)

Following Lieberson's charge, the remainder of this book is devoted to thinking through various strategies for combining data collection approaches that contribute to the social science research process as a whole.

The Study of Cause and Consequence in the Social Sciences

Much of science is consumed with the study of cause and consequence, particularly the fit between theories of causation and empirical observations of the world. The social sciences have experienced a great deal of internal controversy about the feasibility of studying cause and consequence. This controversy has been fueled by the sloppy use of language to interpret results of empirical analyses, the failure to explicitly identify key assumptions, and the inappropriate use of specific analytic techniques. We do not review this controversy here. Instead, we review some of the key analytic approaches to the study of causation in the social sciences and highlight the ways in which mixed method data collection can be used to advance causal reasoning.

Typically, social scientists cannot study causal relationships by randomly assigning subjects to experimental conditions. Instead, they must usually draw causal inference from observing people in social settings. The difficulty in drawing conclusions about causal effects from observational data is that the exposure of interest is usually allocated in some systematic way: The exposed group differs in composition from the unexposed group, and these differences in composition are related to the outcome being studied (Moffitt 2003, 2005; Winship and Morgan 1999). In other words, people are not randomly assigned to the social condition we want to study. This inevitably leads to the problem that there are alternative explanations for the associations between the outcome and the hypothesized cause that we observe. Put yet another way, some factors we do not observe may have influence on the associations we do observe. Sometimes, special circumstances allow the assignment of people to experimental conditions in the social world, usually when some type of special government benefits or programs are to be distributed and those involved desire a "fair" system of distribution. But these circumstances are rare.

An entire literature is devoted to causal modeling in the social sciences. This literature proposes various analytic techniques for estimating models of cause and consequence, critiques those techniques, proposes superior alternatives, and occasionally argues that social scientists should give up altogether efforts to study cause and consequence (Abbott 1998; Bachrach and McNicoll 2003; Freedman 1991; Fricke 1997; Heckman 1978, 2000; Marini and Singer 1988; Marsden 1992; Moffitt 2003, 2005; Raftery 1998; Rubin 1974; Smith 2003; Snijders and Hagenaars 2001; Winship and Morgan 1999). During the past 50 years, a series of hopeful methodological fads emerged and receded, each hoping to solve the problem of studying causal relationships in the social sciences. These include analytic techniques such as selection corrections, instrumental variable approaches, and various model identification procedures. Analytic attention to issues of causal inference is important, but it is rarely satisfactory. Analytic approaches to studying social causes always suffer from either untestable assumptions, limitations of the information available to operationalize these approaches, or both (Heckman 2000; Moffitt 2003, 2005).

Many innovative research designs hold tremendous promise for addressing causal questions because of opportunities to exclude alternative explanations of observed associations in the research design itself (Campbell and Stanley 1963; Cook and Campbell 1979; Rosenbaum 1999, 2001). Studies of twins and other "natural" experiments seem to be among the most promising current design-based approaches, because they are generally thought to have the benefit of removing the chance that unobserved factors produce observed associations between the change and subsequent behavior of the people affected (Card and Krueger 1995; Heckman and Smith 1995; Rosenzweig and Wolpin 2000). That is, they exploit situations in which the exposure of interest was allocated as though it were randomly assigned. However, these approaches also have limitations. First, such situations are rare, and the rarity of these situations dramatically limits the range of topics and settings that can be studied with this approach (Moffitt 2003, 2005). Second, careful examination of exposures that seem to be assigned as though at random often reveal that important unobserved circumstances may still produce the observed empirical associations (Bound and Solon 1999; Heckman 2000; Moffitt 2003, 2005; Winship and Morgan 1999).

Thus, none of the approaches currently available offers a panacea for the problem of causal inference for all subjects, settings, or occasions. In fact, we argue that there are *no* ultimate solutions to the problem of causal inference in the social sciences. The approach we advocate for the study of cause and consequence in the social sciences lies between recognition of the flaws in all available observational approaches and abandonment of the effort. We advocate taking full advantage of every reasonable approach available to build a comprehensive set of evidence for the research question at hand.

We argue that advances in causal reasoning in the social sciences must come from a constant interplay between theory and empirical evidence. In our view, the careful social scientist should try to address the problem of unobserved factors producing observed associations by trying to account for as many factors as possible. This accounting includes (1) theorizing and reasoning regarding possible unobserved factors that may be responsible for observed associations; (2) the construction of research designs to eliminate key rival hypotheses; and (3) the design of measurement strategies to observe as many of the potential causes as possible. Although we believe that no one approach will solve the problem of causal inference, we also believe that these steps advance the social scientific study of cause and consequence.

Our emphasis on measurement strategies for advancing causal reasoning is founded on a specific epistemological view of causal reasoning in social science. In our view, neither social scientific methods nor the data gathered and analyzed by social scientists can demonstrate "proof" of cause. Rather, scientists hypothesize about cause in the theoretical arguments they create. Empirical analyses of data about the social world may be consistent or inconsistent with those arguments, but they cannot prove or demonstrate causation (Marini and Singer 1988). Based on this perspective, the more reliable evidence brought to bear on a theory, the better. Therefore, we espouse an approach to the study of causation that uses multiple sources of evidence to test, or challenge, causal theories – an approach that lies at the foundation of the methods we advocate.

Furthermore, this view of causal inference leads us to emphasize the importance of two specific aspects of measurement in the social sciences. These are the temporal order among measures and the comprehensiveness of the measurement. Temporal ordering of measures is important because most causal reasoning has temporal ordering embedded in it. That is, when we reason that X causes Y, almost always we argue that X occurs before Y. The most common exception to this temporal order is the argument that anticipation of X in the future causes Y now. However, this exception simply identifies a third component to the causal reasoning, Z, where Z is the anticipation of X. If it is possible to observe Z, the temporal order of our reasoning is still quite clear: Z causes Y and Z occurs before Y. This view of the relationship between causal reasoning and temporal order is fundamental to the measurement strategies we describe in Chapters 5 and 6, and the idea that anticipation of events may produce cause is fundamental to the approaches we describe in Chapter 7.

The comprehensiveness of measurement is important for two reasons. First, redundant measures from multiple sources can be used to help reduce the chances that bias associated with the measurement is responsible for observed associations. We argue that the best measurement strategies take advantage of multiple methods to allow the strengths of some methods to compensate for the weaknesses of other methods, thereby reducing the likelihood of replicating bias across measures (Rosenbaum 2001). The effort to avoid replication of measurement bias is particularly important because each specific approach to the study of a specific causal question may be threatened by bias. Replication of investigations into a specific causal question using a variety of different approaches, varying both research design and measurement strategy, holds great promise for advancement of our understanding of the underlying causal relationship (Rosenbaum 2001).

Second, comprehensive measurement can be used to document potential mechanisms responsible for an observed association, lending further evidence for the argument for a causal relationship. Measures of all potential causal factors identified by theory are a fundamental tool for establishing empirical evidence of causal relationships in the social world. Measures of the potential mechanisms responsible for producing an association are particularly important to causal reasoning because empirical evidence of such mechanisms is one tool for establishing a causal relationship (Rosenbaum 2001). Again, mixed method data collection is a particularly useful tool in this endeavor. Readers may associate empirical study of cause and consequence in the social world with statistical analyses of survey data. However, just as we argue that no one data collection method is sufficient for the study of cause and consequence, the leading survey methodologists make the same argument about survey methods. Consider the following quote from Groves et al.'s 2004 monograph on survey methodology:

Surveys are rather blunt instruments for information gathering. They are powerful in producing statistical generalizations to large populations. They are weak in generating rich understanding of the intricate mechanisms that affect human thought and behavior. Other techniques are preferred for that purpose. (Groves et al. 2004, p. 378)

Surveys are powerful for providing evidence of associations, but they are less powerful for discovering the mechanisms responsible for those associations. Less structured methods, such as observation and unstructured interviewing, are more powerful for discovering these mechanisms (Moffitt 2000; Sieber 1973). But once such potential mechanisms are discovered, survey methods are again a powerful tool for establishing associations between these potential mechanisms and the outcome of interest. As a result, mixed method techniques that combine survey data collection with less structured interviewing or observational data collection are extremely powerful for advancing causal reasoning. We devote Chapters 3, 4, and 8 to detailed consideration of these techniques.

Introspection and Involvement

A critical change in the social sciences during the second half of the 20th century has been a massive increase in the creation and availability of data about the social world. Fueled in large part by breakthroughs in statistical sampling and survey methods (Hansen, Hurwitz, and Madow 1953; Kish 1965), this dramatic proliferation of data has been the largest in history. New systems for the mass production of social science data allowed small numbers of researchers to create much greater volumes of data than they could analyze themselves. This, coupled with a technological revolution in the tools available to analyze data – computers – led to large-scale distribution of data to many researchers who were not themselves involved in the data creation. Together, data, computers, and various advances in statistical computation methods have allowed scores of researchers to study the behavior, social interactions, and thoughts of vast numbers of people whom they have never met.

In fact, these shifts to the mass production, large-scale distribution, and computer-based analysis of data have benefited the social sciences in many ways. These changes have allowed social scientists to describe the empirical reality of large fractions of the human population. They have given social scientists the means to address a great breadth of issues of both high theoretical and public policy significance. They have stimulated many more people to become social science researchers, which has brought renewed energy and creativity to these fields. And these changes have given social scientists engaged in the study of cause and consequence enormous access to information for studying the questions at hand. The overall result has been historically unprecedented advances in the quality and influence of social science research.

At the same time, however, the layering of data collection systems and researchers between those being studied and the ultimate analysts of the information collected poses important constraints and limitations on social scientists engaged in the study of cause and consequence. Each of these layers imposes some summarizing or filtering of the original information as it is passed toward the researcher who will ultimately analyze it. Of course, because every researcher engages in summarizing and filtering information, some loss of information and introduction of bias is likely to occur even when researchers analyze data they themselves collect – that is, when no layers separate analysts from the research subjects. However, multiple layers of summary and filtering are likely to both increase the risk of information loss and bias and decrease the data analyst's knowledge of the nature and extent of summary and filtering. These threats impose important limitations on what the researcher can ultimately learn and may produce bias in what is learned (Lieberson 1985, 1992; Sieber 1973). In addition, distance between the collection and analysis of data obscures analysts' knowledge about the process and context of the data collection component, which may impose other limitations on what they can learn.

Recognition of the limitations imposed by the vast expansion of data collection systems leads some scientists to advocate a mixture of data collection methods to advance the study of cause and consequence (Caldwell, Caldwell, and Caldwell 1987; Sieber 1973). Generally, these multimethod approaches include some activities designed to put those responsible for analyzing the data into direct contact with some of the people studied. For analysts, this direct interaction permits greater information on a small number of those being studied as well as greater insight into the data collection process that generates the larger data set.

The field of demography provides a useful example of the evolution of mixed method approaches. By the end of the 20th century, demography had been transformed from primarily a descriptive science to a science increasingly preoccupied with the study of cause and consequence. Unfortunately, many of the research methods created for descriptive demography were not well suited to this new enterprise, which stimulated the development of new approaches for studying demographic phenomena.

John Caldwell is probably the best known advocate of new approaches to demographic research problems in the second half of the 20th century, and he has certainly had a great deal of influence on the discipline. On a number of occasions, Caldwell has argued for explicit combinations of anthropological and demographic research methods.[2] We do not offer a rigorous definition of anthropological methods here,[3] but instead refer to Caldwell, who said these methods involve "local residence, participant observation, and a substantial amount of interviewing with only modest structuring" (Caldwell, Caldwell, and Caldwell, 1987, p. 33).

Generally, Caldwell's promotions of these data collection methods in demography have been coupled with criticisms of the other methods demographers employ (Caldwell 1985; Caldwell, Reddy, and Caldwell 1988a). This critique focuses on a style of research that gained prominence in the 1970s in which demographic survey data were analyzed by researchers uninvolved in the data collection. This style of research became more problematic as demographic surveys were conducted in many countries around the world, as, for example, were the World Fertility Surveys. It became possible for demographers to sit in an office in one country, such as the United States, and analyze data from all over the world without ever visiting the countries they studied. Although few demographers pursued this style in the pure form just described, some came close. This style of research places strong barriers between the researcher and the subjects of that research. Such barriers are problematic for at least two reasons: They limit a researcher's ability to use introspection, and they shield a researcher from insights gained during the data collection process.

Barriers between the researcher and the subject of that research make it difficult for the researcher to use introspection to guide data analyses and interpretation of results. In fact, barriers make introspection a liability rather than an advantage. Some social scientists believe that using introspection to inform theory robs social science of its status as a science. Although we share their concerns about this issue, we advocate its cautious use in social science research and recognize that, at any rate, it is impossible to fully eliminate introspection from the research process.

Almost any data summary about human behavior omits many details, and researchers often find it difficult to avoid using details from their own experiences to fill in the missing data about the lives of others, even when examining social processes taking place among populations they know little about (Blumer 1969). Thus, an American demographer who knows little about Nepal and who is analyzing data from the 1991 Nepal Fertility, Family Planning and Health Survey from an office in the United States is still likely to interpolate missing details in the data using personal experience as a guide. If local cultural and social contexts affect the behavior of individuals, as many social scientists believe they do, then such interpolation is extremely dangerous and generally misleading (H. Becker 1996; Blumer 1969).

Because social science researchers cannot fully avoid bringing their own meanings and interpretations to the research process, we believe that this hazard ought to motivate researchers to work toward making introspection an advantage rather than a liability. In fact, introspection can be a critical part of what we do as social scientists. Although consulting the literature, other scholars' theories, and previous research findings are all important, it is often useful to ask ourselves when formulating a new hypothesis or interpreting analytic results: "Under the same conditions, can I imagine thinking or acting that way?" This isn't a hypothesis test; it's simply a device for exploring how plausible an idea or finding may be. It's an extra tool social scientists can use that chemists and physicists do not have at their disposal. We don't reject an idea just because we don't find it plausible, particularly if we know of someone else who does find it plausible. But when we look into ourselves and find an idea or a result plausible, it becomes easier to begin to consider *why* the idea or result is plausible.

Thus, when ethnographers or anthropologists argue for the importance of living among the people they study, participating in their everyday lives, and conversing with them without a structured agenda, an explicit aim is that researchers should try to put themselves in the informants' shoes (Benedict 1989 [1934]; Geertz 1973). Of course, we cannot completely understand the lives of others through introspection, but interacting with a study population certainly provides insights that interacting with a data set alone cannot. Most social scientists are blessed with vivid imaginations, so lack of direct experience with the study population rarely prevents them from generating hypotheses. But many criticisms of secondary data analysis stem from a concern that hypotheses and conclusions have often been off the mark because researchers have so little direct exposure to the people they are studying.

Research approaches that distance investigators from the research process are problematic for a second reason: They preclude direct involvement in the collection of the data to be analyzed. Direct involvement helps reduce errors and omissions in the data and reveals shortcomings that cannot be avoided. In the past decade or two, anthropologists and ethnographers have been particularly astute in both recognizing researcher bias as a shortcoming and finding ways to use it as a source of insight (Fine 1992; Krieger 1991; Scheper-Hughes 1992). Methodological research on survey design and execution also focuses on the detection and reduction of data collection error and bias (Anderson, Kasper, and Frankel 1979; Groves 1987; Groves et al. 2004; Sudman, Bradburn, and Schwarz 1996). But no single research approach is ever likely to allow investigators to detect or eliminate all potential bias. The integration of multiple methods into a single research design, however, can reduce potential problems by bringing investigators into the data creation process and allowing them to use information from one method to gain insight into the limitations of another.

For example, some research demonstrates that the integration of less structured research methods and the participation of the principal investigator can yield specific improvements in the quality of survey data (Zeller 1993). Our work combining ethnographic and survey methods in Nepal shows that non-survey methods can be used to reduce a variety of non-sampling errors in surveys (Axinn, Fricke, and Thornton 1991). These non-sampling errors include coverage errors, non-response errors, measurement errors arising from the interviewer, measurement errors arising from the respondent, and measurement errors arising from the questionnaire (see Groves 1987 for a discussion of this typology). We also believe that systematic sampling can sometimes improve the design of projects using less structured interviews and observations. We discuss these issues in greater detail in Chapters 3 and 4.

Although steps can be taken to maximize the quality of data resulting from any particular data collection effort, errors and omissions inevitably remain. Investigators who participate directly in the data collection process are much more likely to know about these errors and omissions, and the processes that created them, and to be able to use this knowledge in their analyses of the data. In large-scale survey production, interviewers, supervisors, study managers, and others make scores of day-to-day decisions regarding a study, each of which may alter the data produced by a survey. At best, these decisions will be made the way the principal investigator would have made them – although the investigator may never know about them. At worst, these decisions will run contrary to what the researcher would have done. Just as interaction with the study population yields important insights into the phenomena being studied, interaction with the data collection process provides insights into the limitations of the data. When the data are ready to be analyzed, knowledge about these limitations may be just as useful as insights into the study population.

At this point, it may appear that we believe surveys are a bad source for secondary data analysis. On the contrary, we do not believe survey research itself is problematic, but rather a style of survey research that features little involvement of the principal investigators. Because it reduces information about the shortcomings of the data and the lives of the people being studied, this style robs researchers of opportunities to improve data quality. Instead, we advocate a research style that provides multifaceted and firsthand knowledge of the study population and the data collection process – knowledge that allows researchers to take data limitations into account and use introspection to their advantage.

Even while we argue the benefits of direct involvement, we also recognize that this is not always practical. Many social scientists today are secondary analysts of information that some other investigator or large group of investigators have collected. Our discussions of the importance of direct involvement in the research process are designed to highlight the price investigators may be paying for playing the role of secondary analyst. As we begin the 21st century, to create a data set one can scribble down a sample specification, a list of questions, and a budget; mail them off to any one of dozens of survey research organizations; and wait for a data file to return. Or, to obtain existing data for secondary analysis one can surf Websites for downloadable data or contact one of the country's many data archives and request a CD-ROM. However, this ease of access should not prevent secondary analysts from learning about the process that generated a particular data set. For example, they might obtain a copy of the study questionnaire, use it to interview someone, and have someone else use it to interview them. Secondary analysts might travel to the organization that collected the data and inspect records of original interviews or records of problems and errors that occurred during data collection fieldwork. These steps can dramatically improve a secondary user's insight into the processes responsible for creating the information they will analyze. Likewise, secondary users of survey data willing to travel to the organization that collected the original data can usually obtain permission to view or listen to records of some of the original interviews and learn more about the people involved in the study than publically available numeric summaries of survey data are likely to yield. Involvement in the research process is a matter of degree, and any investigator, including a secondary analyst, can take the initiative to increase that degree. In an effort to encourage this initiative, we describe in later chapters various levels of researcher involvement and point toward ways to increase involvement.

Central Principles in the Creation of Mixed Method Approaches

Mixed method data collection strategies build on the strengths of existing individual methods to construct an approach that has key advantages for some types of research problems. Our comparison of the strengths and weaknesses of various data collection methods reveals that mixed methods are particularly useful when a research problem calls for more than one of the key attributes characterizing individual methods. So when a research problem calls for the combination of high levels of structure to test hypotheses and low levels of structure to discover new hypotheses, mixed methods are particularly appropriate. When a problem calls for the combination of individual responses and group responses, mixed methods are particularly appropriate. Or when a problem calls for the combination of questioning and observation by an interviewer, mixed methods are particularly appropriate. Our review of causal reasoning in the social sciences reveals that mixed method approaches may be particularly useful when either (1) redundant measurement of an association using different methods is useful for assessing the role of method-specific bias in producing that association; or (2) comprehensive measurement is useful for discovering potential mechanisms responsible for producing an association. We also review the role of investigator involvement in the data collection process and the influence of introspection in social research. This review is consistent with the conclusion that mixed method approaches may be particularly useful when high investigator involvement methods can be linked with other methods to ensure that the investigator has substantial exposure to those being studied and to the process of data collection.

On the other hand, our review of the divide between qualitative and quantitative approaches to research in the social sciences reveals that this dichotomy is not particularly useful to our consideration of mixed method strategies. The qualitative/quantitative dichotomy neither reveals key strengths and weaknesses of specific data collection methods nor points toward specific advantages of combining methods into a mixed method approach. As a result, we abandon the qualitative/quantitative labels for the remainder of our presentation of mixed method.

Instead, two overarching themes regarding the foundation of mixed method approaches emerge. The first theme, mixing multiple methods, affords opportunities to use the strengths of some methods to counterbalance the weaknesses of others. Because all methods have strengths and weaknesses, combinations of multiple methods that achieve this counterbalancing aim are particularly valuable. The second theme is that mixing multiple methods is a valuable strategy for producing a comprehensive empirical record about a topic. Empirical documentation combining redundant measurement using radically different approaches has special strengths for reducing errors, discovering new hypotheses, and testing hypotheses. These themes of counterbalancing strengths and weaknesses and comprehensive empirical documentation illuminate a set of common principles in the design of mixed method data collection. We summarize those principles below.

Method Balance

The first theme of mixed method data collection is to design strategies of integration that counterbalance the weaknesses of one method with the strengths of another. This theme overarches three specific principles. The first principle is to balance data collection using highly structured methods with data collection using less structured methods. The structured nature of survey methods and the flexibility of observational or less structured interviewing methods combine to provide, respectively, data useful for testing hypotheses and data useful for learning from informants in their own words and for discovering new hypotheses (Sieber 1973). Less structured methods are also useful for discovering and documenting key causal mechanisms that are responsible for producing the overall causal relationships documented using more highly structured methods. This combined approach is similar to the "triangulation" method as proposed by Denzin (1970, 1978). Chapter 3 focuses on integration of multiple research methods to simultaneously provide data for hypothesis generation and testing. Chapter 4 is devoted to approaches for integrating methods in ways that provide a more systematic application of less structured methods while adding flexibility to the development of models for survey data. Subsequent chapters examine additional approaches for integrating methods. Though every method described in this book aims to use the strengths of some approaches to help compensate for the weaknesses of other approaches, the methods described here are merely examples of this principle. The principle itself has much to offer. It is a fundamental element in the creation of new data collection methods not yet imagined.

The second key principle is to use methods that encourage investigator involvement to balance methods that do not encourage investigator involvement. This principle is aimed at encouraging investigator involvement in all phases of the research process so that introspection can become a beneficial tool rather than a liability. Certainly, methods such as unstructured interviewing and participant observation tend to involve the investigator with the people being studied and the methods being used. But investigator involvement can be enhanced as well in other more structured methods, such as surveys, focus groups, and archival research, promoting more comprehensive understanding of the study population and more comprehensive insight into the strengths and weaknesses of the specific methods being used. Integrated use of multiple methods is an important way to create investigator involvement in these more highly structured methods.

Combining structured and unstructured methods into a single data collection effort allows the investigator to use the openness of unstructured methods to gain new insights into the data collected from structured methods. All the data collection strategies described in this book involve combining methods to accomplish this goal. Some focus on simultaneous or sequential applications of separate methods, as in Chapters 3, 4, and 7. Others focus on hybrid methods that combine elements of distinct methods into a single method, as in Chapters 5 and 6. All aim to improve investigator involvement in the data collection process, and all aim to enhance the investigator's ability to use introspection constructively when designing models of cause and consequence. Introspection is unavoidable in the social sciences. Misused, it is a dangerous liability; used carefully, it provides social scientists with a tool for studying cause and consequence that is not available in most other sciences.

The third key balancing principle for the design of mixed method research is to maintain flexibility in the design and application of data collection methods, allowing new methods and integrative designs to be tailored to the study of cause and consequence. Such flexibility is a common feature of every data collection approach described in this volume, and the examples provided demonstrate how that flexibility has been employed to advance the substantive aims of specific studies. The flexibility imbedded in the methods described here make them ideal for recombination to meet the specific aims of new studies.

Comprehensive Empirical Documentation

The second overarching theme focuses on producing a comprehensive empirical record about a topic. Comprehensive empirical documentation that combines redundant measurement using radically different approaches is a particularly valuable tool in the effort to investigate causal relationships using observational research designs. Three principles are particularly important in the design of mixed method approaches for the investigation of causal questions.

First, comprehensiveness of measurement is especially useful because redundant measurement of an association using different methods is useful for assessing the role of method-specific bias in producing that association. To the extent we can produce consistent evidence of the same association using radically different data collection tools that are likely to be characterized by different forms of bias, our confidence in that association is greatly increased (Rosenbaum 2001). Just as mixed methods can be used for counterbalancing weaknesses of one method with strengths of another to reduce measurement errors, from a causal reasoning perspective varying data collection method-specific biases produces stronger empirical evidence. All data collection methods may be characterized by biases. Varying the method-specific bias by integrating multiple methods reduces the chance that such bias is responsible for observed associations.

Second, from a causal reasoning perspective comprehensive measurement is also useful for discovering potential mechanisms responsible for producing an association. Reasoning that a particular empirical association corresponds to a causal relationship requires reasoning about the mechanisms that produce that causal relationship. Empirical documentation of those mechanisms is, therefore, another important element in producing empirical evidence of a causal relationship. Highly structured methods, such as surveys, have advantages for documenting overall associations; but less structured methods, such as unstructured interviewing and observation, have advantages for discovering the mechanisms responsible for overall associations (Groves et al. 2004). By using mixed method approaches that integrate these different types of data collection methods, investigators have a greater opportunity to both discover and document the mechanisms responsible for causal relationships.

Third, the causal-reasoning perspective highlights the need for comprehensive measures that include the temporal-ordering of measurement. The temporal ordering issue is in no way specific to mixed methods. It is equally important in the application of any one data collection method, if that method is being used to gather measures to test causal hypotheses. Measures of causes are expected to precede measures of consequences. Use of mixed method approaches to study causal relationships also requires attention to these temporal-ordering issues. Because this issue is fundamental to data collection for causal analysis, a substantial portion of the mixed method strategies we describe is devoted to issues of temporal ordering. These issues are the main focus of Chapters 5, 6, and 7. Together, these three causal-reasoning dimensions of a comprehensive empirical record form one of our strongest motivations for the mixed methods data collection strategies described in this book.

Finally, we wish to close this chapter with one more reminder that the methods and strategies described here are tools. As with any collection of tools, the users are expected to understand their aims well, learn their setting, and only then choose an appropriate combination of tools to complete their task. Chapter 2 is devoted to consideration of these issues of matching data collection tools to data collection tasks. Careful consideration of the substantive aims of the specific research project is a necessary precursor to the assembly of an appropriate combination of data collection tools to advance social science. The methods described here can be used to study many different social science topics in a range of settings, but they are not designed to be applied wholesale to new topics and settings without careful consideration of the match between methods and substantive aims.

2 Fitting Data Collection Methods to Research Aims

In the social sciences, data collection methods are tools for measuring human behavior, human beliefs, or other aspects of the human population. In Chapter 1, we described the range of measurement tools commonly used in the social sciences and highlighted some of their similarities and differences. As we argued in Chapter 1, tools are not good or bad. They simply fit the purpose well or poorly. So if you wish to pound a nail into a piece of wood, a hammer fits the task well and a saw fits the job poorly. If, on the other hand, you wish to cut a piece of wood in half, a saw fits the job well and a hammer fits the job poorly. Hammers and saws are not good or bad. They are just more or less useful depending on the job you aim to do.

For many large projects, more than one tool is needed. Continuing with our analogy, using both a hammer and a saw allows you to accomplish things you could not accomplish with only one of these tools. The same is generally true in the research process. As we argued in the previous chapter, using multiple data collection methods usually provides a more comprehensive set of evidence for assessment, often raising the possibility that questions introduced by the use of one method can be answered by data collected with another method (Sieber 1973). However, in choosing either a single method or a mix of multiple methods, like choosing among tools in a toolbox, one must choose each method based on its fit with the task at hand.

In this chapter, we address a series of issues that often arise in the selection of data collection methods in the social sciences (whether conducting a single method or multimethod data collection). First, we address the choice of a study design, including choosing the unit of analysis, selecting cases to study, and choosing between retrospective and prospective measurement strategies. Second, we consider the fit between measurement strategy and measurement aims, including issues surrounding the aggregate level of measurement, the structure of the measurements, abbreviated measurement techniques, and new technologies for measurement and analysis. Third, we discuss a series of common but difficult measurement problems, including translations of measures across languages, measures of sensitive behaviors or beliefs, and reports on others.

There are many other important measurement issues we do not address, but these three types of issues arise often in the social sciences and are common issues regardless of the data collection method. One could choose any single data collection method and encounter each of these issues. A study using only focus group methods is just as likely to face all of these issues as a study using only survey methods. Thus, there is nothing specific to mixed method approaches in the issues presented in this chapter. Rather, we use these common issues to illustrate some of the potential benefits of mixed method approaches. The benefits derive from using the strengths of one method to counterbalance the weaknesses of another method. We introduced this idea as a key principle in the design of mixed method approaches in Chapter 1. In this chapter, we use these common research issues to illustrate this principle. We then expand on the principle to construct the approaches described in subsequent chapters.

Choices Among Research Designs

Every researcher must begin the research process by identifying a research question. Once a specific question has been clearly identified, one must develop a research design before proceeding to collect data. There are key dimensions of any research design that determine its ability to address a given research question (Babbie 2004; Campbell and Stanley 1963; Miller 1983). We feel that four of the most important design issues for studying human beliefs and behaviors are selecting an appropriate unit of analysis, choosing one or more comparison groups, identifying a sampling strategy, and deciding whether to use a retrospective or prospective design.

Unit of Analysis

A researcher's choice of research design begins with the selection of a unit of analysis, defining the object of study. In many social research projects, the unit of analysis is the individual person. This means that the project aims to study people, specifically the variations across individual people. However, individual people can also be aggregated into groups, and many study designs feature a unit of analysis chosen at some higher level of aggregation: family, school, community, county, state or province, organization, ethnic group, or nation-state. The choice depends on the aims of the study.

So research on the spread of sexually transmitted diseases (STDs) frequently focuses on individuals as the units of analysis because STDs are considered an attribute of individuals. Research on revolutions in governance structures focuses on nation-states as the units of analysis because governance structures are considered an attribute of nations. Research on the failure of businesses often focuses on business organizations as the unit of analysis because it is the termination of these organizations that defines ultimate failure of the business. Every choice of research topic has a unit of analysis that best fits the topic. A close match between the substantive aims and the unit of analysis is a strength of a project. A weak match limits the value of the results.

For example, because of data limitations, researchers often use aggregate-level data to study the relationship between individual-level characteristics. Consider unemployment and criminal involvement. When an aggregate relationship is found, such as areas with high unemployment rates also have high crime rates, the researcher may be tempted to conclude that people who are unemployed are more likely to commit crimes than the employed. However, this individual-level relationship does not necessarily follow from the aggregate-level evidence. Making this type of individual-level inference from such an aggregate-level relationship is an example of a type of ecological fallacy (Firebaugh 2001). To test whether being unemployed makes one more likely to commit crimes, the unit of analysis must be individuals. In other words, the evidence required is information about the employment experience of individual persons and whether the same persons have committed a crime.

Sometimes, strong theory or prior research provides an adequate guide to the selection of an appropriate unit of analysis. If this is not the case, some investigation will be necessary to make this choice. It is virtually impossible to arrive at an appropriate unit of analysis for such preresearch design investigation. For example, researchers investigating the forces shaping children's learning in the classroom may have to choose among many possible units of analysis. One could study variation among individual children, variation in teachers, class characteristics, school characteristics, communities, or countries. In situations like these, combinations of unstructured methods, including multiple types of observation and unstructured interviewing, can be valuable tools for investigating the appropriate unit of analysis for a specific research question. These unstructured techniques are ideal for the discovery of new information. They will provide opportunities to learn more about the research problem in ways that improve the likelihood of selecting a unit of analysis that fits the research question well.

Of course, some research questions may lead the investigator to more than one unit of analysis. Multilevel studies simultaneously employ more than one aggregate level of analysis to address their research aims. Because many theories of human beliefs and behavior point toward causal processes that link together multiple levels of aggregation – nations, communities, ethnic groups, schools, families and individuals – multilevel studies are an extremely important part of social research. This book addresses mixed method data collection at multiple levels of aggregation, and these studies simultaneously use units of analysis at more than one level.

The choice of unit of analysis has many consequences for other aspects of research design and data collection strategies. As we discuss below, the choice of the unit of analysis helps to define appropriate comparison groups and levels of measurement.

Comparison Groups

A true experimental design features two or more comparison groups and random assignment of the units being studied to these groups (or to treatments that differentiate the groups) (Campbell and Stanley 1963). Much of the research in the social sciences uses some type of quasi-experimental design, featuring two or more groups to compare *without* random assignment to the groups. There are many different versions of experimental and quasi-experimental designs, and the strengths or weaknesses of these designs are well documented (Campbell and Stanley 1963).

Many descriptive studies in the social sciences do not feature a comparison group – instead, they document something among a single group. In a single-group design, with no comparison group, it is not possible to reach any meaningful conclusions about the differences between the group being studied and any other groups. So, for example, it is not possible to reach conclusions about what makes the rate of marriage lower for African American woman than women of other racial/ethnic groups by only studying African American women. Or, in another example, it is also not possible to learn how men's reaction to divorce is unique, in relation to women's, without studying both men and women. Studies without comparison groups in the design can describe the group investigated, but they cannot place that group in any kind of comparative perspective relative to any other group.

Because of this key design factor, it is essential for most social science research projects to choose a comparison group or groups, and it is essential that the choice of comparison group(s) match the substantive aims. Thus, when studying the relationship between education and earnings, for example, it is essential to compare earnings among those with a high level of education to earnings among those with little education. If one is studying the relationship between the formation of democratic governance and gross domestic product (GDP), it is essential to compare GDP in countries with democratic governments to GDP in countries without democratic governments. If one is studying the relationship between religious beliefs and divorce, it is essential to compare divorce rates across two or more different religious groups. If studying the relationship between parenting practices and number of children, it is essential to compare parenting practices among those who have one child to parenting practices among those who have two children and/or to parenting practices among those who have three or more children. There are an infinite number of potential research questions. For every question, there is one (or more) appropriate comparison group(s).

Selecting Cases for Study

With a unit of analysis defined and appropriate comparison groups identified, the researcher is ready to choose cases to study. The minimum criteria for selecting cases to study are that both the group to be studied and the key comparison group(s) are selected.

When a large number of cases will be studied in a systematic way in order to make an inference to a larger population, we describe the selection of cases as a sample design. The field of sampling is a substantial scientific subfield devoted to systematic procedures for selecting cases to study to ensure that those cases adequately represent some larger population (Kalton 1983; Kish 1965). If you plan to select a large number of cases and use a systematic selection procedure to ensure that your selections are representative of some larger population, consult one of the many available resources on sampling and sample selection. We recommend Chapters 3 and 4 of Groves et al. (2004).

Issues of case selection apply across all data collection methods, including any of the single methods we describe in Chapter 1 and any of the mixed method approaches we describe in the remainder of the book. In the paragraphs below, we discuss common case selection issues, including the scale of representation (national vs. non-national), elimination of undesired variation, and decisions about the number of cases to study. Where appropriate, we draw readers' attention to how these issues typically arise in mixed method studies.

National vs. Non-national   Among studies of individual people designed to represent some larger population, researchers often face difficult choices regarding the appropriate population to represent. Many large-scale research projects are aimed at representing a national population. Representation of a national population is particularly useful if the research aims to create some types of national statistics. This is a common aim for government agencies engaged in social research in many countries. However, representation of a national population is not always necessary for answering particular research questions.

For social scientists engaged in the study of cause and consequence in the human population, there are few occasions when national or political boundaries have any relevance for the study of causal processes. When national laws, policies, or programs constitute an important influence on behaviors or beliefs, national boundaries may form units of analysis or comparison groups, but studies of individual behavior and belief rarely require generalization to a national population to advance our understanding of causal processes. Therefore, most studies of causal processes can choose cases at a smaller scale than the nation and take advantage of intensive data collection methods at multiple contextual levels that may be difficult to apply at a larger scale with huge distances between each respondent.

Nationally representative samples are also expensive, in part because they may require a large number of cases, in part because they may require a complex sample design, and in part because they usually require geographically distributed fieldwork operations that can be expensive to manage (Groves et al. 2004). The decision to represent a large, geographically widespread population, such as a national population, may also limit the researcher's choice of data collection methods and measurement tools. For example, it is difficult to implement direct observations of a large, geographically distributed population. Highly structured survey data collections are more feasible at the national scale.

Issues of scale are likely to place constraints on which of the mixed method data collection strategies we describe are feasible. As we describe in Chapter 8, many new studies are beginning to use mixed method approaches within studies that are run on a national scale. Thus, even if scale is limiting to some extent, it is also possible to formulate mixed method strategies at many different scales. For example, the National Study of Youth and Religion (http://www.youthandreligion.org) employed two different data collection methods. First, a nationally representative sample of 3,370 households including at least one teenager was selected using the random-digit dialing method. A telephone survey was conducted with one teen and one parent in each of these households. To follow up on the information gained in the survey and learn more about youths' lives in their own words, a set of 269 face-to-face, semi-structured interviews were conducted with a sub-sample of the teen survey respondents. It would have been expensive and time consuming to conduct the face-to-face, semi-structured interviews with each teen survey respondent. Moreover, detailed transcriptions from 3,370 semi-structured interviews would produce mountains of text data, challenging the capabilities of even the most skilled qualitative data analysts. Therefore, this study features a combination of methods, with highly structured methods used at a large scale to achieve national representation and less structured methods used at a smaller scale.

Eliminating Undesirable Variation   Cases can also be chosen with the aim of reducing undesired variation across the cases to be studied. Just as important as design choices about what researchers want to study are choices about what researchers do *not* want to study. Comparison groups are necessary to ensure that the selected cases vary across the factors you wish to study. It is also possible to select cases in a way designed to reduce variation across them in factors you do not want to study. So, if one wants to study the relationship between public transportation and unemployment, for example, one may decide that variations between rural and urban areas will confuse the results and that selecting only urban cases is more appropriate. In studying the relationship between religion and fertility, comparing Muslims from one region with Hindus from another region is likely to introduce other unknown and unmeasured differences between the two regions, reducing the investigator's ability to reach reliable conclusions about fertility differences due to religious differences. Focusing on comparisons between Muslims and Hindus in a single region is more likely to identify religious differences. These examples may strike the reader as obvious, but they illustrate an important principle: The selection of cases can be used to eliminate undesirable variation from a study design.

The Number of Cases   Regardless of the data collection method being employed, investigators often request explicit guidance in their choice of the number of cases to study. Unfortunately, there is no universal rule for the correct number of cases. At the low end, if you wish to arrive at any sort of comparative conclusion you must have at least one more point of comparison than you have differences among the units you are comparing. If you are studying political consequences of armed revolutions and your unit of analysis is the nation-state, you will want to have some nations that have experienced armed revolution and some that have not. However, if you only choose one of each, the two countries you choose are likely to be different in other ways besides armed revolution. As a result, it will be difficult to reach any comparative conclusion about the relative importance of the difference in experience of armed revolution versus other differences between the two countries. To accomplish this, the design requires more cases than differences among the cases.

The same point can be made at any other level of aggregation with any other unit of analysis. If one wishes to study the relationship between college attendance and marriage timing, at a minimum one would study at least one person who had attended college and one who had not. However, any two individuals are likely to be different in more ways than just college attendance, so a comparison of two is not likely to be sufficient. If you believe you are comparing people characterized by 100 differences, you will need at least 101 people such that their differences are spread evenly throughout the 101. To the extent that these differences are not spread evenly, you may need many more than 101 people.

The field of sampling statistics has devised a set of systematic procedures for selecting cases to study in order to optimize the number of cases for the topic under study (Groves et al. 2004; Kalton 1983; Kish 1965). These procedures include complex sample designs, estimation of design effects, and power calculations. These approaches are complex and beyond the scope of this book. We urge interested readers to consult Kish (1965) and Groves et al. (2004) for further information. Both of these sources explain how to use your understanding of the relationships or processes under study to choose a number of cases large enough to provide evidence about them.

For those seeking concrete guidance for the design to study a topic about which little is known, however, those procedures may prove unsatisfactory. Unfortunately, these procedures require some estimate of the true magnitude of the underlying relationship the investigator wishes to study. Often, the investigator has little information about the true magnitude, and that lack of information is the reason for launching the study in the first place. This issue creates a chicken-and-egg problem: You cannot know the optimal number of cases for a study without knowing the magnitude of the relationship you wish to study, but you cannot know the magnitude of the relationship you wish to study without conducting the study.

This does not mean that more cases are always better. At the high end, one eventually reaches a level of saturation where new cases do not add any new information. At this point, adding more cases does not advance your research aims. It may be that investigators more often run out of time and resources before they reach this saturation point. However, even with infinite time and resources, continuing to study more cases does not necessarily improve the quality of what is learned.

These two opposing extremes form the bounds of a continuum from not enough cases to too many cases. Investigators must arrive at a number between the extremes that is large enough to detect the relationship the investigators aim to detect. Because of the lack of clear guidance on this topic and limited time and resources, most debate about the correct number of cases revolves around whether the number of cases is large enough to detect the phenomena under study. This process begins at the lower bound and works upward.[1]

Of course, mixed method data collection does not solve this difficult case selection problem. However, preliminary investigation before finalizing the research design can provide more information about the true magnitude of the underlying relationship the investigator wishes to study. This information can improve the quality of guesses about the optimal number of cases needed. Again, combinations of less structured methods, including multiple types of observation and semi-structured interviewing, can be a valuable tool for a preliminary investigation of the magnitude of the underlying relationship because these unstructured techniques are ideal for the discovery of new information. These methods can provide opportunities to learn more about the research problem. Note, however, that one usually needs highly structured measures, such as those associated with survey methods, to arrive at an estimate of the magnitude of the underlying relationship with some precision. Such an investigation is usually beyond the scope of a preliminary investigation, but it can sometimes be obtained through a highly focused pilot study.

Retrospective vs. Prospective Designs

Once the cases to be studied are selected, the researcher begins to face important questions about how the cases will be studied. We use retrospective designs to refer to designs that begin at one point in time and study what happened to the case *before* that time. We use prospective designs to refer to designs that pick a point in time and study what happens to the case *after* that time. Thus, studies of many different kinds of units of analysis may be either retrospective or prospective. Studies of people, communities, businesses, or provinces might look either backward or forward. Again, the choice of design must match the aims of the study, but this choice has substantial implications for measurement strategies.

These measurement implications include both the match between the measures and the object of measurement and the nature of measurement errors likely to accompany a specific measurement. The issue of match between measure and object of measurement frequently arises when the research aim involves studying some type of change. If the change is known to have occurred already, then a retrospective design is appropriate. If it is believed that the change will occur in the future, then a prospective design is appropriate.

The issue of measurement error arises because the nature of retrospective and prospective measurement can be quite different. The study of individuals as the units of analysis provides a good example. When studying what has happened to individuals in the past, interviews are a common measurement strategy, but individuals' reports of the past are known to be characterized by significant recall error (Groves et al. 2004). Moreover, those recall errors are known to vary by subject matter, meaning that the level of error is likely to be higher for some subjects than for others. In Chapter 6, we discuss techniques for reducing errors in retrospective reports from individuals in some detail. In Chapter 5, we discuss retrospective measurement techniques for other units of analysis, such as communities, businesses, programs, or other organizations.

Of course, measuring individual beliefs or behaviors *now*, at the time of the study, greatly reduces the potential for recall errors to shape results. But prospective studies often require multiple measures of the same thing forward in time, and the frequency of these multiple measures raises important issues. If the measures are too far apart, researchers run the risk of missing the events they hoped to study. If the measures are too close together, researchers may significantly increase the burden for participants or influence the behavior or attitudes under study by making them more salient. These issues raise complex measurement trade-offs, which are discussed in detail in Chapter 7.

In data collection for causal analysis, both retrospective and prospective designs afford useful opportunities to match the temporal order of measures to hypotheses being studied. As we said in Chapter 1, this match between the temporal order of measures and the temporal ordering embedded in causal hypotheses is a fundamental element of our philosophy of causal inference from quasi-experimental, observational study designs. Thus, we give issues of temporal ordering a great deal of attention as we discuss the specific techniques described in Chapters 5, 6, and 7.

Matching Measurement Strategy to Aims

The research design choices described above shape choices about measurement strategy. Just as the substantive aims of the research must shape those research design choices, the substantive aims must also shape choices about measurement strategy that are not defined by the research design. In the following paragraphs, we outline a few of the issues related to measurement strategy that are common to most data collections in the social sciences. These include the need for preliminary research, selection of measurement strategies that match the aggregate level of the subject being studied, the possibility of using abbreviated data collection strategies, and options to employ computer-assisted data collection and analysis technologies.

Preliminary Research

Preliminary research is an essential step in the design of an effective data collection procedure. The process of data collection involves ongoing trade-offs between a plan and the constraints realized during implementation. In order to anticipate constraints before launching the main body of a data collection effort, it is essential to conduct significant preliminary research.

The quality and efficiency of data collection improves with more investment in preliminary research, but there is little information about the optimum level of preliminary investment. Nonetheless, the extremes are relatively clear. At one extreme, too high an investment in preliminary research may jeopardize the time and resources available for the main data collection effort. At the other extreme, insufficient investment in preliminary research may result in disaster: completely ineffective main data collection.

One key step in preliminary research is learning everything possible from existing sources about the subject of study. For those planning primary data collection and fieldwork, this includes learning all that is possible about a research location *before* entering the field (e.g., language, norms, practices, history, social stratification, etc.). Often, much of this initial learning can be accomplished by reviewing existing documentation of the study population. However, when existing documentation is sparse or nonexistent, this phase of preliminary research may require immersion in the field to develop firsthand knowledge of a study setting through unstructured observation and interviewing.

A second step is more focused preliminary data collection, for the purpose of gaining foundational information. This includes obtaining the information necessary to select design parameters, as discussed above, as well as information for choosing measurement strategies. This type of preliminary data collection may take the form of a smaller-scale pilot study or a series of case studies. As discussed above, it is common to employ combinations of less structured methods, including multiple types of observation and interviewing, because these less structured techniques are ideal for the discovery of new information necessary to guide research design and measurement decisions. In fact, perhaps the most common integration of multiple data collection methods discussed in the data collection literature is the use of less structured methods in a preliminary phase to assist in the design of highly structured methods (Babbie 2004; Groves et al. 2004). This is a sequential integration of mixed methods, which we discuss relatively little in this book because it receives so much attention elsewhere (e.g., Groves et al. 2004; Morgan 1997; Nassar-McMillan and Borders 2002; O'Brien 1993; Sieber 1973).

A third key step is pretesting the data collection methods. Whether the data collection will include surveys, observations, less structured interviews, or focus groups, pretesting always improves the chances of subsequent success. Pretesting should mimic the plans for the main data collection activity in order to test both the data collection protocols and whatever data collection tools have been designed for the study. This type of pretest gives the investigator firsthand knowledge of the strengths and weaknesses of the data collection plan, it allows the investigator to discover dimensions of the data collection plan that are not working as planned, and it allows investigators to make changes to the data collection plan to ensure that the final implementation is in fact successful. We recommend that every data collection field include at least two preliminary field tests or pretests, but preferably three or four such tests. The investment in these pretests is likely to result in much higher quality procedures during the main data collection.

Defining Theoretical Constructs in Order to Design Measures

A key reason that preliminary research among the subjects of a study is so pivotal is that whatever general theoretical ideas may be guiding a data collection, those general ideas must be translated into setting- and population-specific constructs in order to design reliable and valid measures. Whether the data collection will involve surveys, unstructured interviews, observations, focus groups, archival work, or the type of mixtures we advocate, one of the most common reasons data collection fails is because of mismatches between theoretical constructs and measures. First, general theoretical constructs must be translated into a setting- and study-specific definition. Second, measures must be designed to match the setting-specific definitions as closely as possible. The more clear, precise, and setting-specific the theoretical definitions, the easier it is to design closely matching measures.

Every field in the social sciences has some body of literature addressing the issues of defining theoretical constructs and constructing corresponding measures. Measurement theory in psychology, or psychometrics, offers a particularly rich body of information on these topics (Groves et al. 2004). We will not repeat any of those various literatures here. Instead, we simply argue that setting-specific theoretical constructs are more useful in the design of measures than general constructs; and in order to arrive at precise setting-specific constructs, one needs a detailed understanding of the specific setting and subjects of the study.

Strategies for increasing the power of introspection in this measurement design process include reading as much as possible about the research setting, spending time in the research setting observing and interviewing social actors and interactions, and learning the language of the social actors under study. This may include learning how a language is used differently by the specific group under study.

One example of a theoretical construct most social research data collections aim to measure is socioeconomic status or economic resources. There is considerable debate in the research literature about what these general theoretical constructs mean and a corresponding high variance in how they are measured. But even when a researcher is able to resolve some definition at a purely theoretical level, unless the construct is defined within the context of a specific setting researchers are unlikely to be able to design closely corresponding measures. Suppose we argue that the main socioeconomic status construct that interests us is income. In a highly monetized economy, such as that of the United States, this construct may seem to be easy to measure. In fact, it is not. There is considerable debate within the scientific community about which sources of money should and should not be included in the definition of income; and even when a field within the social sciences can reach agreement, the individual research subjects often do not share the same understanding of income. So when attempting to measure income carefully in settings like the United States, significant effort must be devoted to explaining the investigator's definition of income to the subjects of the study. The measurement is made even more difficult because of the potential cognitive demands on study participants to simultaneously consider multiple possible sources of income and by the potential for respondents to view personal income as a sensitive subject. (We return to measurement of sensitive subjects in more detail below.)

In contrast, consider the measurement of income in a highly non-monetized setting, such as rural Nepal. In this setting, there is some work for pay; but as in rich countries, it is complicated by the potential of multiple simultaneous jobs, varying pay periods (daily, weekly, monthly), and transfer payments. Unlike rich countries, 95% of the rural population of Nepal is engaged in agriculture, small family farms are the most common form of agriculture, and people meet many of their own consumption needs through their own productive activities, greatly minimizing their interactions with markets. As a result, it is difficult for individuals to value their earnings, to know whether it is the value of their production or the value of their consumption that they should consider, or to know what production costs should be subtracted. These issues make measurement of a concept like income extremely difficult in a non-monetized setting. As in the United States, the investigator must provide a clear conceptual definition of income and then invest in communicating the definition to study participants in order to arrive at a measure. This measurement is made even more difficult because of the potential cognitive demands and sensitivity of the subject.

The measurement of income is one example of how setting-specific variation in the definitions of many constructs must drive the design of measures. Issues surrounding the definition of income across settings have been long-standing empirical problems within economics, and other social sciences have their own long-standing measurement challenges. For example, anthropologists struggle with operational definitions of kinship, political scientists with political party membership, social psychologists with depression, and sociologists with employment. Demographers even struggle with the operational definition of a live birth. A scholar from any one of these fields could easily list another 20 such topics. There is no methodological magic that will make the definitions of theoretical constructs easy, for they require long-term, sustained research on the topic from multiple perspectives.

Every data collection project will struggle to establish clear and detailed definitions of theoretical constructs in order to devise reasonable measures. In this struggle, we argue, substantial setting-specific information about both the topic and the people to be studied dramatically enhances the possibility of arriving at a satisfactory measure. Furthermore, we argue that many of the mixed method strategies we describe in subsequent chapters are ideal for generating such setting specific information, even as the measures themselves are being devised. Measures grounded in such setting-specific information are more likely to reflect the theoretical construct that is the object of that measurement.

Matching the Level of Measurement to the Object of Measurement

One of the most fundamental issues in designing appropriate measures is the match in level of aggregation between the measurement and the theoretical construct it is designed to measure, or the object of the measurement. Unfortunately, researchers often fail on this fundamental match. The unit of analysis associated with the object of measurement usually defines an appropriate level of measurement. Within a single domain, many different levels of measurement may be possible. For example, within the domain of exposure to the mass media the levels of individual, household, and neighborhood may all be relevant. If the key issue is how much television someone watches, how often a person listens to the radio, or how often someone sees a movie, the appropriate level of measurement is the individual. On the other hand, if the key issue is whether or not someone has a television or radio in the home, then the appropriate level of measurement is the household. Or if the issue is the level of access someone has to movie theaters, then the appropriate level of measurement is the area in which it would seem reasonable for a person to travel to see a movie. So a thorough study of exposure to the mass media might include individual-level measures of experience with various media, household-level measures of ownership of media, and community-level measures of access to media.

Most substantive domains can be conceptualized at multiple levels of aggregation. Data collection tools can also be used to measure characteristics at multiple levels of aggregation. Because of these many choices about levels of measurement, care in matching the data collection strategy to the aggregate level of the object of that measurement is needed. The match in level of aggregation is essential to provide measures that capture the specific substantive aims of the research.

Context and Length of Interviews

Many social science data collections involve interviews. The methodological literature on data collection includes a great deal of scholarship on techniques for conducting interviews, from multiple methodological perspectives (Babbie 2004; Briggs 1986; Groves et al. 2004; Merton, Fiske, and Kendall 1990; Mishler 1986; Schaeffer 1991; Spradley 1979; Weiss 1994). We do not repeat that literature here. However, the literature points to both the context of an interview and the length of an interview as factors that shape measurement options and the quality of the resulting measures.

The context of an interview includes the place it is conducted, the people who are present, and any information the respondent has been given about the objective of the interview. Many interviews designed to measure personal information require privacy, which may include a location that is private or anonymous and the absence of any other people. Research on variations in respondent cooperation suggests that making it easier for the respondent to cooperate increases the likelihood of participation. This observation often leads interviewers to seek out interview participants in their own homes. But for some respondents and some topics, interviews at home may not afford enough privacy. Examples of sensitive interview situations include teenagers being asked about their sexual behavior, individuals being asked about illegal behaviors, or spouses being asked private information about their relationship. (More discussion of the measurement of sensitive topics follows below.) Discussions of such topics may require privacy, and it is often difficult to find a time when the interview participant is the only person at home. Even if alone in the home, just being there may provide reminders of a parent or partner and thus may make answering some sensitive questions uncomfortable. In these situations, researchers often attempt to conduct interviews at neutral locations, such as a coffee or tea shop, restaurant, public library, or other public location. For example, this strategy was used by the National Study of Youth and Religion for face-to-face, semi-structured interviews. They were typically conducted in a neutral location, where noise and eavesdropping were not likely, but where the participants and interviewers felt at ease and safe.

The length of an interview can influence data quality: Interviews that are too short may not obtain enough information; interviews that are too long may fatigue participants. The level of fatigue increases with the cognitive difficulty of the task: Harder questions require a shorter interview. Thus, long questions or questions that ask respondents to perform difficult recall tasks are better asked earlier in an interview, and an interview primarily composed of these types of questions cannot go on for as long as an interview composed of relatively easy, cognitively undemanding questions. The mode of interview may also limit interview length. For example, it is widely believed that interviews conducted over the telephone should be substantially shorter than interviews conducted face to face (Groves et al. 2004). Even in a face-to-face interview with easy questions, there are upper limits on the length of an interview. In the United States, 2-hour interviews are considered extremely difficult, and 3-hour interviews are exceptionally rare (some respondents might argue not rare enough). This is one reason why the idea that some interviews are "in-depth" and others are not is peculiar. More than 2 hours of interviewing produces substantial respondent fatigue for respondents to both highly structured survey interviews and unstructured interviews. The "depth" of measurement is really a function of the number of questions about any particular topic: A 1-hour interview on a single topic is more of an in-depth interview than a 1-hour interview on ten different topics. Respondents are increasingly being protected from unreasonably long interviews by protection of human subject guidelines (Groves et al. 2004). If the data collection will involve interviews, it will be more successful if careful attention is paid to the appropriate length of the interviews.

Use of Abbreviated Forms of Measurement

Concern about respondent burden and a lack of research time and resources often leads investigators to consider abbreviated forms of measurement, including abbreviated forms of mixed method data collection. Some mixed method data collections, or hybrids of data collection methods, are explicitly designed to take *less* time and resources than the sum of effort for the methods on which they are based. Often the aim is to create a quicker and easier alternative to rigorous implementation of other data collection tools. Such quick and easy tools are not the subject matter of this book. The methods described here are designed to build on rigorous applications of the constituent parts and exceed them by bringing multiples of them together in some way. In this sense, the methods described in this book are designed to be time and resource intensive and to allow researchers to accumulate a rich body of information that is *more* than the sum of what each single method could achieve on its own.

Rapid Rural Appraisal   Nonetheless, abbreviated mixed methods approaches deserve some attention here. One such method is the rapid rural appraisal (RRA) method (Chambers 1983, 1985, 1997; Chambers, Pacey, and Thrupp 1989). Rapid rural appraisal was popularized by researchers working to design and implement social welfare programs aimed at improving living standards among the rural poor (or rural development) in Asia, Africa, and Latin America. During the second half of the 20th century, failure of many such rural development programs led researchers to construct new data collection strategies for finding out more about the people they aimed to help without taking too much time. Rapid rural appraisal is a hybrid of surveys, direct observations, and unstructured interviewing. Researchers visit predetermined research sites, usually with an extensive list of measurement objectives. Standard questions are not provided, so the method is characterized by less structure than a survey. Some measurement objectives are designed to be met by direct observation and others by unstructured interviews with those in the field site. Visits are normally designed to last less than a full day. Notes taken during the field visit are the data product. The structure of these notes varies greatly according to the structure of the list of measurement objectives. A more recent revision of the method is Participatory Rural Appraisal (Chambers 1997, 2002). This revision has many of the same elements, but it is explicitly designed to involve those being studied in the research process by engaging them in the construction of the list of measurement objectives as well as engaging them in answering questions.

  These rapid rural appraisal techniques undoubtedly have merit for providing decision makers with information they might not otherwise have before making decisions. However, we believe the merit of this approach for advancing the study of cause and consequence in the social world is relatively limited. There are many reasons to believe that the levels of measurement error associated with these techniques are likely to be much higher than those associated with rigorous surveys or ethnographies involving extended observation and/or unstructured interviews.

Focus Groups   Although in this book we treat focus groups as a data collection technique that makes special use of the interaction of multiple individuals in the measurement process, some researchers use focus groups as an abbreviated form of unstructured interviewing. The aim here is to use a focus group as an efficient way of collecting textual data from which to extract quotations, often to accompany a statistical analysis of survey data (Knodel 1997, 1998; Knodel et al. 1987). Once again, we believe the primary emphasis on saving time makes this approach likely to be less valuable than the alternative of a more intensive application of unstructured interviews and direct observations. The levels of measurement error are likely to be greater, and the insights into causal mechanisms are likely to be fewer. Thus, in our discussions we reserve focus groups for those measurement tasks that explicitly require interactions among the subjects of a study in order to meet the measurement objectives, and we do not advocate the use of focus groups to save time.

New Technologies for Data Collection and Analysis

Most books about the analysis of social science data address the many analytic revolutions over the past half century made possible by the invention of computers. Computer-driven revolutions in social science data collection have been more recent. In the past 10–15 years, computers have begun to dramatically change the options available for data collection methods. In turn, these advances have expanded the range of measurement strategies available to meet study aims.

Computer-Assisted Interviewing   The biggest example of these technological changes in data collection is computer-assisted interviewing, or CAI (Saris 1991). Within survey research, Computer-Assisted Personal Interviewing (CAPI) and Computer-Assisted Telephone Interviewing (CATI) have transformed the ways that questionnaires are designed and that interviewing is conducted (Groves et al. 2004). Now, instead of typing questions onto paper to construct a questionnaire, survey researchers often program questions into a computer. Instead of using a paper-and-pencil questionnaire to conduct survey interviews, interviewers use laptop computers to follow along with the appropriate questions. This change has revolutionized the amount of tailoring of question wording to specific respondents that can be done within the context of a highly structured questionnaire (Couper 1996; Groves et al. 2004). That is, based on answers to previous questions, computer programs can generate somewhat different versions of the same question matched more closely to the respondent's specific situation. This tailoring has the advantage of building much more flexibility into a highly structured questionnaire, but it also has the disadvantage of reducing the overall level of standardization of questions across respondents.

Audio Computer-Assisted Self-Interviewing Technological advances in the use of computers to collect data have also transformed the possibility for self-report-based data collection. The most important example here is Audio Computer-Assisted Self-Interviewing, or ACASI (Couper and Rowe 1996; Groves et al. 2004). The ACASI technology uses audio recordings on laptop computers and headphones to allow respondents to interview themselves. The respondent wears headphones connected to the computer, and the computer plays audio recordings of questions. The respondent can then type answers directly into the computer so that no private information needs to be shared with an interviewer. As we discuss below, self-interviewing has been seen as a potential remedy for problems associated with reporting potentially sensitive behaviors or beliefs. By increasing the confidentiality of responses, self-interviewing is believed to increase respondents' reporting of such sensitive matters (Groves et al. 2004). The shift of self-reporting technology to a computerized form provides a great deal of flexibility and increases the opportunity for question tailoring, just as with CAPI and CATI described above.

The Internet and Interactive Voice Response Recent substantial advances in the application of Internet and Interactive Voice Response (IVR) technologies to survey data collection have made these two technologies feasible for data collection as well (Couper 2000, 2001, 2002; Groves et al. 2004; Sills and Song 2002). Of course, there are trade-offs involved in using either Internet or IVR modes for data collection. The key drawback of the Internet is the relatively low level of access and, in particular, differential access by race, socioeconomic status, and related characteristics (NTIA 2000, 2001). These problems are greatly reduced in the study of younger people in countries like the United States. For example, the National Longitudinal Study of Adolescent Health (Wave 3) data indicate that 96% of 18-year-olds have computer access and 81% have an e-mail account. Another drawback of the Internet is that it is primarily text-based, requiring literacy and a modicum of experience. On the other hand, the advantages include the fact that it is inexpensive, is not constrained by location, and, like other forms of computer-assisted interviewing, permits complex survey instrument design, such as fills, skips, and edit checks (see Couper 2000).

One advantage of IVR is that the only technology required to implement it is access to a Touch-Tone telephone. In rich countries such as the United States, coverage is of little concern, especially with mobile phones replacing the loss in landline coverage (Blumberg et al. 2004). Costs to study participants can be minimized by providing a toll-free telephone number. One disadvantage of IVR is the fact that complex instruments are harder to develop, given the need to produce customized voice files. In addition, IVR surveys generally take longer because of the need to play each question and all response options in sequence, thereby increasing the risk of break-off (see Tourangeau et al. 2002). Another disadvantage of IVR is the difficulty of generating automated prompts to respond.

Qualitative (Non-numeric) Data Analysis Software   In the last few decades, many software programs have been created to assist with the analysis of qualitative (non-numeric) data. These programs are primarily designed to ease the management and analysis of textual data, such as interview transcripts or field notes, but some programs also feature ways to manage and code photo, video, or audio files. These programs are designed to help with the management of complex data. They usually feature standard tools for coding, keeping track of codes, and mapping relationships between codes. There are ways for multiple analysts to document and share coding or memos written in the process of analysis. There are also tools designed to assist in the construction of theory or argument building. It is not clear whether these larger qualitative data analysis programs came before or after the recent tendency for qualitative studies to collect more data from more subjects, but in any event, the existence of the programs facilitates more large-scale qualitative data collection. For further review, discussion, and comparisons of qualitative analysis software, see Lee and Fielding (1991), Richards and Richards (1998), and Weitzman and Miles (1995).

Special Measurement Problems

Before we turn to demonstrating mixed method data collection strategies, we review a few common measurement problems that often arise in social research for both single method and multimethod projects. Of course, every measurement objective presents specific problems of its own; and because there is an infinite number of potential objectives, we are not able to address all the potential measurement problems here. Instead, we review a small number of common problems in order to illustrate the types of solutions currently available. We consider problems related to translation across languages, measurement of sensitive topics, and measurement of reports from one individual about other individuals.

Translation Across Languages

No two people are the same. Even if they share a common language, culture, and many other attributes, the same question, answer, or observation may not mean the same thing to two different people. This is a well-known problem in social science measurement, and it has formed the basis for important critiques of standardized measurement strategies (Briggs 1986; Groves et al. 2004). Even when questions are standardized, they do not necessarily produce comparable measures because the same question may mean something quite different to two different people.

When the people you study do not share the same language, this problem is even greater. Imagine asking a person who speaks only Japanese a question in English. Either the question will be completely meaningless to this Japanese speaker, or the sounds themselves will have a completely different meaning than they do to an English speaker.

Therefore, we need to translate the English question into Japanese. The more we translate, the clearer the question becomes to the person who speaks only Japanese. At the same time, the more we translate, the more the question varies from the question in English. As the question becomes more meaningful in Japanese, it also becomes less comparable to the original question.

Creating comparable measures across different languages is a truly daunting task filled with many pitfalls. Just translating questions from one language to another for use in the study of a new population creates tremendous obstacles. Keep in mind that our use of the term "language" is not limited to just foreign languages, but also refers to different uses of the same language across age, social class, race/ethnicity, or region. For example, when designing interview questions about romantic relationships for adolescents, middle-aged researchers must work to find the appropriate terminology for that age group. There are no easy solutions to language translation and meaning problems, but there are useful strategies to follow. In particular, lessons from survey methodology offer useful insights into the process of translating measures across languages.

Strategies for Translating Measures Across Languages   The field of survey methodology has learned a great deal over the past four decades about how the design of questions and questionnaires influence answers and therefore measures of concepts that are based on those answers (Groves et al. 2004; Schaeffer and Presser 2003). A thorough body of research documents how the context, order, and wording of questions and response alternatives can shape individual responses to questions (Groves et al. 2004; Sanchez 1992; Schuman and Presser 1996; Schwarz 1999; Schwarz and Sudman 1992, 1996; Tourangeau 1999; Tourangeau, Rips, and Rasinski 2000). Similarly, extensive research has shown how language differences and the differential meanings of the same words in different settings can affect the ways that respondents interpret and respond to what appears to be comparable questions (Harkness et al. 2003; Harkness and Schoua-Glusberg 1998; Schwarz 2003). Thus, efforts to translate concepts into survey measures must include careful attention to the specific details of the questions themselves.

Methodologists have also established techniques to facilitate the matching of survey questions to the concepts they are intended to measure and that they do so similarly across different societies and languages. Some of these techniques are aimed at the initial design of questions, some at assessing the external validity of the questions, and some at refining questions to ensure that they work well. Survey methodologists often use (or team up with others to use) focus groups, qualitative interviews, and ethnography to inform the initial design of questionnaire items (Axinn, Fricke, and Thornton 1991; Groves et al. 2004; Krueger and Casey 2000). Techniques for refining questions include field pretesting, respondent behavior coding, and randomized questionnaire experiments (Fowler 2004; Fowler and Cannell 1996; Groves et al. 2004; Oksenberg, Cannell, and Kalton 1991; Tourangeau 2004). Key techniques for assessing external validity of items include expert review, focus groups, cognitive interviews, field pretests, and respondent behavior coding (Fowler and Cannell 1996; Graesser et al. 1996; Groves et al. 2004; Schuman and Presser 1981; Sudman and Bradburn 1982). Also useful for ensuring comparability across cultural groups are vignette studies that examine question comprehension and comparability by asking respondents to categorize concrete situations in the language of the proposed survey questions (Martin 2004).

A process designed to translate measurements across languages will benefit from taking advantage of as many as possible of the following steps: (1) the use of an expert advisory group; (2) less structured interview and observational data collection to explore meanings and understandings; (3) designing and pretesting questionnaires or other measurement strategies; (4) conducting pilot studies; and (5) evaluating pilot data. Note that an appropriate expert advisory group for a translation process includes experts in the subject matter to be studied who are native speakers of the language to which the measures are being translated, as well as native speakers of the language from which the measures are being translated.

Measuring Sensitive Topics

Many studies aim to measure beliefs or behaviors in areas that are believed to be particularly sensitive among those who will be studied. In fact, concern over the sensitivity of certain topics has fueled a substantial subfield of methodological research on scientific integrity and the protection of human subjects (Groves et al. 2004). In addition to these concerns, however, potentially sensitive subjects introduce special measurement error problems.

The greatest methodological concern about measures of sensitive topics is that study participants may systematically underreport behavior and beliefs in sensitive areas (Groves et al. 2004; Tourangeau and Smith 1996; Tourangeau, Rips, and Rasinski 2000). Reporting on illegal behaviors is a clear example of this potential problem. Study participants are expected to underreport illegal behaviors to researchers because they are likely to fear that some type of penalty may follow. However, research on sensitive topics demonstrates that, even when the topic is not illegal, if the study participant perceives significant social prohibitions on his/her behavior or belief, underreporting is likely. Examples include racial stereotyping and abortion behaviors and beliefs. Likewise, if the participant feels the topic is of a highly private or personal nature, underreporting is likely. Examples include financial earnings and sexual behavior.

Confidentiality   Methods designed to improve the reporting of these sensitive behaviors and beliefs focus on maximizing the level of confidentiality afforded to study participants. Most studies pledge confidentiality to respondents and work extremely hard to honor that pledge. In fact, the pledge of confidentiality in some studies has legal standing that helps to protect study participants. Within the context of a specific study, researchers have devised a number of techniques to increase the level of confidentiality (Groves et al. 2004). Many of the most popular techniques involve some type of self-reporting, so that the study participant can provide a report directly to some confidential media, such as a booklet in an envelope or a computerized recording, without speaking to an interviewer. As discussed above, computer-assisted data collection techniques have revolutionized this type of self-reporting through Audio Computer-Assisted Self-Interviewing (ACASI). It is widely believed that ACASI improves reporting of potentially sensitive beliefs and behavior (Groves et al. 2004).

Note that although ACASI has tremendous potential to improve reporting of sensitive behaviors and beliefs, it does not always succeed. An important example is the case of abortion reporting. Responses to survey questions are well known to substantially underreport the incidence of abortion as compared to data compiled from abortion providers (Jones and Forrest 1992). Although it was hoped that the use of ACASI would remedy this problem, ACASI measurement produces only slightly higher reports of abortion, leaving the gap between survey reports and provider data still quite substantial (Fu et al. 1998). This example is important because it illustrates the possibility that some topics may be so sensitive that even substantial efforts to enhance confidentiality do not eliminate the underreporting problem.

The Form of Measures   For some topics, researchers attempt to reduce the sensitivity of the topic by altering the form of the question. For example, in the United States survey respondents are notoriously reluctant to provide answers to questions about income. Although most studies aim to collect precise measures of income, many now offer respondents some type of categorical alternative to disclosing their precise income. That is, if respondents refuse to answer a question about their precise income, they are offered a categorical alternative, such as "Would you say your income is less than $25,000,

$25,000–$50,000, $50,000–$100,000, or more than $100,000?" The idea here is that the categories reduce the sensitivity of the measure and make it easier for respondents to answer.

A useful alternative to this type of categorical question is a series of questions, sometimes referred to as a "fold-out," designed to measure the same information in an even somewhat less invasive way. Thus, following the categorical example provided above, when a respondent refuses to provide precise information about income, researchers might ask: "Would you say your income is greater than $50,000 or less than $50,000?" Responses to this question would then drive a second series of questions such that if the respondent replied "greater than $50,000" researchers would ask: "Would you say that your income is greater than $100,000 or less than $100,000?" If, on the other hand, the respondent replied "less than $50,000" to the initial question, in the second series researchers would ask: "Would you say that your income is greater than $25,000 or less than $25,000?" The resulting series of answers provides the same information, but under some circumstances the latter alternative may be easier for some respondents to answer.

Note that the cognitive burden of the questions is also reduced in this interlinked series of questions. In general, respondents' ability to provide complete and accurate responses depends on the cognitive difficulty of the task (Eisenhower, Mathiowetz, and Morganstein 1991; Groves et al. 2004; Sudman, Bradburn, and Schwarz 1996). The technique described here can help reduce the cognitive difficulty of reporting and increase complete, accurate responses. Reporting on the timing of events is generally considered a more cognitively demanding task than reporting on the occurrence of events (Eisenhower, Mathiowetz, and Morganstein 1991; Means et al. 1991). So these types of question series may be particularly useful when studying the timing of events. We return to this issue in Chapter 6, which is devoted to improving the quality of reporting on the timing of events.

Although questions about income are often considered sensitive in highly monetized economies like that of the United States, in agrarian settings that are not highly monetized, other financial dimensions, such as land ownership, may be sensitive. The key issue is that sensitivity of questions is likely to be highly context specific, so that substantial information about the local context of the study is often needed to design appropriate questions. For example, in Nepal the setting is characterized by a significant history of land-reform-driven land redistributions. In this context, it is extremely difficult to obtain accurate answers to questions about land ownership. On the other hand, farmers are quite comfortable answering questions about how much land they farm and how much they rent. This alternative strategy is important because it still provides a great deal of information about the farmer's overall scale of production and his relative position of ownership within that specific scale of production, even though it does not provide direct information about ownership. This example illustrates the point that each specific context may generate both sensitive questions unique to that setting and alternative avenues of measurement. Of course, such alternative measurement strategies must be tailored to the aims and the setting of the specific research project.

Social Desirability

All research involving human subjects may be affected whenever the conditions or topic of the study can potentially encourage the subject to want to present him- or herself more positively to the researcher. Social desirability, or "the tendency of people to deny socially undesirable traits or qualities and to admit socially desirable ones" (Phillips and Clancy 1972, p. 923), is a well-known threat to the measurement of behavior and attitudes in many domains (Belli et al. 1999; Bishop, Tuchfarber, and Oldendick 1986; Crowne and Marlowe 1964; Phillips and Clancy 1972; Press and Townsley 1998; Presser 1990; Rossiter and Robertson 1975; Theriault and Holmberg 1998). In fact, although studies have shown that the problem of social desirability may be present in mail-in surveys or self-reports where the interviewer is not present (Press and Townsley 1998), it is believed that the presence of the researcher or interviewer in a face-to-face interview also influences subjects to report themselves in an equally (if not considerably more) socially desirable way (Aquilino and Lo Sciuto 1990; Finkel, Guterbock, and Borg 1991; Krysan et al. 1994). In addition, social desirability is frequently considered a threat to the validity of findings when what is being measured is of a slightly controversial or sensitive nature, such as racial attitudes or premarital sexual behavior (Aquilino and Lo Sciuto 1990; Krysan 1998; MacCorquodale and DeLamater 1979).

For example, as gender role attitudes have become more egalitarian in the United States, there is growing recognition that it is socially desirable to present no gender double standard when asked about courtship choices for young men and women (Thornton and Young-DeMarco 2001). Without explicit steps designed to address the issue of social desirability in responses, research is likely to underestimate the true magnitude of the gender double standard. To address this obstacle, research designed to measure the gender double standard uses random assignment experiments that alternate asking first about men and then about women with asking first about women and then about men. This technique provides measures of the level of social desirability and can be used to account for that social desirability in estimates of the magnitude of the gender double standard (Axinn, Young-DeMarco, and Caponi 2003).

Such explicit measurement design features are needed whenever social desirability may compromise the accuracy of a measure. Again, the specific nature of social desirability is quite likely to be setting-specific. Likewise, the specific nature of the design feature that can be used to mitigate each specific form of social desirability is likely to be setting specific. The integration of multiple data collection methods can be a substantial asset in discovering these setting-specific measurement issues. We provide examples using mixed method strategies to address such measurement issues in Chapter 3.

Reports About Others

Many research projects ask individuals to provide reports about other individuals. This may occur in individual-level studies when information on multiple individuals, such as a family or a social network, is believed to be important to the behavior or beliefs of the individual being studied. It is even more likely to occur in studies with a unit of analysis that aggregates individuals, such as a family, a neighborhood, a business, or a community. In these types of studies, individuals are frequently asked to report on the behavior or beliefs of other individuals.

Asking study participants to report on the behavior or beliefs of others presents special methodological problems. Reporting quality depends on both the cognitive difficulty of the reporting task and the level of information available to the person reporting. In the case of reports on others, individuals may simply never have had the information on others needed to make such reports. This, of course, makes it unlikely that these reports will be complete or accurate. In general, problems associated with a lack of knowledge about others are likely to be more common for measures of beliefs than for measures of behaviors.

Even though there has been relatively little research on methodological issues involved in gathering reports on others, some evidence indicates that there are systematic differences in the quality of reports on others. In some situations, it appears that informants can provide very complete and accurate data regarding the behavior of others (Axinn et al. 2002). This ability depends on the relationship between informants and the persons about whom they are reporting. For example, mothers and their children generally have close, positive relationships (Rossi and Rossi, 1990; Thornton, Orbuch, and Axinn 1995), and empirical evidence demonstrates that mothers are capable of providing extremely complete and accurate reports about their children's behavior (Axinn et al. 2002). But even in this situation, the quality of mothers' reports about their children depends on the subject matter being reported. Mothers provide somewhat lower-quality reports of behaviors of which they disapprove (Axinn et al. 2002). This phenomenon is likely to characterize the quality of any informant's reports of some other person's behavior. Reporting quality is likely to be highest for subjects that the two individuals in question are highly motivated to discuss and of which the informant approves.

Research about reports on others also demonstrates that flexibility in the reporting metric offered to informants can improve the quality of reports on others (Axinn et al. 2002). Giving informants a choice of response formats for their reports on others improves the informants' ability to present the facts they know in a report. Thus, flexibility in the response alternatives offered to informants is a desirable feature in research designs aimed at using informants to provide reports about others.

Conclusion

In this chapter, we have reviewed a handful of common issues most data collections face. The research design issues we review – choice of unit of analysis, of comparison groups, of cases to study, and retrospective versus prospective designs – are common to all social science data collection aimed at studying cause and consequence. We also address a general series of issues surrounding the choice of measurement strategy that most data collections must face. These include the need for preliminary research, the advantages of matching the aggregate level of the measurements and the object of those measurements, the possibility of using abbreviated measurement strategies, and options for using computer technologies in data collection. Finally, we reviewed a few common measurement problems many studies face: translation across languages, measurement of sensitive topics, and reports on others. This list of topics is by no means exhaustive, but these issues help to set the stage for our discussion of specific mixed method data collection approaches in the chapters that follow.

Our approach to mixed method data collection focuses on the creation and implementation of new tools for measurement of the human population. The choice of data collection method, including all single method as well as mixed method alternatives, must fit the specific research aims in order to be effective. Because the potential research aims vary infinitely, we did not attempt to match aims to methods here. Instead, by discussing some of the most common issues, we hope to illuminate the choices available and the trade-offs among those choices so that individual researchers might match their aims to the data collection methods. One of the great advantages of mixed method data collection approaches is that they offer more data collection alternatives – thus, more options for making these choices. Mixing multiple methods also gives researchers opportunities to address trade-offs among choices by using the strengths of some methods to compensate for the weaknesses of others. Finally, mixing methods helps researchers create a comprehensive empirical record by integrating multiple approaches. Each of the chapters that follow details specific mixed method strategies that provide concrete examples of these themes.

3   The Micro-Demographic Community
Study Approach

In this chapter, we discuss a research model that combines multiple data collection methods simultaneously to study cause and consequence. This model, referred to as the "micro-demographic community study approach," combines survey methods, observational methods, and less structured interview methods in a dialectic manner. The method began to spread in demographic research late in the last century, and it has been used to study many different topics across a wide range of settings (Back and Stycos 1967; Bracher, Santow, and Watkins 2004; Caldwell, Hill, and Hull 1988; Kaler and Watkins 2001; Kertzer and Hogan 1989; Kohler, Behrman, and Watkins 2001; Massey et al. 1987; Rutenberg and Watkins 1997; Stycos 1955; Watkins 2000). This simultaneous combination of methods has many advantages, including (1) promoting the investigator's direct involvement at the study site, which improves data quality and enhances the researcher's grasp of the social context; (2) providing multiple types of data, adding depth to the layers of evidence available for testing hypotheses; and (3) fostering a flexibility in the research process, producing insights and possibilities one method alone could not (Axinn, Fricke, and Thornton 1991). We draw on a specific application of the micro-demographic community study approach employed to study social change and the family in Nepal to highlight concrete examples of the three main benefits we see in this method of data collection.

The specific approach described here combines a formal, structured survey operation with a complete, intensive ethnographic investigation throughout every phase of the data collection process. We believe that this fully integrated approach represents a useful model for other community studies of social change across a broad range of settings. The data generated by this type of multimethod approach retain the full advantages one might obtain from either a standard survey or a standard ethnography, while adding new capacities for quality control, discovery, triangulation, and verification.

Portions of this chapter are based on the following previously published article: Axinn, William G., Thomas E. Fricke, and Arland Thornton. 1991. "The Microdemographic Community-Study Approach: Improving Survey Data by Integrating the Ethnographic Method." *Sociological Methods and Research* 20(2): 187–217.

Tamang Family Research Project

The application we discuss comes from the Tamang Family Research Project (TFRP), a study of social change, family process, and fertility among a single ethnic group in Nepal. The data collection described here took place during 1987 and 1988 in two communities inhabited by the Tamang ethnic group.[1] The project was explicitly designed to overcome numerous obstacles to the collection of high-quality data, including some level of mistrust toward outsiders, a high level of illiteracy among the study population, and extremely low levels of transportation and communication infrastructure in the local setting. The data collection techniques employed were designed to address known issues regarding social change and the family and to be flexible enough to address other emergent issues, all the while collecting the data needed for tests of specific causal hypotheses.

Theoretical Model

This project's substantive hypotheses arose from a causal model in which family structure and relationships influence subsequent fertility behavior. At the same time, social and economic changes have dramatic influences on aspects of family life. The survey instrument design grew from our definition of the individual life course as the unit of analysis, with three culturally relevant periods of life critical to the nature of family and household relationships. In this setting, these periods are early socialization embodied in childhood and adolescence (from birth until marriage becomes acceptable), early adulthood (the period centering on marriage), and adulthood (the period of establishing independent households and building families). Each of these life periods occurs within definite contexts: village, family, and the constraints and opportunities posed by past actions in the individual life course.

Figure 3.1 presents a schematic representation of this model. It identifies the classes of important contextual and behavioral variables gathered and examined in this research. Although a dynamic perspective implies three dimensions of change (village, family, and individual) corresponding to historical, family, and individual time, we have simplified the diagram to represent features of village and family that remain fairly constant throughout the individual life course periods of primary interest.

Two Tamang Communities

Comparison of village context was a crucial design element of the research aimed at testing this model.[2] The study compared two settings: Timling, a remote settlement near the border with Tibet, and Sangila, a cluster of villages

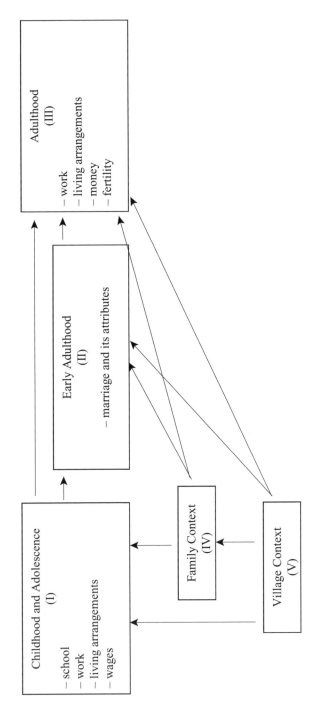

Figure 3.1. Heuristic causal model to be examined among Tamang

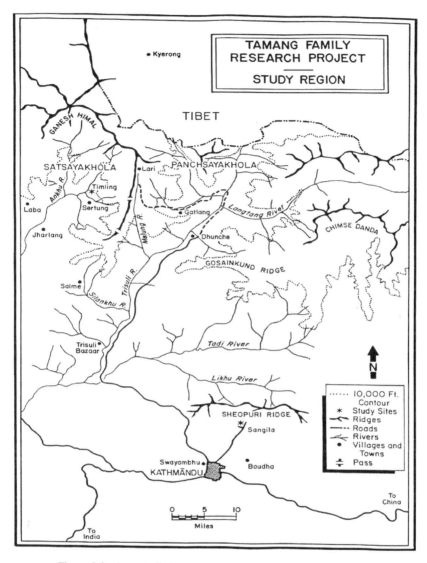

Figure 3.2. Area studied

near Kathmandu (Figure 3.2). Key differences between these settings are historical relations, proximity to Kathmandu, and the extent of educational and wage
labor opportunities. Timling was chosen as a relatively subsistence-oriented setting. Although wage earning was not entirely absent in the past, its importance
to the overall economy was extremely attenuated.

Even with changes in the wage labor participation of Timling's population, the village lies a 5- to 6-day walk from the nearest drivable road and bazaar. Timling's households rely most heavily on local production, and immersion in the wage labor market is yet incipient.

If Timling can be said to represent a subsistence setting, Sangila is representative of the monetized end of the continuum for the Tamang people. This setting consists of a cluster of villages and hamlets at the north edge of the Kathmandu Valley, near a drivable road to Kathmandu served by buses and taxis (Figure 3.3). Many households within Sangila (which extends in a 3-mile arc centering on the main paved road from the city) are minutes from the bus stop, while others are a brisk hour's walk from the road.

This setting's stable agrarian system continued more or less undisturbed from the early 19th century until 1950–1, when Nepal's borders opened to foreigners after a century and a half of closed feudal rule. Schools were built in the dispersed collection of settlements beginning in the early 1960s. An earlier temple school that taught reading for religious purposes to a very few students was converted to a public school in the mid-1950s. These earliest schools provided classes up to grade 3, but rapid expansion to keep up with the level of village students followed and four schools now provide education at various levels through grade 10.

Wage labor participation is extensive and various (Fricke and Thornton 1989). Although wage labor in Timling tends to be in the limited form of seasonal work at road construction or portering, the Sangila area provides a spectrum including government service jobs, carpentry, work in stores and various factories, and road work and hauling loads. At the same time, nearly all households continue to have some component of their domestic economy tied to farming in their village fields. As with Timling, extensive participation in the wage economy has increased within the lifetime of the oldest respondents.

Survey Instrument Design

The research team designed two types of data collection instruments they considered appropriate for trained interviewers. The first type was a household census and family genealogy that enumerated all household members and the network of kin relationships for each member, up to three previous generations. Parental and sibling information on these instruments may also be considered as family context measures.

The second type was an individual questionnaire. The theoretical orientation determined the classes of data elicited in this instrument. These domains are described in Figure 3.4, along with the theoretically motivated categories to which specific sections relate in Figure 3.1. Additional sheets triggered by

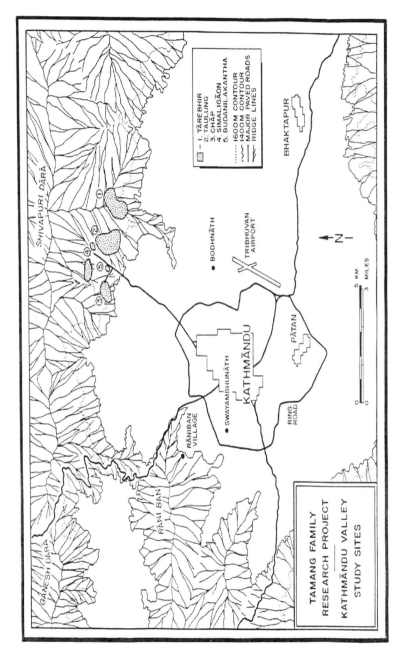

Figure 3.3. Kathmandu Valley study site

59

Section	Contents	Model Categories
A	Education: respondent's schooling; reasons for leaving; literacy	I
B	Residence: residence history outside of natal village; relationship of coresidents; ages at first events; visits to natal villages	I, II
C	Parental background: education; wage-labor employment; literacy of respondent's parents	IV
D	Marriage: timing; autonomy of decision; transactions; relationship between spouses before marriage; ceremony; residence; dissolution timing and decisions (for 1st, 2nd, and last marriages)	II, III, IV
E	Fertility and contraception: timing of births; breastfeeding; survival of children, ages at death, and education and marriage for each	III
F	Employment: formal and informal economy participation; ages at first time and first time after marriage; wage work and amounts in 12 months preceding interview	I, III
G	Inheritance: contents of and timing for men and women	III
H	Media exposure: exposure to movies, print media, and television; ages at first exposure; levels of exposure in 12 months preceding interview	I, III
I	Networks: relationship of people relied on when sick; relationship of people helped in last 12 months; mode of payment; relationships of people in informal work groups	IV
J	Household economy: crops planted; animals owned and sold in last 12 months; number of those providing help from outside of household and their relationship to household head (section asked of household head only)	IV
K	Interviewer observations: household quality and possessions	IV

Figure 3.4. Summary of primary survey instrument

appropriate responses in relevant sections gathered data on former spouses and on each child ever born alive.

Several steps were taken to ensure that interviewers using these formal instruments would gather accurate and reliable data. Most important, the investigators who designed the instruments spoke the language of the study population fluently and had lived with the study population and related communities. This issue is often taken for granted when studying one's own society, but it is crucial in a study of another society (Briggs 1986). Linguistic fluency is essential to questionnaire construction, which assumes shared interpretation by respondents and investigators. But the issue is even more complex, because the flow of questions must itself be designed to allay the respondent's natural anxiety in an unfamiliar context. These issues certainly require attention in cross-national or cross-cultural research, but they also deserve attention in studies of one's own society, particularly with regard to subpopulations with whom investigators do not have shared experience.

In the current case, the investigators' prior knowledge of the Tamang and Nepalese languages and of the Tamang communities in Nepal were essential background for designing structured survey instruments, but they were confronted with an additional problem because Tamang is an unwritten language. Although it may be roughly transcribed in the national alphabet, the dialect differences that appear from village to village together with the low probability of hiring sufficient numbers of educated Tamang-speaking interviewers led the team to formulate the instruments in Nepali, the national language. This allowed the research team to be reasonably certain that the questions elicited standard meanings across settings. A side effect of this, however, was a decision to keep questions at a largely behavioral rather than attitudinal level.

Thus, the aim was the creation of a Nepalese-language questionnaire. Individual questions were originally constructed in both English and Nepalese. Drafts of these instruments were translated from English into Nepalese by native Nepalese speakers. They were then translated back to cross-check the meaning of each question. This process was repeated over several iterations. Investigators also used previous research findings and their own knowledge of the setting to locate questions in an appropriate sequence within the questionnaire. Indeed, the sorts of questions asked were likely to find their way into trailside conversations throughout Nepal. Finally, the formal instruments were taken to Nepal and pretested in a Tamang village similar to those to be studied later. This pretest was critical in the effort to ensure that the questionnaires were linguistically appropriate to the local population. Once the pretest was completed, instruments were again revised with the input of both native Nepalese scholars and investigators. Additional steps taken during the data collection to ensure that these questions held a shared meaning for investigators and respondents are described below.

Survey Interviewer Training and Management

Interviewers were recruited in Nepal from survey research organizations, university campuses, and Tamang communities similar to those being studied. The investigators made special efforts to hire native Tamang interviewers, because some respondents in Timling were likely to require questions to be translated from Nepalese to Tamang. The team also recruited female interviewers, because many previous surveys in Nepal limited the sex of interviewers for convenience but with unknown results (Axinn 1989, 1991).

Candidates were originally screened on their reading and writing abilities. A pool of 32 were then given a 1-week intensive training course in interviewing techniques modeled after the course used at the Survey Research Center of the University of Michigan (Survey Research Center 1976). This course was followed by training in an actual field context: a Tamang village not a part of the study.[3] The best 16 of these interviewers were hired.

Interviewers and investigators lived under one roof for the entire 3-month period of data collection at the Sangila site where work commenced. The stay began with 3 more days of intensive interviewer training and continued visits by the project anthropologist to community households.[4] Ethnographic data collection began as a part of this rapport building, and the survey operation was initiated only after each household had been visited. Moreover, the first instruments administered were the least threatening census and genealogy sheets. Investigators accompanied interviewers to the field each day to supervise. While one investigator gathered ethnographic data, the other circulated through the village supervising and assisting interviewers who had problems.

Because the investigators lived with the interviewers in the field, supervision was nearly constant. Every evening, investigators read every interview completed that day. This allowed investigators to examine work for errors and omissions throughout the data collection. Responses on questionnaires were cross-checked during the ethnographic data collection for additional continuous monitoring of the interviewers' performance. Because more interviewers than necessary were hired, those who did not perform adequately could be released; during the first 3 months of data collection, four such interviewers were let go. The firing of interviewers who clearly failed to follow protocols had a considerable positive effect on the morale of interviewers who had worked hard to follow study protocols, as well as reinforcing the rules themselves. Finally, frequent training refreshers for the interviewers were easily incorporated into the daily regimen in response to issues the investigators noted while reading completed questionnaires.

After completing the data collection in Sangila, investigators and a group of the demonstrably best interviewers moved data collection to Timling, where the same procedures organized activities.

Less Structured Data Collection Techniques

In addition to the data gathered through formally structured survey instruments, the combination of fieldwork strategies allowed the investigators to gather a wealth of other material. Historical material for the villages allowed the team to establish important local watershed dates: the building of schools and roads; the availability of particular categories of work, such as participation in the British army's Gurkha regiments; and the like. In addition, extremely detailed patriline histories were gathered. These are important for the analysis of enduring relationships among clans and patrilines as well as in establishing the specific cultural and social organizational context of marital events.

Extensive informal interviews were conducted with selected informants on a range of topics related to family organization and relationships, marriage, village histories, and other relevant topics. Many of these were taped on audiocassettes in the field and produced more than one thousand pages of transcript. Of particular interest for the purposes of the TFRP, for example, are transcriptions of spontaneous informant comments on the tension surrounding household fission in the newly emergent wage labor economy and the expectations of wealth flows from children's wage labor jobs. Both of these are useful for fleshing out the cultural meaning of trends revealed by the behavioral data from the questionnaires.

Finally, case history materials were gathered that focused on specific life course and family transitions and the value context within which they occurred. Case materials existed for (1) relationships between parents and children working for wages away from the villages; (2) marriages and elopements; (3) the process of household formation and fission from parental households; (4) reactions and consequences of deaths for children and adults; and (5) the organization of work on road crews and in the markets of Kathmandu. Extensive social structural information has been collected, especially that having to do with auspicious and forbidden categories of marriage and culturally expected behavior among various categories of relatives. All of this information not only provides important context for statistical analyses but also redresses those criticisms of research on family and demographic change that suggest that too much is inferred from behavioral data alone (Kertzer 1984; Stone and Campbell 1984).

Benefits from Researchers' Involvement in the Field

Increased Knowledge of the Local Context

The advantages derived from a researcher being present and active in data collection at the field site are a by-product of the intensive local knowledge available to her or him and relate to issues of data quality and accuracy. As the investigator inevitably grows more familiar with personal and community histories, she or he is increasingly able to ask questions with concrete references and to observe behavior with knowledge of their local context. Knowledge of local context means that behavior can be placed into an expanded and meaningful frame with enhanced significance for the study as dictated by the case study method (Fricke 1990; Mitchell 1983). For example, a child gleaning potatoes from an already harvested field is not simply an unknown child of about 12 years in an unknown field. He becomes the son of a particular person, living in a family of known economic status and structure, given permission to glean potatoes in the field of a person with a particular kin or friend or landlord relationship to his family. At the least, this density of knowledge provides apt illustrations for the more general social processes determined through other means. More fruitfully, the unforeseen events of village life can provide theoretical insights and deepen the interpretation of standardized data gathered through questionnaires.

Reduction of Survey Error

A micro-demographic community study approach can also be useful in minimizing survey errors. Groves (1987) divides survey errors that affect data quality into two kinds: errors of non-observation and measurement errors. Errors of non-observation include coverage errors, non-response and sampling errors, and measurement errors include errors arising from the interviewer, the respondent, and the questionnaire. Here we use the categories of errors suggested by Groves (1987) to discuss the ways survey research can benefit from integration with an ethnographic approach.

Errors of Non-Observation   The TFRP aimed to interview every resident over age 11 in each of the two communities being studied. Because this was a study of the total population and not a study of a representative sample of the population, sampling error was not a concern.[5] Thus, coverage errors and non-response are the two possible sources of non-observation errors in this study.

The combined approach helped investigators minimize coverage errors by allowing them to live in the community and become familiar with all of its households, collect genealogical information that could be used to locate every living relative of someone residing in the village, and visit each dwelling unit repeatedly to discover unrelated residents. This depth of information generated by ethnographic techniques was used to ensure that every dwelling unit and individual residing in the community was contacted. The combined approach also minimized non-response. A number of rapport-building techniques common for ethnographic data collection were used to generate a high level of respondent cooperation. These techniques included living among the respondents, becoming involved in casual conversations revolving around the sharing of tea or snacks, taking pictures for respondents, and providing some first-aid medical assistance to respondents.

In the primary data collection effort, the TFRP obtained data for 1,520 out of 1,521 respondents identified as eligible for interview in the two settings, virtually a 100% response rate. Of the 1,521 total eligible respondents, 1,415 (93%) were interviewed in face-to-face visits. These included both residents who were present in the community and those who migrated to take temporary jobs. In both settings, the TFRP tracked such migrants, sought out their temporary residences, and interviewed them face-to-face whenever possible. There were no refusals in either setting. However, 7% of the interviews were conducted with proxy respondents because the respondent was either physically unable to participate or TFRP staff were unable to track down the respondent. Most proxy interviews were conducted with spouses or parents, if they were available, and secondarily with siblings. Because the questionnaires focused on behavioral information, these knowledgeable sources were generally able to provide adequate detail. Furthermore, for some analyses the definition of a household member included only those who regularly ate and slept at the house, so individuals who were away for extended periods were not considered among those eligible for the study.

Nonetheless, the investigators took a number of measures to reduce the percentage of proxy interviews in both settings. Where possible, interviewers attempted to visit respondents at their places of work, such as the carpet factories of the Kathmandu Valley. From Timling, interviewers traveled to road-building work camps, a 2-day walk over extremely rugged country. Where respondents were unavailable at the initial interviewer visit, interviewers were required to make callbacks at frequent intervals, at different times of the day, to meet them. These callbacks were virtually daily events. In both settings, proxies were not authorized until the final 2 weeks of data collection, when the opportunities for meeting the actual respondent were exhausted.

The effort given to meeting eligible members of the population resulted in a very high percentage of questionnaires administered to the respondents themselves. There were no large differences in the percentages of young or old and male or female respondents met in face-to-face interviews. Thus, the study obtained regular interviews with the respondents themselves for 1,103 out of 1,166 (94%) of the ever-married respondents and 312 out of 354 (88%) of the never-married respondents. Similarly, 91% of the male and 96% of the female interviews were regular interviews with respondents.

Discussions with local residents indicate that the interview experience was enjoyed by the respondents, which enhanced the data quality. In the village setting, an unpleasant encounter would be impossible to conceal, yet, far from having people avoid interviews, the TFRP team experienced respondents in both settings seeking out interviewers to have their interview taken. Part of the explanation for this is the real appreciation among residents for a study of the Tamang, a sense among the Tamang themselves that it was important to see how they lived and how they were changing. Certainly, there was a strong sense of sincerity communicated by the very fact of investigators' residence in the study areas for lengthy periods. This occasioned many approving remarks and effectively built and maintained rapport between the Tamang villagers and the researchers.

Thus, the less structured research methods employed by the TFRP helped the more structured data collection efforts to avoid errors of non-observation. This coverage of the population ensures that non-response is not a serious threat to the integrity of the study results.

Measurement Errors   Measurement errors resulting from interviewer effects can be minimized by the careful training and supervision of the interviewer staff (Couper and Groves 1992; Fowler 1991; Fowler and Mangione 1990). As described above, the TFRP took great care to train interviewers before sending them to the field. These efforts also went beyond pre–field training, and here we describe the advantages of the researchers being resident in the community while survey data collection is ongoing. The work of the interviewers was supervised constantly. Interviews were observed in progress, and all questionnaires were read by the researchers every day. Because the researchers resided with the interviewers, there was daily opportunity to comment on individual work. Periodic training sessions were scheduled during the data collection to deal with problems and keep interviewers thinking about their technique. Because the team overhired interviewers at the outset, those who did not perform acceptably could be released without hampering the data collection. Along with evaluating individual interviewer performance, the intensive interviewer supervision was used to evaluate the effects of interviewer characteristics on data quality. The results of these investigations are described in detail elsewhere (Axinn 1989, 1991), so we do not discuss them here. In sum, supervision of the data collection process allows the researcher to deal with sources of measurement error as they arise, improving the quality of data.

Prior knowledge of the study population and intensive knowledge of the local community also helped investigators reduce measurement errors arising from respondents. Questions of timing and recall provide an important example. From previous work, investigators knew that the Tamang used a special calendar based on the Tibetan system of counting cycles of 12 years, each year associated with the name of an animal. Although the system's usefulness is fully realized in the aging of respondents, the TFRP team also incorporated it into key timing questions in the questionnaire to aid respondent recall of event timings. Similarly, historical data collected using ethnographic methods could be used to estimate the timing of particularly memorable historical events. Such events could then be used by investigators or interviewers to help respondents recall the timing of particular events in their own lives.

It should also be pointed out that cross-checks of responses with respondents, their families, their neighbors, and public documents were used as a check not only on respondents but on interviewers as well. Because investigators resided in the village, discrepancies discovered after an interview could be reconciled with the respondent and corrected. A good example of this might be a marriage timing. A man might report in error that he married at a particular age. But as the data collection proceeded, investigators had the opportunity to ask his wife, his parents, his wife's parents, and others about the timing of that marriage. Discrepancies of this type could then be and were reconciled and resolved in the field.

Linguistic incomprehensibility and unfamiliarity with the structured interview situation are important sources of measurement errors arising from the questionnaire (Briggs 1986; Stone and Campbell 1984). Because the investigators spoke the local languages fluently before designing the questionnaire, some questions were written directly in one of those languages and others were easily translated. As described earlier, other steps taken to increase the comprehensibility of the questions included translations by native speakers and pretests. Ultimately, however, the aim was to ensure that respondents interpreted the questions as having the same meaning that investigators intended. Because investigators were present in the community as the survey was administered, they were able to examine responses immediately for misinterpretations. These examinations allowed investigators to make adjustments in wording or interviewers' techniques and re-administer questions to the entire population without perceptibly slowing down the study. Only a small number of such adjustments were necessary, and most of them were carried out very early in the survey, but the presence and involvement of senior study staff allowed the changes to be made during the data collection.

These have been examples of the ways in which the full integration of ethnographic and survey data collection, carried out simultaneously in the field, gave researchers unique opportunities to minimize measurement errors. Now we turn to the ways in which multiple types of data speak to each other and increase the depth of evidence available.

Benefits from Obtaining Multiple Types of Evidence

Any well-developed survey approach will, of course, construct instruments based on knowledge of the population being studied. In the TFRP case, instruments were designed from prior knowledge of one segment of the population in addition to extensive reading of comparative ethnographic material from other Tamang communities in Nepal. Similarly, surveys devised for studies that are explicitly without a community focus can include "culture-specific" question sets intended to be generally appropriate to the particular ethnic group or society being studied. Community studies introduce a new order of complexity in the range of data that can be gathered. Recent work in anthropology, for example, suggests that highly localized historical events and relationships among families may have important implications for behavior (Greenhalgh 1990; Roseberry 1989). Here we discuss the value of ethnographic knowledge for understanding the meaning of relationships between measures within community contexts. Our example comes from an analysis of historical patterns in marriage alliance in a remote setting (Fricke 1990).

Consider clan membership. By itself, it is little more than an indicator of extended family identity that would have no more place in typical analyses than a surname. A relationship between such an identifier and other measures would generally not be analytically useful and would create rather than solve a puzzle. An analyst would want to know what forces are proxied by clan identity, so using a more ethnographic approach in which the nature of clan identity can reveal itself is most beneficial. In the remote TFRP setting of Timling, extensive informal discussions with members of the community revealed that clan membership was an important component of village political history. Moreover, the reasons for these relationships had to do with the particular past of this village and were not generalizable to the Kathmandu setting. The collection of historical details from the recent past as well as legends of village settlement were combined with an understanding of the structure of marriage alliance among the Tamang to develop hypotheses about the relationship between clan and the form of a daughter's first marriage.

Table 3.1 shows that membership in a particular clan was powerfully related to the form of alliance entered into or renewed by a daughter's first marriage.[6] Moreover, clan is shown to be more than a proxy for differential wealth because, in this setting, land is the single most important indicator of wealth (Fricke 1986), and a measure for such differences between families is included in the model. The understanding of specific clan political histories allows clan to be incorporated into the model, resulting in an additional 6% of explained variance. Not only were we able to test specific hypotheses related to very specific community political relationships and marriage as a result of findings from our ethnographic research, but we have been alerted to an important control to be inserted into subsequent survey analyses with data from this setting.

Survey analyses alone would not have brought to light the significance of these context-dependent relationships. Further, the finding of these relationships in Timling caused the investigators to explore the data from the other TFRP setting for similar relationships that may have resulted from such political family histories. Ethnographic work in that area suggested that none would be found because dominant families had long since lost their political control of the area and no such relationships were found in the data.

This is just one example of how findings from analysis of the data obtained from less structured methods led to increased predictive power of survey data models. The result is a richer theoretical discussion of the processes as well as empirical evidence supporting the ideas. These layers of evidence tell a stronger story than one method alone could.

Table 3.1. *Multiple classifications of proportion of women in reciprocal alliance marriage by background characteristics*

Characteristic	(N)	Unadjusted mean	Adjusted mean[a]	Adjusted mean[b]
Wife's birth order				
First	(30)	.27	.34	.35
Later	(82)	.48	.45	.45
(Eta^2)		(.04)	(.01)	(.01)
Marital decision making for wife				
Mostly seniors	(53)	.60	.62	.62
Jointly	(15)	.27	.24	.27
Mostly wife	(44)	.25	.24	.23
(Eta^2)		(.12)	(.14)	(.14)
Affinal kin geographic proximity				
In Timling	(78)	.47	.49	.50
Outside Timling	(34)	.29	.25	.24
(Eta^2)		(.03)	(.05)	(.06)
Premarital land holdings				
Equal/husband more	(72)	.47	.50	.49
Wife family more	(40)	.33	.28	.30
(Eta^2)		(.02)	(.04)	(.03)
Wife's clan				
Tamang	(60)	.53	—	.53
Ghale	(52)	.29	—	.29
(Eta^2)			—	(.06)
Grand mean			.42	.42
Total cases	(112)			
R^2			.22	.28

[a] Adjusted for effects of all variables except wife's clan.
[b] Adjusted for effects of all variables including wife's clan.

Benefits from Incorporating Flexibility in the Process

Earlier, we described the types of less structured data collection methods that the TFRP used, including historical materials, informal interviews, and case studies. These data provided information on issues that were not represented in the main questionnaire. This included information on events or activities that investigators were unaware of at the time the questionnaire was designed, but about which they ideally would have liked questions to be asked of every member of the study population. When such information was discovered via ethnographic methods during fieldwork, it was then possible for the TFRP to obtain measures using supplementary procedures. This is a key way in which the flexible nature of using multiple methods to inform one another leads to richer results. One example of this reflexive process from the TFRP was the discovery of a unit of social organization, called *memekhor*, specific to the local area of the Kathmandu setting and historically important to the definition of eligible marriage partners. Because marriage was a focal subject in the TFRP study, it was essential to know the *memekhor* of each married member of the study population, even though the instruments included no reference to this unit of organization because it was discovered after investigators were already in the field. However, the strategy of living in the community for an extended period made it possible to gather this material in an additional one-page questionnaire that was developed to gather information on other aspects of the marriage process specific to this setting. Thus, potentially important information discovered as a result of the residence of primary investigators in the community was not missed.

Another important example of how the reflexive interchange between methods improved the research process was the discovery, through observations and unstructured interviews, of a development project that operated in parts of the Sangila research site. The project, called the Small Farmers Development Program (SFDP), is active in many parts of Nepal, but its activities are highly localized. The SFDP provides production credit to poor farmers in part of the Sangila community. The project also carries out a number of other activities likely to affect fertility behavior, particularly contraceptive use (Axinn 1992). Because fertility behavior was one focus of the TFRP, the questionnaire was designed to measure important factors linked to fertility. Yet the questionnaire did not contain measures of participation in the SFDP. It was only discovered through informal ethnographic interviews conducted in the field.

Moreover, membership in the SFDP is also related to other key factors that were measured in the questionnaire and that were predicted to affect fertility behavior. For example, women whose husbands were involved in non-family wage work were expected to be more likely to contracept than other women. But wage work considerably reduces the chances of participating in the SFDP because one requirement for membership is that the household's income comes from farming. So, theory predicts a positive effect of SFDP membership on contraceptive use, a positive effect of wage work on contraceptive use, and a negative effect of wage work on SFDP membership. Thus, tests estimating the effects of wage work, which was measured, on contraceptive use would be biased by excluding SFDP membership, which was not measured.

The discovery of SFDP activities in the area, while data collection was in the field, gave investigators an opportunity to collect records of residents' participation in this program. These records were linked to data collected with questionnaires and provided the means to test hypotheses concerning contraceptive use without omitting a critical measure and mis-specifying the model.

Below are estimates testing the effects of husbands' wage work on contraceptive use, with and without SFDP membership in the model, to demonstrate the

Table 3.2. *Logistic regression estimates of the effects of husbands' non-family work experiences on couples' contraceptive use: asked of currently married women ages 35 to 44*

	Excluding information on the SFDP	Including information on the SFDP
Husband had a non-family work experience before his first marriage	.98	1.32*
Household participated in the Small Farmers Development Program (SFDP)		1.83*
Controls		
Interviewer was female	.80	.99
Household was located outside project site	−1.97*	−1.38*
Years in the married state	−.01	.02
Age at marriage	−.08	−.03
Chi-square	9.79	14.92*
(d.f.)	(5)	(6)
N	59	59

*p < .05, one-tailed.

effects of omitting this variable. For this purpose, we borrow models of contraceptive use from Axinn (1991, 1992), where a more detailed description of the measures used can be found. The dependent variable is a dichotomy: coded 1 if a woman has ever done anything to avoid or delay becoming pregnant and 0 if not. Because the variable is dichotomous, logistic regression procedures were used to estimate the multivariate models (Kmenta 1986; Morgan and Teachman 1988). Husbands' non-family wage work is also measured with a dichotomy: coded 1 if they ever had this experience before marriage and 0 if not. Whether or not the household participated in the SFDP was measured by a dichotomy: coded 1 if the household had participated in the SFDP. Finally, the multivariate models of contraceptive use contain four important control variables. They are a dichotomy coded 1 if the interviewer was female, a dichotomy coded 1 if the household was located outside the SFDP project site, a continuous measure of the number of years women had lived as a married person, and a continuous measure of women's age at marriage in years.

Logistic regression estimates of these multivariate models are displayed in Table 3.2. The first model estimates the effect of husbands' non-family wage work experiences on subsequent contraceptive use without including participation in the SFDP. In this model, wage work does have a positive effect on contraceptive use, but this effect is not statistically significant. Indeed, the overall model chi-square also fails the significance test; the results from tests of this model thus provide only weak support for the hypothesis predicting a positive effect of wage work on contraceptive use.

When information on the SFDP is included in the model, however, the picture changes dramatically. The second model in Table 3.2 estimates the effect of wage work controlling for SFDP participation. Here the effect of wage work on contraceptive use is positive, larger than before, and statistically significant. As expected, the effect of participation in the SFDP is also positive and statistically significant. In fact, in this model the overall chi-square statistic is also statistically significant. Thus, omitting information on SFDP membership leads to a downward bias of the estimate of the effect of wage work. This downward bias might lead researchers to conclude that wage work has no significant effect on contraceptive use, but models including SFDP membership would lead researchers to conclude the opposite.

Clearly, information on the SFDP, discovered during ethnographic data collection in the field, was critical to the task of evaluating the effect of wage work on contraceptive use with survey data. A standard survey, with questionnaires completely determined before beginning the fieldwork, would not have measured this experience. Such an oversight would have left researchers with no alternative but to use what data were available to construct mis-specified models. Tests of such mis-specified models might easily result in researchers drawing incorrect conclusions with regard to a number of hypotheses. Instead, a combined ethnographic and survey approach helps researchers discover and incorporate information that standard surveys may miss. This flexibility and exchange between methods allows for a degree of theoretical and analytical model refinement often unattainable when only one method of data collection is engaged and there are no opportunities to reenter the field and recover missing information.

This SFDP example also illustrates the ways this mixed method approach can advance causal reasoning about a process by discovering new causal mechanisms. Unstructured interviews and direct observations led researchers to believe that participation in the SFDP was likely to influence contraceptive use (see also Axinn 1992 and Barber et al. 2002 on this substantive issue). By adding standardized measurement of participation to the data collection and linking this measurement to the more highly structured survey data, researchers were able to demonstrate that associations across a large population were consistent with this mechanism. Thus, simultaneous application of mixed methods fueled identification of potential causal mechanisms and an initial verification of the plausibility of those mechanisms.

Conclusion

The crucial features of the approach described are the simultaneous use of rigorous survey and ethnographic methods, integrated in the field throughout the data collection. This approach goes beyond other attempts to combine structured and open-ended data collection techniques. For example, some approaches focus on survey data collection and seek to supplement survey data with textual information gathered using other methods. But a full-fledged ethnographic data collection is aimed at a holistic understanding of the social, cultural, and historical context within which individuals act. As discussed above, this holistic aim allowed investigators to both gather information they had not foreseen and interpret context-specific relationships in the data.

Likewise, approaches designed more explicitly to collect open-ended data often add surveys to check the extent of specific behaviors or opinions only after they have been discovered in the field. Such an approach robs the survey of important aspects of its contribution to the data collection. One aspect is the structured questionnaire, with standardized questions designed before the fieldwork specifically to measure theoretically critical variables. This type of instrument can be used by interviewers trained to read the questions with a standardized technique to gather data from a complete population or a fully representative sample of that population. Such a thorough survey approach provides the standardized data needed to specify and test complex causal models using statistical tools. As mentioned earlier, such tests provide the means of evaluating the theoretical questions a specific data collection is designed to answer.

Finally, it is the integration of this intensive ethnographic data gathering and high-quality survey data collection that provides the methodological innovation advocated here. Integration at every phase of the data collection process requires investigators to have strong ethnographic knowledge of the study population before designing the survey instruments. Investigators must be in the field gathering ethnographic data on individuals and the local context throughout the survey's field period. Also, investigators need to supervise the interviewers, read the questionnaires as they are completed, collect redundant information ethnographically, and be prepared to alter either the survey or the ethnographic questioning depending on what they learn from the other source. The examples provided above are intended to illustrate the many ways this integration can enhance the quality of the final data set. The combined approach can reduce non-sampling errors from common sources, such as non-observation, non-response, and measurement errors arising from the interviewer, the respondent, or the questionnaire. It also provides a way of collecting contextual information that can be employed to better specify our individual-level hypothesis tests. Last, and perhaps most important, the integrated approach can allow for the discovery and collection of data on issues or events the investigators were unaware of at the time they designed the survey element of the study.

Thus, an integration of ethnographic and survey techniques must not be an excuse for doing less than a complete job with each of the components. Much of the mutually reinforcing benefit is only possible when both methods are treated rigorously. The survey questionnaire must be designed carefully, interviewers need to be thoroughly trained and meticulously supervised, and the study population, or sample of that population, should be chosen scientifically. The extensive coverage of the population of interest and the comparability of questions are two important strengths that the survey adds to the ethnography. Likewise, the ethnographer needs to have an intensive exposure to the group to be studied before the study begins. In cross-national research, this exposure may need to include learning a new language and becoming familiar with a foreign culture.

This investment is not trivial. Together, the investigators had several years' experience working with rural Nepalese before embarking on the study described here. Such a large investment of time may not always be necessary, but separate field experience with the group to be studied, before the study, certainly contributes to the successful merger of the two approaches. During the field phase, the ethnographer must reside in the community being studied, participate in local activities over an extended period, and collect information using a variety of unstandardized techniques. This intensive knowledge and the unstructured approach are two important strengths that the ethnography adds to the survey. Thus, we argue that the benefits of this multimethod strategy are only fully realized when rigorous survey and ethnographic techniques are applied simultaneously and integrated at every phase of the data collection process.

Furthermore, many of the benefits arising from the method we describe result from its application to a finite population, small enough for the simultaneous survey and ethnographic work to constantly rub up against one another. It is the contact between the two approaches that allows the strengths of each to compensate for the weaknesses of the other. So, although studies might undertake to sample a number of communities, we advocate applying this simultaneous mixture of survey and ethnography one community at a time.

We wish to emphasize that the micro-demographic community study data collection strategy is not intended as a replacement for national-level sample surveys. Rather, the combined survey and ethnographic approach is a potentially useful supplement to national-level data collections. The methods described here involve a high level of investment by investigators just to collect data on one community. The level of investment needed for a national data collection of this type could easily be prohibitive. For some research problems, such as estimating national levels of some behavior or opinion, the combined ethnographic and survey approach may be less appropriate than national sample surveys. However, research problems that require context-specific measures and community-level information in order to test specific theories or hypotheses may well benefit from using the approach we described here.

Finally, a fully integrated combination of survey and ethnographic methods, what we call the micro-demographic community study approach, may be a useful data collection tool in a variety of settings. The examples we provided point toward its utility in cross-cultural studies. However, the heightened quality control, collection of both individual and contextual information, measurement of factors unforeseen at the study's onset, and insight into the meaning of measures that this method can generate are assets in any setting. Below, we offer suggestions for issues faced in applications of this approach to other settings and topics.

Issues of Application

Perhaps the most common issue identified in the simultaneous use of multiple methods is that the use of different methods heightens the opportunity to create conflicting results. Although the discovery of congruent results using quite different data collection methods can strengthen the investigators' conviction in those results, often, of course, different methods will produce different results. We argue that this conflict among empirical results, and therefore the theoretical framework guiding data collection, is the essence of the scientific process these methods are aimed to achieve. When multiple methods each produce results consistent with a theoretical framework or hypotheses, it may increase confidence in that element of theory, but it certainly does not produce new theoretical insights. By contrast, when we arrive at conflicting empirical results, we are forced to carefully re-examine either our methods, our theory, or both. In this sense, mixed method approaches are designed to create conflicting empirical results and therefore stimulate continuous research progress. This design encourages discovery and innovation and makes the documentation of consistent results all the more remarkable. Redundancy of results is an aim of the mixed methods approach, but conflicting empirical results are a likely part of the process.

Obviously, most micro-demographic community studies like the Tamang Family Research Project are intensive, multi-investigator endeavors that require many resources. If one is planning a smaller-scale study or a dissertation, this model may not be feasible. However, there are key features that can be adapted for smaller-scale projects. For example, in conducting either a community- or institution-based study, using a mix of more and less structured data collection methods has benefits. This mix facilitates both a standardized data record of the members of the community/institution and the richer detailed records that emerge from less structured data collection. This combination of information can provide insight into both the context you are studying and the meanings study participants convey regarding the concepts you hope to measure.

Nevertheless, we highly recommend either composing or joining a collaborative team to conduct such a study. Having collaborators who bring their own perspectives and skills provides another useful set of contrasts to the research process. Some balk at collaboration because collaborators may arrive at different interpretations from the same sets of data, creating disagreements and potentially conflict. However, just as we recommend multiple data collection methods to avoid replicating bias, the involvement of multiple researchers can also help the study team avoid replicating individual bias in the interpretation of empirical results.

Multidisciplinary teams can provide especially fruitful collaborations. In these types of mixed method projects, having strong specialists in all design, data collection, analytical, and substantive domains involved in the project will help ensure high quality in every phase. A mixed method research project is only as strong as its weakest part. Of course, the challenge to a multidisciplinary team approach is that team members often have different standards, languages, or strategies for dealing with the issues at hand. Multidisciplinary team members must work harder than other teams to communicate and resolve disagreements or misunderstandings. Nevertheless, the payoffs from this variation in perspective are likely to outweigh the costs.

Both the setting and subject matter of the study will shape any particular application of the micro-demographic community study approach. In rural Nepal, family life is organized within small rural villages, and these communities provide an important structure to social relationships. Given the aims of this study, focused on family formation processes in this setting, rural village communities provided an ideal application of the micro-demographic community study approach. The same approach might not prove to be useful for the study of family formation in another setting, like the United States, in which family relationships may be spread over much greater geographic distances. However, the same intensive combination of data collection methods could be applied to many other topics in a wide range of settings. For example, a study of organizational interaction might harness these intensive methods within the context of a single business. This approach may be productive even in a context where most daily activities and social interactions are not limited to a confined geographical space, if the particular relationships under study are concentrated in a single place. Many other examples are possible. The key to successful application of this approach is achieving substantial overlap among the subjects being studied across multiple data collection methods.

This overlap can be more difficult to achieve in applications attempting to scale the method up to reach a larger study population. The technique has been used successfully in comparative studies of a small number of communities (Caldwell, Hill, and Hull 1988; Morgan and Niraula 1995; Niraula and Morgan 1996a, 1996b). Scaling the method up to a large number of communities is likely to reduce the synergies of a single-community study. Nevertheless, efforts to collect highly structured interview measures simultaneously with unstructured interviews and direct observations at a large scale are becoming more common in the social sciences. There are several examples. By the beginning of the 21st century, these examples include some of the most influential studies of specific substantive areas. The Fragile Families study of poverty and family formation is one example (Carlson, McLanahan, and England 2004; Garfinkel and McLanahan 2003; Harknett and McLanahan 2004; McLanahan forthcoming). Another example is the project Welfare, Children, and Families: A Three-City Study, a study of family and child well-being in low-income settings (Burton et al. 2001; Burton, Hurt, and Avenilla 2002; Cherlin et al. 2004; Cherlin, Fomby, and Moffit 2002). A third example is the National Study of Youth and Religion (Denton 2003; Smith 2003). Undoubtedly, increasing scale produces important trade-offs in the level of synergy across simultaneously conducted mixed methods. However, these studies illustrate that the important advantages of integrated mixed method data collection can be realized on a larger scale.

Scaling up mixed method data collection raises many interesting issues regarding exactly how multiple methods are to be integrated with each other. In the single-community study described in this chapter, investigators could conduct unstructured interviews and direct observations by day and read the results of structured survey interviews by night. At a large scale, such daily integration is difficult to implement. In the following chapter, we will discuss techniques useful for scaling up the application of mixed method data collection: statistical analyses of survey results for the systematic selection of unstructured interview informants. We then return to the general issue of scale in the final chapter of this book.

Illustrations of Principles

The micro-demographic community study approach provides a nice illustration of the mixed method data collection principles identified in Chapter 1. The illustration includes both principles closely tied to the theme of using strengths of some methods to counterbalance weaknesses of other methods and principles closely tied to the theme of comprehensive empirical documentation. The micro-demographic community study approach uses highly structured surveys in simultaneous combination with less structured interviewing and direct observation – combining methods to counterbalance strengths and weaknesses. Through this counterbalancing, the method also provides greater flexibility, allowing the measures to adapt to the local setting and change midstream to document key beliefs or behaviors discovered through the data collection process. The counterbalancing elements of this approach also encourage a high level of investigator involvement with the study population – as discussed above, a factor most likely to be successful when applied one community at a time.

The micro-demographic community study approach clearly has the capability to provide extremely comprehensive empirical documentation. Although the level of temporal order measured using this technique is a function of the specific instruments and protocols designed for each individual application, the simultaneous multiple methods provide high variation in potential sources of measurement bias. By combining quite different measurement strategies simultaneously, investigators can gather redundant measures to check results from data collected in different ways. This comprehensive measurement also provides substantial opportunities to document mechanisms that may be responsible for producing causal relationships. As in the example of the Small Farmers' Development Program (SFDP), unstructured methods can be used to discover and identify causal mechanisms and corresponding structured surveys can be used to test for the overall association expected to result from those mechanisms. The use of both strategies at the same time, in the same setting, to study the same topic facilitates this discovery and documentation process.

4   Systematic Anomalous Case Analysis

Like the previous chapter, this chapter describes a specific application of mixed method research. This application is less an overall project model and more a piece of the research project in which existing data facilitate a fieldwork project that produces findings with the potential for informing further survey analyses and data collections. It is a focused description of the back and forth between more structured and less structured research methods that can develop progress toward understanding certain social processes further than one method alone might achieve (Sieber 1973). This chapter also differs from the first in that it could more realistically be applied to other questions and settings by one researcher on a smaller scale than the previous chapter's example. However, having existing survey data to use and permission to recontact respondents is necessary, and these issues are addressed at the end of this chapter.

The approach we present here is rooted in ideas about the social scientific process that have been around for some time. Kendall and Wolf (1949) suggest: "Through careful analysis of the cases that do not exhibit the expected behavior, the researcher recognizes the oversimplification of his or her theoretical structure and becomes aware of the need for incorporating further variables into the predictive scheme" (pp. 153–4). Commenting on this, Sieber (1973) writes: "But often the researcher does not have in hand the additional information necessary for measuring the further variables. Since it is extremely rare for a survey researcher to reenter the field for intensive interviewing after the completion of a survey, the needed information is almost never collected." Examination of anomalous cases often leads to refinements of social theories and measurement strategies (Kendall and Wolf 1949; Lazarsfeld and Rosenberg 1949–50). The approach of studying anomalous cases has been called *deviant case analysis*. The majority of studies employing the logic of deviant case analysis to improve theories are of an intensive nature, focusing on one or two individuals, groups, organizations, and/or countries. In this chapter, we suggest new applications of

Portions of this chapter are based on the following previously published article: Pearce, Lisa D. 2002. "Integrating Survey and Ethnographic Methods for Systematic Anomalous Case Analysis." *Sociological Methodology* 32(1): 103–132.

deviant case analysis that can be developed by combining survey data analysis and purposive sampling strategies with less structured methods to identify and study anomalous cases.

Our approach uses information available from regression diagnostic techniques employed during initial survey analyses to identify anomalous cases. These cases are then sampled and studied with intensive, unstructured methods. Our methods of identifying anomalous cases from representative survey data provide a unique way for researchers to pinpoint subgroups of a population that are difficult to locate. The rich information provided by in-depth analysis of these anomalous cases adds a new layer of evidence to the research process and therefore an enhanced understanding unlikely to be achieved by standard survey research methods alone. This is not to say that other approaches to studying deviant cases or to combining survey and less structured methods are flawed. Instead, this chapter is meant to inspire new methodological possibilities that can widen the range of options for studying social dynamics, especially by mixing methods.

The procedures discussed here are illustrated with a study of fertility preferences in Nepal, but the approach itself can be tailored to fit many substantive research interests. Although the study described in this chapter ultimately uses insights from semi-structured interviews to modify survey measures and models, other situations may call for different less structured methods to be used. Likewise, alternative applications of this approach may focus on the ethnographic analysis itself, using information from surveys to enrich that analysis. So, although we describe only one specific application of this combined approach in detail, the basic elements of the approach we describe here can be modified and applied to a wide range of research problems.

Below, we first briefly describe the background for the specific research project discussed throughout the chapter. Second, we explain the mechanics and benefits of systematically sampling anomalous cases from survey data analyses for further investigation. Third, we describe the types of less structured methods used. Fourth, we illustrate three types of useful insights that can be drawn from this manner of studying anomalous cases. We show how findings from the less structured data collection and analysis can help revise theory, suggest new measurement strategies for subsequent survey analyses, and reveal sources of measurement error. Finally, we conclude with suggestions for how this approach can be applied to new topics in a wide variety of settings.

A Study of Religion and Family Size Preferences in Nepal

The research discussed in this chapter examines the influence of religion and other factors on family size preferences in Nepal. The beginning theoretical framework for this investigation integrated sociological developments in the conceptualization of religious influence, findings from previous studies in other settings on religion's relationship to fertility behavior, and prior fieldwork in this setting designed to better understand religious influence in Nepal. The Chitwan Valley Family Study (CVFS) survey data provided an excellent source with which to test the hypotheses derived from the theoretical framework, but one round of analysis can never be taken as the final word on a topic. Thus, we sought to identify a systematic way to infuse the process with less structured data collection and exploration to offer new ideas and richer details about suspected processes.

The basic sequence of methods in this approach is as follows. First, multivariate models of factors affecting family size preferences were designed and tested using survey data. Second, regression diagnostic tests of these models were used to identify a list of statistical outliers as potential informants. From this list, 28 informants were selected using systematic sampling techniques. Next, semi-structured interviews and observations were carried out with these informants. Insights gained from the interviews and observations were then used to recode survey data and to suggest additional predictors in multivariate survey analyses.

The survey data used in the survey analyses described here are from the 1996 Chitwan Valley Family Study. These data come from a survey administered to a probability sample of 5,271 men and women between the ages of 15 and 59 living in the Chitwan Valley of south central Nepal. The survey collected data on current attitudes and preferences as well as past experiences and behaviors regarding a variety of demographic and social processes.

For the study here, we focus on two groups among the CVFS survey respondents: a *pre–family formation group* of unmarried men and women, aged 16–25 years ($n = 959$), and a *completed fertility group* of married men and women, aged 45–59 years, who had at least one child ($n = 864$). For each group, we specified a preliminary model to predict family size preferences.

The dependent variable for both preliminary models was a scale created from a set of questions designed by Lolagene Coombs (1974) to ascertain ideal family size. The first item in the Coombs Scale measure was as follows: "People often do not have exactly the same number of children they want to have. If you could have exactly the number of children you want, how many children would you want to have?" Using this ideal number as a basis, subsequent questions attempted to further delineate preferences. The second item asks: "If you could not have exactly [the number the respondent gave] children, would you want to have [one number lower] or [one number higher]?" The answer to the second question was then used in a third question: "If you could not have [the second-choice number] of children, would you want to have [one number lower] or [one number higher]?" Figure 4.1 displays the options a respondent has when answering the Coombs Scale questions. Depending on the path a respondent followed in answering these questions, the responses were coded as somewhere between 1, representing the lowest underlying ideal family size

82

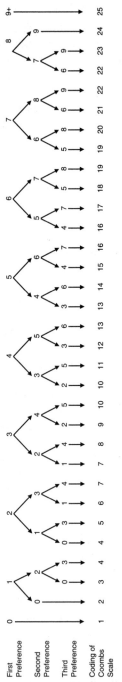

Figure 4.1. Response alternatives and coding scheme for Coombs Scale family size preference measure

preference, and 25, representing the highest underlying family size preference. Treating the Coombs Scale as an interval level measure, ordinary least squares (OLS) regression models were designed to predict Coombs Scale scores for each of these two groups.

For the pre–family formation group, the initial model includes religio-ethnic identity, the importance of religion, gender, age, number of siblings, parents' ability to read, education, media exposure, travel to the capital city or another country, expectance of an inheritance, and the hours from the home to the nearest urban area. The estimates from this model are displayed in the first column of Table 4.1.

The preliminary model used to predict family size preferences among the completed fertility group of CVFS respondents is displayed in the second column of Table 4.1. The predictors used in this model are similar to those used in the model for younger, unmarried respondents, except that age at marriage and number of children ever born to the respondent are included as control variables.

In developing these preliminary models, a variety of models were tested to arrive at one that best explained the relationship between religion and child-bearing preferences for each group. This process began with simple models and then moved on to model the influence of religion as a combination of one's religio-ethnic identity and the importance of religion in one's life. In the end, two dummy variables were created for each of the five religio-ethnic groups in these models, one representing those in each group that felt religion was very important and a second for those who placed little or no importance on religion. The reference category in this model is high caste Hindus, who find religion very important. The other variables in the models are controls selected on the basis of theories of fertility preferences and results of previous research. The adjusted R^2 is .09 for the pre–family formation group model and .12 for the completed fertility group model. Because the focus of this chapter is not on these substantive results, they are not discussed in detail here. The focus is instead given to how this multimethod approach for studying childbearing preferences was conducted.

Systematic Sampling of Anomalous Cases

Researchers wanting to reliably generalize findings from any type of study to a larger population must achieve a representative sample of that population (Kish 1965). For many ethnographic studies, a representative sample is not the goal, and other types of sampling procedures are useful (Babbie 2004; Strauss and Corbin 1990). However, when the ability to safely generalize about the anomalous cases in a study is desirable, we advocate systematic selection of a sample of these deviant cases using regression diagnostic tests from survey data analyses to provide a sampling frame. Information available from the data and

Table 4.1. *Preliminary OLS estimates from models of family size preferences among two subsamples of the Chitwan Valley Family Study*

Religio-ethnic group by importance of religion[a]		Coombs Family Size Preference Scale	
		Pre–family formation group (unmarried, ages 15–29)	Completed fertility group (married, ages 45–59)
High Caste Hindu	Finds religion unimportant (0,1)	−.20 (1.22)[b]	−.26 (.65)
Low Caste Hindu	Finds religion important (0,1)	−.74* (2.18)	−.34 (.93)
	Finds religion unimportant (0,1)	−.75** (2.42)	−.76 (1.29)
Hill Tibeto-Burmese	Finds religion important (0,1)	−.56* (2.18)	−.22 (.70)
	Finds religion unimportant (0,1)	−.20 (.88)	.39 (.72)
Newar	Finds religion important (0,1)	.17 (.45)	.49 (1.09)
	Finds religion unimportant (0,1)	−.14 (.50)	−.35 (.41)
Terai Tibeto-Burmese	Finds religion important (0,1)	.22 (.86)	1.18*** (3.22)
	Finds religion unimportant (0,1)	.19 (.75)	2.61*** (4.97)
Controls			
Gender (1 = female)		−.59*** (4.68)	.03 (.11)
Respondent's age		−.05* (1.98)	.05* (2.07)
Number of mother's children		.06* (1.93)	.05 (1.46)
Mother and/or father could read (1 = yes, 0 = no)		−.04 (.38)	−.45* (1.90)
Education (highest grade completed)		−.11*** (4.80)	.01 (.27)
Age at marriage			.03 (1.21)
Number of respondent's children ever born			.16*** (3.49)
Newspaper and radio exposure scale		−.19* (2.28)	−.33* (1.92)
Travel to Kathmandu or to other country (1 = yes, 0 = no)		−.19 (1.48)	−.22 (1.01)
Expecting inheritance from parents (1 = yes, 0 = no)		.00 (.01)	−.43* (1.86)
Travel time to Narayanghat		−.05 (.78)	.22* (1.86)
Intercept		8.05	3.61
Adj R-squared		.09	.12
N		959	864

[a] Reference group is high caste Hindus who find religion important.

[b] T-ratios in parentheses.

*p < .05, **p < .01, ***p < .001 for one-tailed t-tests.

diagnostic tests of its analysis can help identify subgroups of the population that are of great interest and that are otherwise difficult to locate.

The aim of this project was to gain a deeper understanding of the relationship between religion and childbearing preferences by identifying cases that were incorrectly predicted and studying these cases in depth to look for limitations in theory, measures, and methods. Although data analysts may view statistical outliers as dubious in value and may even exclude them from their analyses, we show here that outlier respondents may offer information that can help researchers improve preliminary models and increase their scope of applicability. Therefore, for this study a set of informants drawn from CVFS survey respondent outliers was systematically selected, interviewed, and observed with the intent of uncovering new factors linked to religion and family size preferences in this region.

For all CVFS respondents in both the pre–family formation and completed fertility groups, we computed residual values, or the difference between the Coombs Scale score predicted by the preliminary model and their actual answers to the survey questions. The residual value distributions for both models were graphed. Figure 4.2 displays the distribution of residual values for the pre–family formation group.

We were particularly interested in learning more about respondents in both groups who desired more children than the preliminary statistical model predicted. Therefore, respondents from the right tail of the residual distribution were selected for further study. For both groups, respondents whose residual values were approximately 2 or more standard deviations to the right of the mean residual, 0, were identified as outliers. Among the pre–family formation group, the outliers consisted of 31 respondents with residual values of +3 or higher, or those who scored at least 3 points higher on the Coombs Scale than the statistical model predicted. Among the completed fertility group, the outliers consisted of 31 respondents with residual values of +6 or higher.

To generate systematic samples from each of the preliminary regression models, each group of outliers was categorized by gender. The outliers were then listed in order of the magnitude of their residual value. Seven men and seven women were then selected from each of the two groups. These 28 informants served as the sample of ethnographic informants used to learn more about religion and childbearing preferences from the perspective of model outliers.

In addition to providing a sampling frame, another way that survey data can be a useful tool for beginning less structured fieldwork is by providing a source of valuable information about informants. This can help in preparing for interviews by suggesting important topics to discuss, making it easier to physically locate informants, and providing a pre-established rapport with the informants. For example, before meeting informants we examined and made notes about their completed questionnaires and life history calendars from the

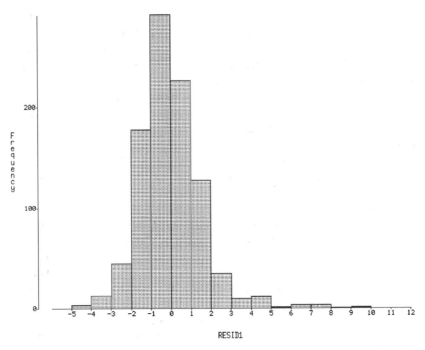

Figure 4.2. SAS graph displaying the distribution of residual values for Coombs Scale measure of family size preference among pre–family formation group (ages 15–29)

1996 CVFS survey. Although spending time with informants and members of their social world is vital to understanding the dynamics of their lives and certainly influences the direction and shape of the interview, the availability of biographical information before an interview allows for useful preparation. A life history calendar, for instance, reveals such past events as moves, parental separations, or periods of school dropout that can be explored in greater detail during an interview.

The maps and records kept by the survey project staff made locating respondents relatively easy. Also, the selected informants were familiar with the staff interviewers who accompanied us to the field and served as interviewing assistants. Because a good rapport had been established with the informants during previous CVFS data collection projects, the informants were more open and at ease during the semi-structured interviews. We also worked at continuing to build rapport by respecting and working around our participants' busy lives to schedule the visits and interviews, by describing the aim of our study, and by answering any questions they had. For this type of integrated mixed method design, it is important that all phases of a project, whether using surveys or other methods, follow the highest standards and build strong rapport with respondents/informants.

Implementing Less Structured Methods

Once the anomalous cases are sampled, the less structured data collection begins. This provides cases who have not been predicted correctly an opportunity to speak back to the process and suggest improvements in theory, measures, and methods (Horst 1955). A variety of intensive methods – such as participant observation, unstructured interviews, content analysis, focus groups, and archival studies – can be employed at this stage to gain a full, rich understanding of the factors involved with these anomalous cases.

For the project discussed here, one of the authors spent 5 months living in the field, observing, and carrying out semi-structured interviews. Analysis of these interviews is the main focus here. Averaging about 90 minutes, the interviews took place in Nepali with both the European American researcher and a native Nepali research assistant present at each interview. The researcher and assistant developed a typed interview guide in both English and Nepali that they carried to each interview. Each interview began with the three structured survey questions on ideal family size that make up the Coombs Scale, the dependent variable from the analyses of CVFS survey data. This technique measured the extent to which informants' answers to these questions in this interview varied from their answers during the original survey, nearly 2 years earlier. After this structured inquiry, semi-structured interviewing about the informant's personal family size preferences, childbearing issues, religious beliefs and practices, and family and friends' views on family size and religious beliefs and practices followed, with the interviewers referring to the interview guide occasionally, but not asking questions in any particular order or with any particular wording. In all, 27 of the 28 selected informants were interviewed.

During and immediately after each interview, detailed notes were taken. Another option would have been to take audio or video recordings of the interviews. In this case, the decision was made that a recorder was too disruptive to the interview process, because the participants seemed uneasy with the recorder. One way to overcome such uneasiness might be to demonstrate how a recorder works to interviewees who might never have seen one before – for example, record some general conversation with the participant and play it back for him or her to hear and to get comfortable with the process. In addition, it often helps to place a towel or handkerchief over the recorder once you have shown the recorder and obtained permission to record the interview, making the recorder less visible and reducing some of the interviewee's anxiety.

Interview notes, a form of field notes, have two important uses. First, the researcher can examine the notes many times during and following the interview phase, exploring content for themes and meanings common among the anomalous cases (Agar 1996; Spradley 1979; Strauss and Corbin 1990). In a comparative approach, non-deviant cases could be selected for in-depth analysis as well, allowing researchers the opportunity to compare and contrast the themes and meanings found when studying both types of cases. Second, researchers can code and count themes found in the notes and/or transcripts to quantify various meanings or phenomena (Emerson, Fretz, and Shaw 1995; Miles and Huberman 1984). For example, in this study notes were used to count the number of times a particular phrase was used or idea mentioned to gauge the strength of attitudes, beliefs, or behaviors. This combination of analysis types, both free-form textual analysis and structured coding and counting of themes and phrases, helped identify undiscovered issues and the common language with which informants discuss these matters.

The goal of conducting these semi-structured interviews or other ethnographic methods to study deviant cases was to reveal knowledge necessary to further refine theories, measures, and/or methods for continued progress toward understanding a causal process. Based on this aim, one alternative would be to summarize and present the findings from the fieldwork as the product of this phase of research and call for future research of multiple kinds. However, in the case described here we inserted one more round of iteration in the process. We took the findings from the fieldwork and used them to suggest a round of revisions to our survey models and methods.

Using Ethnographic Insights to Revise Theories, Measures, and Methods

The in-depth study of anomalous cases can provide meaningful insights on three levels. First, researchers may be able to uncover additional factors that had not previously been considered (Kendall and Wolf 1949; Sieber 1973). Second, intensive deviant case analysis can reveal ideas for refining the measurement of key variables if further survey data analyses will be conducted (Kendall and Wolf 1949). Third, using less structured methods to study anomalous cases can reveal methodological phenomena responsible for the cases' deviance and suggest ways to correct for these problems in the future (Horst 1955).

Gathering and analyzing field notes sharpened the project examined here in several ways. First, these processes informed the research team about the dynamics of religious influence in Nepal; and from this deepened understanding, new, more informed measures of religion were coded from the survey data for further analyses. Second, the processes identified the pervasive effect of family planning media messages on individuals in Nepal, which also led to new measurement strategies in the statistical analyses. Finally, these processes illustrated the importance of methodological issues and how they can influence the fit of survey data to a statistical model. As a result, we developed a better understanding of sources of error and what they mean for the study of anomalous cases.

Revising Theories: New Dimensions of Religion

For the preliminary survey data analyses of religion and childbearing preferences, relying on existing theories of the impact of religion, we had hypothesized about how various dimensions of religion would influence childbearing preferences. First, we expected that each different religio-ethnic group was characterized by a distinct formulation of religious meanings. Next, we hypothesized that respondents in all religio-ethnic groups would vary in the extent to which religion was a salient part of their identity. We also reasoned that, above and beyond an individual's religious identity, the level of religious belief and activity within the community in which the respondent lived would have an influence on childbearing preferences. Initial findings did not support the hypothesis about community-level effects. Also, individual-level beliefs and practices did not have the hypothesized effect among the younger respondents. Therefore, one priority of the less structured approach was to ask questions and explore issues around the form, function, and meaning of religion in the study area.

Throughout the interviews and observations, the influence of the religious beliefs and practices of senior members of households became apparent. Especially during the interviews with the pre–family formation group, young people defined their religious identity mostly as a reflection of their mother, father, or a grandparent. If a young person visited a temple or performed a religious rite in the home, it was often with other family members. When informants were asked where they learned their religious beliefs or why they worshiped a particular god or goddess, they most often cited the traditional beliefs and practices of their parents and other family members. When asked if they saw themselves as more religious or less religious than their parents, all the pre–family formation informants responded that one or both of their parents were more religious. The majority of religious activity was either led or practiced alone by the matriarchs of the family, although in many cases patriarchs were also religiously active.

Shanti,[1] an 18-year-old high caste Hindu, described how religious worship of Hindu gods and goddesses within her home were a form of religious education:

My parents teach *dharma* (religion) to me. Each morning I do *puja* (worship) with my mother to *Ganesh* (a Hindu god). Then, in the evening, I worship five *devis* (gods) with my father. When I pray with my mother or father, *ghan* (knowledge of religion) comes to me.

Conversations like this one illustrated that religion in this setting is very family centered and that young family members are expected to gradually learn from

Table 4.2. *Revised OLS estimates from models predicting family size preferences among two subsamples of the Chitwan Valley Family Study*

Religio-ethnic group by importance of religion[a]	Coombs Family Size Preference Scale			
	Pre-family formation group (unmarried, ages 15–29)		Completed fertility group (married, ages 45–59)	
	Model 1	Model 2	Model 3	Model 4
High Caste Hindu	−.05	−.01	−.20	−.19
Finds religion unimportant (0,1)	(.31)[b]	(.07)	(.50)	(.48)
Low Caste Hindu	−.65*	−.69*	−.30	−.26
Finds religion important (0,1)	(1.91)	(2.04)	(.76)	(.65)
Finds religion unimportant (0,1)	−.52*	−.57*	−.72	−.26
	(1.67)	(1.83)	(1.20)	(.65)
Hill Tibeto-Burmese	−.49*	−.50*	−.12	−.09
Finds religion important (0,1)	(1.91)	(1.94)	(.39)	(.28)
Finds religion unimportant (0,1)	.01	.03	.48	.46
	(.03)	(.13)	(.87)	(.83)
Newar	.27	.29	.50	.49
Finds religion important (0,1)	(.67)	(.77)	(1.10)	(1.09)
Finds religion unimportant (0,1)	.02	.05	−.40	−.42
	(.07)	(.17)	(.46)	(.49)
Terai Tibeto-Burmese	.49*	.55*	1.29***	1.21***
Finds religion important (0,1)	(1.84)	(2.08)	(3.32)	(3.07)
Finds religion unimportant (0,1)	.56*	.03	2.74***	2.25***
	(2.07)	(.13)	(4.93)	(3.82)
Household Religiosity				
Household members' average temple visits per month	.68***	.70***	.30	.40
	(3.76)	(3.87)	(1.00)	(1.32)
Household members' average importance of death rites	.43*	.45*	−.13	−.17
	(1.70)	(1.79)	(.30)	(.40)
Controls				
Gender (1 = female)	−.60***	−.62***	.01	.03
	(4.74)	(4.89)	(.05)	(.10)
Respondent's age	−.05*	−.06*	.05	.05*
	(1.95)	(2.14)	(2.00)	(1.81)
Number of mother's children ever born	.05*	.05*	.05	.05
	(1.85)	(1.89)	(1.34)	(1.30)
Mother and/or father could read (1 = yes, 0 = no)	−.04	−.05	−.48*	−.46*
	(.33)	(.39)	(2.03)	(1.91)
Education (highest grade completed)	−.12***	−.11***	.01	.00
	(4.75)	(4.80)	(.18)	(.03)
Age at marriage			.03	.03
			(1.24)	(1.21)
Number of respondent's children ever born			.16***	.17***
			(3.58)	(3.63)
Newspaper and radio exposure scale	−.23**		−.33*	
	(2.76)		(1.89)	

Table 4.2 *(cont.)*

Religio-ethnic group by importance of religion[a]	Coombs Family Size Preference Scale			
	Pre-family formation group (unmarried, ages 15–29)		Completed fertility group (married, ages 45–59)	
	Model 1	Model 2	Model 3	Model 4
Newspaper, radio, and TV exposure scale		−.33***		−.34*
		(3.40)		(1.77)
Travel to Kathmandu or to other country	−.19	−.17	−.23	−.22
(1 = yes, 0 = no)	(1.48)	(1.36)	(1.06)	(1.01)
Received/expects inheritance	−.02	−.03	−.45	−.45*
(1 = yes, 0 = no)	(.10)	(.16)	(1.93)	(1.91)
Travel time to Narayanghat	−.02	−.02	.24*	.20*
	(.28)	(.27)	(1.99)	(1.67)
Intercept	6.90	7.16	3.45	3.68
Adj R-squared	.11	.12	.12	.10
N	958	953	859	827

[a] Reference group is high caste Hindus who find religion important.
[b] T-ratios in parentheses.
*p < .05, **p < .01, ***p < .001 for one-tailed t-tests.

time to time rather than always being preoccupied with religious activities or thoughts. Particularly for young adults in this setting, religious identity seems to be based largely on the religious practices and beliefs demonstrated in their families. This led to a re-evaluation of the theoretical framework and the incorporation of more ideas about the levels of religious influence above individuals' own religiosity, especially about the impact of family members' religiosity.

Discovering the importance of religion at the family level, we used the survey data to create measures reflecting the household religious environment. Because the CVFS contains interviews with all members of a household between the ages of 15 and 59, it was possible to use the survey responses of all family members on their religious practices and beliefs to create average household-level measures. For example, household measures were created for the average frequency of visiting religious temples and the average importance given to death rituals.[2] They were then used to predict childbearing preferences.

Model 1 in Table 4.2 displays the results from a revised model, predicting family size preferences among the younger age group, which includes measures of the average frequency with which household members visit religious temples and the average importance of death rituals among household members. Both measures have a positive and statistically significant effect on family size preferences – that is, the more often family members visit temples and the more strongly they believe in the importance of death rituals, the more children an

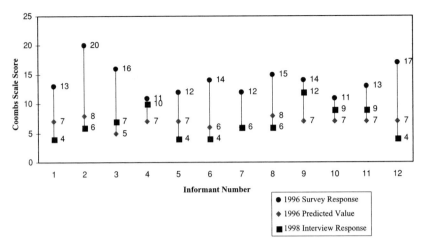

Figure 4.3. Comparison of Coombs Scale scores for 1996 survey responses, 1996 predicted values, and 1998 interview responses of unmarried informants (ages 16–25)

individual desires. These measures contribute to the higher adjusted R^2 for this model (.11) than for the preliminary model in Table 4.1 (.09), suggesting that these measures help explain the influence of religion on childbearing preferences. An F-test comparing these two models confirms that the revised model is a statistically significant improvement over the initial model at the $p < .001$ level.

Model 3 in Table 4.2 displays the revised model of family size preference for the married, older respondents. Including the household-level measures of temple visits and the importance of death rituals did not change the adjusted R^2 (.12) and thus does not improve the predictive value of this model over the preliminary model. This is not particularly surprising given that interviews with the pre–family formation group brought the influence of elder relatives' religiosity to our attention.

Revising Existing Measures: Media Influence

Every informant in both groups who responded to the Coombs Scale questions during the semi-structured interview (22 of the 27 interviewed) gave an answer lower than the response she or he had given 2 years earlier. In many cases, the answer given was close to what the statistical model predicted. Figure 4.3 plots three scores for 12 of the 14 members of the pre–family formation group:[3] The original score derived from their responses to the Coombs Scale questions on the 1996 survey, the predicted score derived from the preliminary model (found in Table 4.1), and the score derived from their responses to the Coombs

Table 4.3. *Mean Coombs Scale responses for two subsamples of outliers: 1996 survey response, 1996 predicted value, and 1998 interview response*

	Coombs Scale score (1–25)		
	1996 survey response mean	1996 predicted value mean	1998 interview response mean
Pre–family formation group	13.64	6.86	6.75
Completed fertility group	22.86	10.64	9

Scale questions in the 1998 interview. The 1998 Coombs Scale scores for all these informants are substantially lower than those calculated from the 1996 survey data and match much more closely the score predicted by the preliminary model. Table 4.3, which presents group means for the three scores, provides an overall picture of this pattern.

Figure 4.4 plots the three Coombs Scale scores (1996 survey score, predicted score, and 1998 interview score) for 10 of the 14 members of the completed fertility group.[4] The same pattern is evident for these respondents: Their scores fall substantially 2 years after the survey, coming very close to the score that the statistical model predicted for them. The means for the three Coombs Scales scores, presented in the bottom row of Table 4.3, illustrate this. Drawing on analysis of the interview notes, we determined that one possible cause of this uniform decrease in preferences might be the influence of recent family planning media campaigns.

During the unstructured portion of the interviews, there were discussions with informants about ideal family size and the changes in their responses over time. Noticeable were the similarities in how informants described their reasons for wanting a small number of children. For instance, 5 of the 13 unmarried young adults used exactly the same phrase, *dui jana thikai chha* (two children are good), and several other informants used similar phrases. One informant remarked, "Having two children will bring me happiness." Several unmarried informants who had taken English-language courses used the words "quality versus quantity" in the midst of sentences in Nepali. One informant spoke of a teacher at her school who had explained the benefits of investing in fewer children; another stated that she wanted only two children who would both be *thulo manche* (important people). Overall, 20 of the informants discussed the financial advantages of raising fewer children, such as cutting down on the cost of food, clothes, and schooling and distributing land among fewer adult children.

In probing the source and significance of these phrases and common language, it became obvious that informants were aware of family planning slogans featured in newspapers and magazines, on billboards, and on radio or

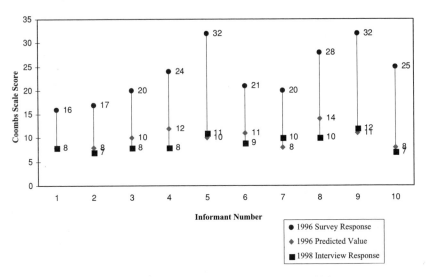

Figure 4.4. Comparison of Coombs Scale scores from 1996 survey responses, 1996 predicted values, and 1998 interview responses for married respondents with children (ages 45–59)

television. These messages overtly encourage families to limit their family size to two children. The message that was most often quoted word for word during the interviews was the one mentioned above: *Dui jana thikai chha*. Three other messages that were common in the media and expressed in several variants during the interviews were *Dui bhanda badi santan dhann dhau dhau parchha* (It is difficult to raise more than two children), *Buddhiman babu ama le dui bhanda badi santan janmaudainan* (Wise parents do not give birth to more than two children), and *Dui bhai thikka; dherai bhai dikka* (Two children are just right; many children mean trouble). On the radio, a thrice-weekly drama promoted small families as happier than large families because more can be invested in each child and it is easier to feed them, send them to school, and keep them healthy.

It is logical to posit that if exposure to these kinds of messages influenced the language with which informants discussed their attitudes about family size, it might also have influenced their responses to the Coombs Scale questions. And if media exposure to these messages affected responses, then perhaps the outliers had less exposure in 1996 than they did in 1998. Therefore, the ethnographic findings suggested going back to examine more survey data for answers.

The CVFS survey data provide evidence that outlier respondents had less media exposure than other survey respondents in 1996. Table 4.4 reports the

Table 4.4. *Average media exposure of the outliers and non-outliers from preliminary models of family size preferences*

	Outliers (N = 62)	Non-outliers (N = 1,792)	Difference of means t-test results
Frequency of reading the newspaper (0–3)	0.82	1.04	+
Frequency of listening to the radio (0–3)	2.06	2.21	+
Ever listened to family planning programs (0,1)	0.63	.72	+
Frequency of watching television (0–3)	1.34	1.64	*
Household owns a radio (0,1)	0.42	.48	

means and statistical tests of difference for various media-related measures for the original group of all outliers from which informants were sampled and for all other CVFS respondents. The outlier respondents had significantly less exposure than all other CVFS respondents on four of the five measures. Outliers read newspapers less often, listened to the radio less often, watched television less often, and were less likely to listen to family planning programs on the radio. Their households were also less likely to own a radio, but this difference was not statistically different. Therefore, it is possible that the media campaigns promoting small families – two-children families in particular – had less influence on these outlier respondents than on other participants in the 1996 survey. Another possibility is that the frequency of family planning messages in the media increased from 1996 to 1998; and so even if these respondents' frequency of media exposure was unchanged, they became exposed to more messages about fertility limitation.

No survey data are available to examine changes in media content or exposure among outlier respondents during the 2 years between the CVFS survey and the less structured interviews. However, given the wide use of phrases and rationales for small families in our interviews that echoed those in the family planning media, it is likely that media exposure had some reductive influence on their Coombs Scale scores in 1998.

Although the preliminary models included measures of newspaper reading and radio listening, the interviews and observations of television programming convinced us to expand the measure of media exposure to include data on the frequency of television watching. It had not initially been included in the media measure because we did not know how common it was to watch television in this area, nor did we realize that there were such overt messages on television regarding ideal family size. This is an example of how direct observation and exploratory interviewing in the field can correct false assumptions. This is one of the most valuable benefits less structured methods bring to the research process: Being able to put the researcher more directly in the shoes of those being studied helps avoid fatal biases (Becker 1996; Blumer 1969).

Models 2 and 4 in Table 4.2 incorporate the revised measure of media exposure. As shown in Model 2, when television watching is added to media exposure for the pre–family formation group, the coefficient increases from $-.23$ to $-.33$, and the adjusted R^2 increases from .11 to .12, suggesting that this revised measure improves the predictive value of the model for the unmarried group. For the completed fertility group, however, adding television viewing to the measure increases the coefficient only slightly, from $-.33$ to $-.34$, and decreases the adjusted R^2 from .12 to .10. Overall, this age group may watch less television than the younger group, which would lessen the impact of adding it to the media exposure measure.

At this point, some would argue it was not necessary to have used multiple research methods to arrive at the findings about the importance of family members' religion and the wide reach of media campaigns. It is possible that these ideas could have emerged from an independent ethnographic study in a Nepalese village or from running survey data analyses on every possible variable in the data set, but the possibility remains that they would not. In fact, an experiment by Sieber (1973) indicates that both surveys and ethnographic fieldwork tend to miss findings that the other type of method can more easily bring to light. For example, high-quality survey research provides the power to do a variety of comparisons across large groups, but it is limited in its ability to find new ideas or suggest misunderstandings of concepts. Less structured methods are better at revealing new information and the rich context of issues under study (Brannen 1992).

Understanding the Methods: Sources of Error

When considering other reasons for obtaining different responses to the same questions at two points in time, another factor to be weighed is survey error and its various sources. Survey data are subject to errors in validity, errors in reliability, and interviewer effects. These different types of error hold important implications for studying extreme cases from survey data.

Validity   A survey item is considered valid if it measures what it is intended to measure (Carmines and Zeller 1979). Problems of differential validity arise when some respondents have a different way of understanding a survey question than other respondents. For example, some respondents may misunderstand the question or may not be used to the cognitive process involved in formulating an answer (Caldwell 1985; Caldwell, Hill, and Hull 1988; Sudman and Bradburn 1974).

Evidence from the interviews conducted here suggests that a few of the outlier respondents from the survey did not fully understand the Coombs Scale questions or how to formulate responses. For a few of the older completed fertility group informants, the confusion over the questions seemed to be based on their skepticism that fertility could (or should) be planned. This may emanate from both the fatalistic nature of the dominant Hindu culture in Nepal (Bista 1994) and the relative novelty of modern birth control methods in this setting. An older man named Shyam typified the response of five other older informants to the questions about family size preference. He chuckled and replied: "People cannot have the exact number of children they want. It is not up to us. We have the number of children that we have." When these informants were asked to consider whether they would want one more or one less child if they could not have the number they had in reality, they seemed uninterested in rethinking their past and how they would do it differently if they could. Even those who formulated a response to the Coombs Scale questions often added a condition. This happened in 5 out of 14 cases. For example, an older high caste Hindu woman said that she would choose two sons and one daughter as her ideal, but that "people do not usually get what they wish."

When members of the completed fertility group had a difficult time answering questions about the ideal number of children to have, they were asked about their own children and what it was like raising them. During these discussions, a few informants said that they would have done things differently if they could have or if they had known what they know now. In fact, some of them said they now advise their adult children to have smaller families and use family planning methods. Therefore, some of these informants were probably outliers in the original survey because they had not completely understood what researchers were trying to ask in the survey question about the ideal number of children or felt that it was acceptable to conclude a number different from their own completed family size. However, further into the semi-structured interviews, once they discussed many of the issues surrounding childbearing in their own words, they were more comfortable discussing the possibility of a family size different from the one that they had.

In the larger research process, one benefit that can emanate from this mixed method approach is the researcher's ability to use the intensive interviews as an opportunity for detecting problems of differential validity. During fieldwork, a researcher can adapt the interview process to make the measuring tool more valid for all respondents and incorporate this in subsequent surveys or interviews. This is an example of how the flexibility inherent in a well-designed mixed method approach can be beneficial. This is demonstrated in other studies where focus groups or individual interviews are used to develop culturally appropriate survey items (O'Brian 1993; Zeller 1993).

Reliability   The reliability of a survey item is the degree to which repeated measures will yield similar responses. Some reliability problems come from random errors. Sometimes a random shock will result in an unexpected response to a particular survey item (Carmines and Zeller 1979). For example, a respondent may be tired or not pay attention to a question and give a nonsensical answer, or a coder might make an error. For some of the outliers selected in the project described here, the high residual value may have been due to a random shock causing an accurate measurement of an atypical state in the subject, an inaccurate measurement of a typical state in the subject, or a combination of both. Revisiting these types of outlying respondents, either with a repeated survey or ethnographic interviews, helps us to understand how to reduce these types of random error.

For the research project discussed in this chapter, one explanation for the change in family size preferences given between the two interviews may be the phenomenon of regression to the mean. This occurs when a random shock causes an extreme value response once, but repeated observations result in more expected or consistent results. For example, among our informants there may have been some who misheard the question and thought they were being asked to state the number of children they actually had, which may have been more than they now feel is ideal. In one case, it seems, a respondent's history of alcoholism may have introduced substantial random measurement error. An interviewer may have heard the response wrong or written down the wrong number. There are multiple possible sources of random shocks resulting in outlying responses. In biomedical clinical trials, researchers have found that subjects selected on the basis of having unusually high or low values of a particular measurement will tend to have values closer to the population mean in subsequent measurements (Beath and Dobson 1991). To test this effect among the outliers, similar interviews would need to be conducted with a subset of CVFS left-tail outliers whose family size preferences were much lower than predicted in 1996. If an increase in media exposure was playing a role, one would expect to see still lower Coombs Scale scores. If regression to the mean was at work, one would expect these left-tail outliers to have higher scores that were closer to the population mean. A test of this effect is beyond the scope of our current discussion, but it is plausible that both factors are at work, meaning that there may be some regression to the mean *and* increased media exposure may be lowering fertility preferences in this context.

The possibility that regression to the mean is partly responsible here suggests that a more complex sample design is desirable for systematically sampling anomalous cases. The limit to the particular sampling approach used in the case described here resulted in no informants selected from the opposite tail of the residual distribution or from the small size of residual cases. This limited the ability for comparisons between the informants interviewed and others who wanted *fewer* children than the model predicted or others who wanted exactly the number of children the model predicted. For future studies of this kind, unequal probability sampling may be a useful approach. One could pick respondents for ethnographic re-examination by randomly sampling the original survey data cases, giving each case a sample selection probability proportional to the error (or squared error) of its residual in the statistical model. This type of approach would generate ample extreme cases, from both ends of the continuum, while simultaneously including cases with less extreme residual values that would make it possible to distinguish regression to the mean effects from other types of change.

Interviewer Effects   Research methods that require face-to-face inter-action inherently involve interviewer effects (Bradburn 1983; Lyberg and Kasprzyk 1991). Interviewer effects can lead to response bias. Therefore, another hypothesis predicting why all 22 informants who responded gave lower answers during the 1998 interviews than they did 2 years earlier is that differen-tial interviewer characteristics had an effect. The 1996 CVFS survey interviews were conducted in person by a trained staff of local Nepali interviewers. On the other hand, the semi-structured follow-up interviews in 1998 were all conducted by a European American woman from the United States who speaks Nepali. In the case of the semi-structured interviews, the informants probably had few, if any, prior interactions with a woman from the United States, which may have made them feel less open with their responses. Also, any similar interac-tions would probably have been with Westerners working for nongovernmental organizations promoting family planning and/or development projects, which may have motivated them to describe a low family size preference. In addition, whether or not they had any such previous interactions, the informants may have known about low fertility rates in countries such as the United States, and they were probably aware that the interviewer was studying population issues. Following standard interviewing techniques, the interviewer took steps to help establish a nonjudgmental presence, such as emphasizing a desire to learn about how things really are and counteracting any belief that there were any "right" or expected answers, but the outlier informants may have been affected by the interviewers' inherent characteristics (Bradburn 1983; DeMaio 1984). The result may have been that they felt that the appropriate response was to express preference for a smaller number of children.

   When methodological errors produce outlier respondents in survey data, sub-sequent less structured interactions with these respondents may provide little substantive insight for theoretical or analytical revisions of the sort discussed earlier. However, these cases do identify important options for improving sam-pling, survey instruments, and data collection efforts in the future. This infor-mation about methodological issues and options is an important reason to study various types of deviant cases. Because methodological problems create deviant cases through potentially much different processes than theoretical or measurement limitations, it is extremely important to identify the processes producing each particular anomalous case before reaching strong conclusions regarding its implications.

Conclusion

As described in this chapter, there are several benefits to integrating survey and less structured methods to learn from anomalous cases in a population. First, a large-scale survey can provide a useful sampling frame from which to systematically select deviant cases as ethnographic informants. Regression diagnostics are a powerful way to identify a sampling frame from which one can systematically select a sample of ethnographic informants who can provide much theoretical and methodological insight. Second, access to informant characteristics measured in the survey data enables researchers to learn valuable information prior to observations or interviews. This information can help researchers prepare for interviews by suggesting conversation topics or probes and by providing background and contextual characteristics. Also, survey data collections can help by establishing prior rapport with informants and providing records explaining where to locate them. Finally, the insights that emerge from less structured methods lead to improved theories, measures, and methods that can then inform subsequent survey data collection and/or analysis. In the example used here, developing new measures of religion and media exposure significantly improved the ability of a regression model to explain variance in family size preferences among the young, unmarried adults in the sample.

Issues of Application

This chapter is designed to encourage readers to consider new mixed method ways to tackle other research topics and questions with a sequential, systematic application of methods. The lessons learned from this specific study can benefit those interested in using a similar approach for their own work. First, careful attention must be given to the sampling procedures. We advocate unequal probability sampling to obtain informants from both extremes as well as from the pool of cases for which a particular model works well. The unequal probability sampling approach allows for comparisons that are necessary to understand the processes creating each anomalous case. Second, while carrying out the less structured methods to study the selected informants, effort should be made to distinguish which cases are anomalous because theories were mis-specified and which cases are results of errors in validity, reliability, or interviewer influence. There is much to be learned from the multiple types of outliers.

In this study, anomalous cases were selected based on their residual values. In other words, these are cases in which the observed value of the dependent variable was very different from the value predicted by the model. These are the types of cases examined in most standard deviant case analyses. However, using a comprehensive regression diagnostics modeling framework, cases can also warrant investigation when their independent variable values give them undue influence over the model.[5] Future systematic analyses of anomalous cases should sample cases with both large residuals and values for independent variables that have disproportionate influence. This is because a large residual is not as much a concern if the values of the independent variables do not exert undue influence on the model and disproportional influence of independent variable values is not worrisome when the case's residual is low. Selecting anomalous cases requires careful consideration of the statistical issues surrounding extreme cases.

Another key feature of the approach described here is having a level of involvement in a research project that allows both access to the survey data and the permission to recontact survey respondents for re-interview. This is a requirement for longitudinal data collection, whether it is a mixed method application or just two waves of a purely survey or interview study. In any case, those involved in primary data collection are at an advantage for being able to conduct this kind of project. That being said, there are ways to modify the approach that may still maintain some of the benefits. For example, one might use a secondary data set to conduct survey analyses, perform regression diagnostics, and search to find common characteristics of residual cases that could guide the selection of a separate sample for interviews (individual or focus group) or observations that might offer insights into a process that models based on survey measures alone may still be missing. In this example, perhaps one gender, age, or ethnic group will be overrepresented in the anomalous cases, suggesting that a sample for follow-up should focus more heavily on that group. This is another way of using analyses of survey data to help guide the systematic selection of informants.

Illustrations of Principles

The sequential, systematic mixed method approach described here illustrates several of the themes and principles of mixed method data collection presented in Chapter 1. First, this method uses the strengths of structured survey methods and observational and semi-structured interviewing methods to provide balance. Survey methods provide standardized measures of sample cases that can be used to test theory, estimate models, or yield description as required by the research project. Survey analyses also provide tools to empirically test new hypotheses that emerge from the less structured data collection methods. Use of observations and semi-structured interviews enhances inductive exploration of reasons why models are not predicting well for some individuals.

By combining the less structured methods with the analyses of existing survey data, this approach requires the investigators to move from their office into the field to hear from people in their own words and observe their actions. As described in this chapter, by placing the researchers in the field they have access to new insights about the meaning of survey questions to particular individuals and groups that stimulate a new understanding of the survey measures. All these field experiences and new insights increase the extent to which a researcher can reliably draw on his or her introspection to think through issues that arise in the research process.

This application also highlights the value of flexibility in a sequential mixed method approach that ultimately leads to improvement in the theory guiding and results produced by a research project. In the study described in this chapter, adding observations and semi-structured interviewing produced better specified theory and models of family size preferences.

Regarding the production of a comprehensive empirical record, the approach described in this chapter adds less structured data (field notes and interview transcripts) about the same topics covered in the structured survey, so that the themes and meanings derived from the less structured methods can be compared to the conclusions reached through analysis of more standardized measures. Where new hypotheses emerged, they could be tested with new analyses of the existing survey measures. This step-by-step compilation and checking of various forms of empirical evidence provides a more comprehensive record as the basis for findings, increasing one's confidence in the conclusions.

5   Neighborhood History Calendars

The previous chapters discussed mixed method approaches that integrate multiple methods, sequentially, into a single data collection strategy that has several separate steps. In this chapter and the next, we discuss a different type of mixed method approach, one that uses elements from several different methods to create a new, single hybrid method. The resulting hybrid methods have some characteristics of more structured methods, such as surveys, and other characteristics of less structured methods, such as unstructured interviewing or observation. Each specific combination that creates a new hybrid method is designed to achieve specific measurement goals, and each comes with its own strengths and weaknesses. In this chapter, we focus on Neighborhood History Calendar (NHC) methods as an example of such a hybrid method.

Both Neighborhood History Calendars and Life History Calendars, the subject of the next chapter, are designed to measure the timing and sequencing of changes occurring sometime in the past. The emphasis on measurement of timing is consistent with a strategy of studying causal relationships that focuses on the relative timing of various circumstances and events. As discussed in Chapter 1, our strategy for creating new empirical evidence to study cause and consequence in the social sciences relies heavily on the idea that the timing of measures should correspond to the timing implied in causal hypotheses. That is, if X causes Y, then X should precede Y in time, and our measure of X should specify timing well enough to know whether or not X preceded Y.[1] The calendar methods described in Chapters 5 and 6 are designed to achieve such timing measurement based on retrospective reports. These methods collect information now to measure the timing of events or changes in the past.

Throughout the social sciences, important streams of research focus on the relationship between the individual and the community, organizational, and ecological contexts within which individuals live their daily lives. For example,

Portions of this chapter are based on the following previously published article: Axinn, William G., Jennifer S. Barber, and Dirgha J. Ghimire 1997. "The Neighborhood History Calendar: A Data Collection Method Designed for Dynamic Multilevel Modeling." *Sociological Methodology* 27: 355–392.

the relationship between macro-level social changes and micro-level individual behaviors has been a focal theme in both classic and modern sociological theory (Alexander 1988; Coleman 1990; Durkheim 1984 [1933]; Smith 1989). This theme is not only a theoretical issue, it has practical significance as well. Recent studies indicate that macro-level characteristics play an important role in shaping micro-level behavior in a broad range of substantive areas, including demography, gender relations, child health and development, criminology, and education (Brooks-Gunn et al. 1993; Entwisle and Mason 1985; Huber 1991; Raudenbush 1988; Rountree et al. 1994; Sampson, Morenoff, and Gannon-Rowley 2002). Macro-level characteristics, sometimes called "contextual characteristics," do affect individual-level behaviors, and the continued exploration of these effects is likely to be an important area of social science inquiry for some time to come. This chapter discusses how the hybrid contextual history calendar methods can be used to collect detailed, dynamic, retrospective data about the social contexts within which individuals live.

Recent advances in multilevel modeling have dramatically improved efforts to include macro-level contextual characteristics, sometimes called "ecological characteristics," in models of individual-level behavior (Brooks-Gunn et al. 1997a, 1997b; Bryk and Raudenbush 1992; DiPrete and Forristal 1994; Goldstein 1995; Raudenbush and Sampson 1999; Ringdal 1992; Sampson et al. 2002). Advances in event history, or hazard, modeling have also helped researchers formulate increasingly dynamic models of individual behavior (Allison 1984; Petersen 1991; Yamaguchi 1991). However, few researchers have successfully combined multilevel modeling approaches with dynamic models. Some have incorporated static measures of contextual features into dynamic individual-level models (Brewster 1994; Sastry 1996), but incorporation of dynamic measures at both the contextual and individual levels poses many problems. Among them, such models require data that include dynamic event history measures of contextual change over time, dynamic measures of individuals' lives, and a detailed migration/mobility history to link individuals with contexts. The methods discussed in this chapter are designed to overcome common obstacles in data collection; innovative analytic methods to analyze these types of multilevel data are being developed elsewhere (Barber et al. 2000; Maples, Murphy, and Axinn 2002).

In this chapter, we outline a method for collecting contextual event history data. Our method integrates reliance on a calendar instrument with a combination of survey, ethnographic, and archival techniques for gathering data. The method extends the Life History Calendar technique (discussed in further detail in the next chapter), which was designed to gather individual-level event histories, to data collection at contextual levels. The method follows the principles of efforts to combine standardized, extensive data collection methods and unstandardized, intensive data collection methods into a single coherent data collection effort based on the same principles undergirding the mixed method approaches described in Chapters 3 and 4. Instead of a sequential mix of methods, this approach uses one hybrid data collection method that takes its design from both less and more structured approaches simultaneously. The resulting approach is flexible enough to collect contextual data from a wide range of settings for a broad range of substantive uses. This method has several important advantages, including direct collection of contextual characteristics rather than aggregation of individual-level characteristics; collection of sequences of contextual changes so that researchers can differentiate among contexts that may look the same now but have arrived at that outcome via different paths; documentation of a contextual event history that can be linked to individual life histories to create truly dynamic multilevel models.

Contextual Event History Data

Collection of contextual event history data poses important obstacles, including obtaining accurate information on timing and sequencing of contextual change and measuring the most important contextual changes. To overcome these obstacles, the technique we describe combines the structure of a calendar with a wide-open search for data that includes in-depth interviews with key informants, group interviews, and consultation with archival sources.

The methods we describe were designed to meet the specific needs of a particular study, described elsewhere in this volume, called the Chitwan Valley Family Study (CVFS). The CVFS was designed to measure dynamic changes in the socioeconomic context of 171 neighborhoods in south central Nepal and to link these changes to individual-level life histories for the purpose of explaining changes in marriage timing, childbearing, and contraceptive use. Because rural Nepal is the setting for the CVFS, the methods were designed to overcome several setting-specific obstacles. However, the design and implementation of these methods address many issues that will confront any effort to gather standardized dynamic contextual history data, regardless of subject matter or setting. Below, we discuss these issues, the design alternatives researchers face, and the specific solutions chosen in the CVFS.

Neighborhood History Calendar Design and Implementation

The CVFS Neighborhood History Calendars are designed to measure contextual changes most relevant to the study's setting and substantive aims. However, we begin describing the method by addressing issues facing all such calendar instrument design efforts, including the choice of time units, substantive domains, and an accompanying questionnaire.

Design of the Instruments

Specifying Time Units and Choosing Timing Cues   As in applications of calendar methods to individual life histories, the choice of time units
used in the calendar must depend on both the substantive aims of the study
and methodological constraints created by the issues being studied. One might
choose days, weeks, months, or years:

> The investigator must choose a time unit that is small enough to ascertain with adequate
> precision the sequence and temporal interrelation of events. To record events that occur
> fairly frequently or quite close together, it is necessary to divide time rather finely. At
> the same time, one must consider the respondent's ability to make fine time distinctions
> and the feasibility of fitting the desired time unit over the required time span of the study
> onto a calendar of manageable size. (Freedman et al. 1988, p. 44)

Although one of our objectives was to determine the sequence of contextual
changes over time, the contextual events of interest in the CVFS did not occur
frequently. The study design also required that we collect histories for a period
of 42 years – from when the Chitwan Valley was settled, in 1954, to the year
the data collection was completed, 1996. For this combination of reasons, we
chose years as the time unit for our Neighborhood History Calendars. Figure 5.1
presents an English translation of our Nepalese Neighborhood History Calendar. The years run across the top row of the calendar and form the column
headings. These year demarcations provide respondents with time references
to aid in their recall of the timing and sequencing of changes around their
neighborhood.

Because of the relatively long period of recall and the fact that many Nepalese
do not use calendars to mark time in their daily lives, we believed that additional timing cues would be needed to aid respondents' recall of event timing.
Therefore, we created a second row of timing cues, below the row of years,
for major events we believed individuals might find memorable. We chose two
types of events to put in this line. The first type was regional or national events
that would have occurred at the same time for everyone in our study population.
It was essential to our purpose that the timing of these events be quite salient
so that respondents could use the timing of these events to help them recall
the timing of neighborhood changes. We conducted semi-structured interviews
with a non-systematic sample of the study population to determine a set of such
events. In this process, it is important to interview respondents from several different cohorts because they are likely to remember different important events
(Schuman and Scott 1989). The set of events we chose included earthquakes,
floods, national elections, and the deposition of Nepal's king. These events
were printed in the second row of the calendar (the locations of these events are
represented by an asterisk in Figure 5.1).

The second type of event we chose was neighborhood-specific events that were extremely salient to local residents but were not germane to the study and therefore not included elsewhere on the calendar. For example, in one neighborhood many residents could recall quite clearly the year in which one resident had been mauled by a crocodile. Because such neighborhood-specific events did not pertain to the entire population, these events were written on the calendar, in Line 2, during the data collection process. We also attempted to put our questions in an order beginning with neighborhood changes that we believed would be quite salient – for example, electrification.

As a result of this strategy, respondents were able to use visual cues on the calendar – years, national events, and local events – to help them recall the timing of local events and changes they found difficult to remember. For example, when faced with the task of recalling an important change in bus service to the neighborhood, from dry season only to year-round, respondents could draw on the calendar years, national events such as elections, or local events that were already recorded on the calendar. This strategy was particularly important among some ethnic groups (Tharu, Kumal, and Derai) who use neither age nor calendar years to mark time.[2] Among these groups, the timing of salient local and national events provided the most important cues for the timing of neighborhood changes.

Choosing Domains   The choice of domains is also a function of the substantive aims of the study and the setting being studied. For the purposes of the CVFS, the research team was mainly interested in those neighborhood-level contextual changes that theory suggested should influence marriage timing, childbearing, or contraceptive use. These included such changes as new schooling opportunities, changing employment opportunities, and improvements in the health care infrastructure (Caldwell 1982; Smith 1989). However, we also conducted a series of unstructured interviews with members of the study population to explore the possibility that other local events (either not predicted by theory or unknown outside the study area) might be important determinants of these family formation changes. These unstructured interviews helped us develop a list of nearly 50 different types of neighborhood characteristics and changes that residents mentioned when describing their neighborhood. We then worked to reduce this list by focusing on only those characteristics that seemed most likely to influence changes in marriage timing, childbearing, or contraceptive use. Examples of these include changes in agricultural services (mills, cooperatives, and dairies), the formation of local women's groups, the existence of local youth groups, and the introduction of public banks.

One useful consequence of our multiple-interview strategy is that new, locally important domains could be added to the calendar while in the field. In order

Neighborhood ID: 09-15-178

Name of the Neighborhood: Momogau

Year / Event	54	55	56	57	58	59	60	61	62	63	64	65	66	67	68	69	70	71	72	73	74	75	76	77	78	79	80	81	82	83	84	85	86	87	88	89	90	91	92	93	94	95	96
1. Electricity						*							*														*	*	X							*	*						
2. School		3		2														1																							1		
3. Health Service			3				2																																			1	
4. Bus Service Any Season											2																								1								
5. Bus Service Rainy Season										2																													1	1			

Year / Event	54	55	56	57	58	59	60	61	62	63	64	65	66	67	68	69	70	71	72	73	74	75	76	77	78	79	80	81	82	83	84	85	86	87	88	89	90	91	92	93	94	95	96
6. Mill						*							*														*	*						3		*	*						
7. Co-operative											3							2									1											2			1		
8. Dairy																																						1					
9. Market							2								1																										1		
10. Bank															1																												

Year	54	55	56	57	58	59	60	61	62	63	64	65	66	67	68	69	70	71	72	73	74	75	76	77	78	79	80	81	82	83	84	85	86	87	88	89	90	91	92	93	94	95	96	Year
Event						*							*															*								*	*							Event
11. Employment Opp.							3			2						1																												11. Employment Opp.
12. Small Farmers Group																																												12. Small Farmers Group
13. Women's Group																																												13. Women's Group
14. Temple																																												14. Temple
15. Police Station																																												15. Police Station
Year	54	55	56	57	58	59	60	61	62	63	64	65	66	67	68	69	70	71	72	73	74	75	76	77	78	79	80	81	82	83	84	85	86	87	88	89	90	91	92	93	94	95	96	Year

Key:

* National and regional events entered on calendars to aid respondent recall. Examples: First national election, Rapti River flood, Nepal's king resigned.

X (in Line 1) Indicates the year electricity became available in the neighborhood. A blank line indicates that electricity was still not available at the time of the interview.

1 Respondents were asked, "Where is the nearest ___ (name of service, e.g., bank, school, health service, etc.)?" They then were asked, "In what year did that open?" Field workers recorded "1" in the column of the year the service first opened.

2 Respondents were asked, "Before ___ (service mentioned in #1) opened, what was the closest one? And "In what year did that open?" Field workers entered "2" in the column of the year the service first opened.

3 Respondents were asked, "Before ___ (service mentioned in #2) opened, what was the closest one? And "In what year did that open?" Field workers entered "3" in the column of the year the service first opened.

Blank Lines Indicate that the service did not exist. (Interviewers were required to respond to opening questions about the existence of each service in the accompanying questionnaire.)

Note: Names and identifiers have been changed to protect the anonymity of the neighborhood. Nepali years were used in the data collection. Western year 1996 = Nepali year 2052/2053.

Figure 5.1. An example of a completed Neighborhood History Calendar from the Chitwan Valley Family Study

to accommodate spontaneous additions of new categories, we left blank a few lines at the bottom of the calendar. In practice, the addition of a new domain is useful only if it has been collected from every neighborhood in the study. To accomplish this, we divided our data collection into three stages, or three visits to each neighborhood. None of the second visits were made until all the first visits were complete; none of the third visits were made until all of the second visits were complete; and no new domains were added during the third visit. This strategy gave us the opportunity to discover new domains of questioning during the first and second visits and ensure that they were collected from all the neighborhoods in the second and third visits.

As with Life History Calendars, substantive areas must be limited in number and precisely defined (Freedman et al. 1988). Collecting history data over a long period of retrospection and over many domains can produce a high respondent burden that may reduce respondent rapport and cooperation. Limiting the number of domains and providing precise definitions helps reduce the respondent burden. Another useful consequence of our multiple-interview strategy is that this respondent burden can be distributed across multiple respondents during multiple visits.

Often, the key informant for one domain of a history calendar may not be knowledgeable about other domains. For example, although residents of a neighborhood were quite able to identify the school nearest to that neighborhood, they often did not know exactly when the school first opened or how many teachers worked there. Officials at the school or school records were much more likely to provide these data.[3] Such problems were a major motivation for a mixed method data collection strategy that included some interviews in the neighborhood, some interviews with local officials, and as much consultation of written records as possible. However, these issues may also influence the selection of domains included in the Neighborhood History Calendar. This is particularly true in a data collection that includes multiple types of contextual history calendars, such as the CVFS. We used other history calendars, such as school and health service calendars, to supplement our Neighborhood History Calendar (discussed in greater detail below). In general, respondents' inability to provide reliable timing in response to some questions may also influence the choice of domains included in any one particular calendar instrument.

Designing the Accompanying Questionnaires   The research team also designed a questionnaire to accompany the Neighborhood History Calendar, one that provided a structure of suggested question wordings and standardized probes. Interviewers were not required to follow the question wordings exactly; instead, the printed questions constituted a tool to which interviewers could refer during the interview. This tool proved most useful for training the interviewers in the appropriate wordings and sequences for questions and probes. It also provided a crutch to interviewers when they could not recall the question sequences or wording.

Accompanying questionnaires also provide greater flexibility for recording information. Although the calendar instruments were designed to record the timing and sequencing of important community events, we used the questionnaire to obtain additional information about community events that could not easily be recorded on the calendar. For example, in the neighborhood histories we asked for the location of the nearest school, when it first opened, the location of the nearest school before that one opened, and when this other school opened, for up to three schools. These timing issues were recorded on the calendar. For each school, we also asked residents about the availability of bus service to the school, the time it took to reach the school by bus and by foot, and the cost of bus service to the school. The responses to these questions were all recorded in the questionnaire.

We used a similar strategy in our histories of other dimensions of context. For example, when collecting histories of schools and health services, we recorded the timing of changes in the services provided by the specific school or health service on the calendar. In the questionnaire, we recorded responses to additional items, such as open-ended questions about how the money to construct the school or health service had been raised. Thus, by using the questionnaire to supplement the calendars, we had the flexibility to record a variety of information that was not easily incorporated into the calendar format. This also helped keep the calendar focused on the timing and sequencing of contextual changes.

Data Collection

Although our data collection procedures included some structure, they were not as structured as many standardized individual-level survey interviews (Kahn and Cannell 1957). The calendar itself provided a good deal of structure, defining both the areas of questioning and a suggested sequence of inquiry (Freedman et al. 1988). The accompanying questionnaire also provided the structure of suggested question wordings and standardized probes. However, interviewers were not required to ask questions exactly as worded or follow the sequence of questions.

This strategy has both limitations and strengths. On the one hand, variations in question wording and order are known to affect responses (Biemer et al. 1991; Bradburn 1983; Sudman and Bradburn 1974). On the other hand, flexibility in the interviewing process allows the interview to take on a more natural character, which helps the respondent to provide more accurate and detailed information (Belli 1998; Briggs 1986; Caldwell et al. 1987; Schaeffer 1991; Suchman and Jordan 1990). We believe the combination of our calendars' structure, the supplemental questionnaire wording, and the flexible interviewing protocol minimized large sources of response error while allowing the interviewer to interact more naturally with respondents. This style of contextual data collection parallels a flexible style of collecting data on individual-level demographic behavior that has been applied in a number of studies and is discussed in previous chapters (Axinn et al. 1991; Back and Stycos 1967; Massey 1987a). Note that this flexibility should be accompanied by high levels of interviewer training and supervision in order to produce high-quality data (Fowler 1991).

Our data collection procedures also differed from standardized individual-level surveys because of our multiple-interview format. In each neighborhood, we required interviewers to collect contextual data from at least two different sources, and they often consulted three or four. Further, each of these interviews was not constrained to be an individual interview, and group interviews were common. These group interview situations paralleled the Participatory Rural Appraisal technique, encouraging the assembled neighborhood residents to correct each other and come to some collective agreement about the dates of important neighborhood changes (Chambers 1985). Even when these group interviews were used, we counted the group interview as one source and required interviewers to collect at least one more group interview about the same neighborhood information before leaving the neighborhood. We also cross-checked information provided by neighborhood residents against archival sources whenever possible. In fact, this was often possible, and most dates of changes – like new schools, health services, electrification, and bus services – were cross-checked against archival sources.

Boundary Issues   Every effort to collect contextual data faces the issue of defining boundaries for the context. This issue can be particularly difficult in research on neighborhoods, because they rarely have commonly agreed-upon or well-defined boundaries (Sampson et al. 2002). In the CVFS, a neighborhood was defined as a cluster of 5–15 households. This definition fit the settlement pattern in Chitwan. When the valley was deforested in the mid-1950s, the Nepalese government distributed land parcels to settlers systematically around a prepared road grid. The result was that most farmers settled in small clusters of households surrounded by farm lands.[4] Our approach is likely to work well in any setting with a similar settlement pattern. However, by the time of our study some of these settlements had grown large enough so that our upper limit constituted only part of a larger residential community. In fact, our design included sampling eight clusters from a small city in one corner of Chitwan (Barber et al. 1997). This situation was one reason we chose to ask residents about their context without reference to boundaries, as described below. By avoiding the use of boundaries, residents were able to tell us about any aspect of their context that they considered relevant to their lives, no matter how distant. Because our approach worked well in this situation, we are confident it can be used to gather data on contextual change over time in many different settings, characterized by a wide range of settlement patterns.

Our system for selecting neighborhood clusters was designed to use natural boundaries, such as farmlands, roads, streams, and irrigation canals to identify selected clusters. However, we worked to make our contextual measurements completely independent of our neighborhood boundaries. We accomplished this by visiting each cluster of households and asking residents about their neighborhood context without reference to any boundaries. Our sampling boundaries defined only which residents we asked (although we occasionally spoke with informants who lived near our selected households). As we asked about each domain, respondents were free to tell about any aspect of that domain they felt was relevant, and we asked about time and distance to the characteristic in question. For example, within the school domain, residents were asked about the location of the nearest school and then time and distance to reach that school. No boundaries were used to eliminate some schools. So our neighborhood contextual histories are histories of changes in and around the neighborhood that are salient to residents, not just changes within neighborhood boundaries.

Choosing Informants   As mentioned earlier, we interviewed multiple informants about the same information, sometimes in group interviews. The residents of households located within the selected neighborhoods constituted our set of eligible informants, but no attempt was made to represent the residents of the neighborhood. Interviewers attempted to vary the informants they spoke with in each neighborhood, particularly in terms of age, gender, and education. In general, older informants were particularly helpful because they tended to be more knowledgeable about early events.[5] More-educated informants also tended to be more knowledgeable about some types of changes, such as schools and health services. Those who traveled often were more knowledgeable about bus services and related transportation issues. Thus, interviewing a variety of informants helped us gather reliable information across a variety of domains.

Interviewers also tried to involve a diverse set of informants in group interviews.[6] The participants in group interviews were usually self-selected from those around the neighborhood at the time of the interviewer's visit. However, interviewers encouraged women to join the discussion with their husbands; older, uneducated residents to join discussions with young, educated residents; and residents of various ethnicities to join in discussions. This diversity of perspectives helped to ensure that group interactions brought together many viewpoints about the same contextual changes. This helped us gain insights into the neighborhood changes, get a more complete record of those changes, and generate reliable estimates of the timing of changes.

Consulting Records   In addition to interviewing, we also consulted archival sources whenever possible. Many features of neighborhood contextual change are recorded in public records, either at the local or the regional level. These include features like construction of public schools or health service facilities, electrification, and provision of special economic development programs. Following our general strategy of collecting redundant information, we checked local and regional government agencies for such records, even in cases where interviews had already provided the information. This cross-checking helped identify unreliable information on event timing.

Note that whenever redundant information is collected, discrepancies are likely to occur. We found many discrepancies between reports of construction timing from neighborhood residents and reports in official government documents (discussed in detail below). Furthermore, government documents are not necessarily a more accurate source of information. Many government administrators are motivated to misrepresent construction completion dates. Sometimes, purely bureaucratic issues create discrepancies. For example, the date a school opens for classes may differ from the date government records show the school opened because of a time lag in registering the school with the government. In general, based on a combination of redundant interviews and record checks, we found local records to be more reliable sources of timing information than regional administrative records. For example, a school's own records often proved to be the most reliable source of information on the date a school opened, as many sources of error intervene between local records and regional sources of information.

Recording Techniques   A variety of design features on the neighborhood calendar were created to improve the accuracy of recording. These included repeating both the "year" and "local events" lines multiple times throughout the calendar, shading every other line in the calendar, adding a bold vertical line every ten lines, and repeating the row category in the right-hand margin (see Figure 5.1). Each of these features was designed to reduce the chance that interviewers would record responses in the wrong row or column of the calendar.

For all the neighborhood-level characteristics, we recorded (1) the beginning date for the nearest facility; (2) the beginning date for the nearest facility before that one opened; and (3) the beginning date for the nearest facility before that. These were identified on the calendar with the numerals 1, 2, and 3 (Figure 5.1). Missing data were recorded on the calendar as "NA." Additional information about each of these services (name, time to reach, etc.) was recorded in the accompanying questionnaire. Blank lines on the calendar indicate residents had no access to the service in question. (In addition, interviewers marked that the service did not exist in response to an opening question in the accompanying questionnaire.) We also took complete histories of each of the facilities directly from the facility itself. Each facility was assigned a unique ID number for use in linking data about that facility gathered on different instruments.

In our collection of other contextual histories, we used a broader range of recording devices. For example, in our school and health service history calendars, we recorded numbers of staff and numbers of rooms with up to three-digit integers. We also recorded the existence of services using X's in a starting or ending year. A continuation of the same service is indicated by the line connecting the X's in the first and last years of that service. Examples of these recording techniques are provided in Figures 5.2 and 5.3.

Data Coding and Computer Entry

The coding, data entry, and data management of Neighborhood History Calendar data can be complex. The calendar method produces as many variables as units of time within each substantive domain. As a result, the total number of variables can be as high as the number of substantive domains times the number of time units. Within each domain, data can be entered as a new variable for each new time unit, or data can be entered as spells. Data entry in spells can reduce the data entry tasks when events (or changes in the coded values) are uncommon in each line. However, data entry in spells increases the data entry tasks when these events are quite common.

For example, in our Neighborhood History Calendar, the nearest school could be entered as a spell of points coded 1 going from the year 1971 to the year 1996 (Figure 5.1). This requires entry of both the value of the spell (in this case, 1 for nearest school to the neighborhood) and the entry of the time the spell began and the time the spell ended (years in our case.) This data entry strategy worked well for our Neighborhood History Calendar, where the number of events per line was quite low.

However, this strategy did not work as well for our School History Calendar (described in detail below). That calendar features a number of substantive domains that change value every year. Examples include the number of teachers, the total number of students, and the number of female students. Because these values change every year, data entry in spells becomes quite cumbersome. When the event values change often, it is much more expedient to set up the data entry as a new variable for each time unit (year) and enter a new variable for each time.

In general, we recommend coding and entering the data while in the field. This maximizes the opportunity to reconcile and correct data errors discovered during the coding and entry processes. If coding and data entry take place in the field, when errors or omissions are discovered, it is quite straightforward to return to the data source in question to make corrections. Although this slows the data processing somewhat, the result is a more complete and reliable data set.

Table 5.1. *Number of neighborhoods*
with a school within a 15-minute walk

By year	Number	Percentage
1964	76	44
1974	137	80
1984	142	83
1994	153	90
1996	153	90

Examples of Data Gathered with Neighborhood Calendars

The data from the Neighborhood History Calendar provide a dynamic record of local contextual changes from the neighborhood's point of view. Because these data are collected as independent series of event timings, they can be reorganized into a wide range of useful contextual measures. In this section, we review three ways analysts might use these contextual event history data: (1) as measures of historical change; (2) as measures of exposure to specific characteristics; and (3) as measures of time-varying contextual-level covariates in multilevel hazards models.

Measures of Historical Change   The data from these neighborhood histories can easily be aggregated to provide measures of change over time in the geographic unit from which the neighborhoods were selected. In our case, these data provide a historical account of change over time in the Chitwan Valley of southern Nepal. Because our data include timing to the year, we can assemble an annual history of neighborhood changes in the Chitwan Valley. To simplify presentation of this example, however, we have instead assembled a history of decennial changes beginning in 1964. The first example is presented in Table 5.1.

This table presents the cumulative number of neighborhoods in our sample having any type of school (even if it offers only 1 year of schooling) within a 15-minute walk of the neighborhood. The data come from our Neighborhood History Calendar data collection in our sample of 171 neighborhoods. Because our sample is chosen to be representative of all the neighborhoods in Chitwan Valley, these figures give us measures of the change over time in schooling opportunities in the valley. Fewer than half of the neighborhoods had a school within a 15-minute walk in 1964, but by 1994 a full 90% of the neighborhoods had a school nearby. Note that because we ask for the time to the nearest school, the data could be used to recalibrate these historical change measures for any specific radius, (e.g., 30-minute walk, 1-hour walk).

Table 5.2. *Number of neighborhoods with*
a health service within a 15-minute walk

By year	Number	Percentage
1964	16	9
1974	42	25
1984	57	33
1994	92	54
1996	94	55

Table 5.2 presents the cumulative number of neighborhoods that had some type of health service outlet (ranging from pharmacies to clinics) within a 15-minute walk. Again, the data are presented in decennial increments beginning in the year 1964. Here we see that only 9% of the neighborhoods had a health service outlet within a 15-minute walk by 1964. By 1994, however, more than half of the neighborhoods had nearby health services.

The neighborhood event history data also allow researchers to reconstruct the sequences of changes across a number of different domains. For example, comparing the data in Table 5.1 to those in Table 5.2, it becomes clear that the 1964–1973 decade was a time of dramatic expansion of schooling opportunities in Chitwan, but it is not until the 1984–1993 decade that we see a dramatic expansion in health services. By adding data from our other substantive domains, we could examine the relative timing of the expansion of transportation, employment opportunities, or development programs (see, e.g., Axinn and Yabiku 2001).

Measures of Exposure   Analysts who are most interested in the impact of a particular neighborhood characteristic on some other outcome may use these data to determine the length of time neighborhoods have been exposed to the characteristic in question. For example, in studies of contraceptive use researchers might need to know how long neighborhoods have been exposed to the presence of a nearby school or health service. Table 5.3 provides an example of reorganizing our neighborhood history data into these types of measures.

For each block of years of exposure, Table 5.3 indicates the number of neighborhoods associated with that much exposure to schools or health services. Nearly half of the neighborhoods in Chitwan have had more than 30 years of exposure to a school within a 15-minute walk. Another third have had 21–30 years of exposure to a nearby school, but less than 10% have had no exposure to a nearby school. The picture of exposure to health services is quite different. About a quarter of the neighborhoods had more than 20 years of exposure to

Table 5.3. *Years of exposure to school or health service within a 15-minute walk*

	School		Health service	
Years of exposure	Number of neighborhoods	Percentage of neighborhoods	Number of neighborhoods	Percentage of neighborhoods
31+	81	47	18	10.5
21–30	61	36	27	16
11–20	6	3.5	29	17
Less than 11	7	4.1	26	15
None	16	9.3	71	41.5
Total	171	100	171	100

health services within a 15-minute walk, but nearly half have had no exposure to such services within a 15-minute walk.

Measures of Contextual-Level Time-Varying Covariates   Perhaps the most exciting use of the neighborhood event history data is as measures of contextual-level time-varying covariates for use in dynamic multilevel models. Consider a multilevel model focusing on a dynamic outcome, such as marriage timing. To estimate a dynamic model of marriage timing examining individual-level covariates (such as educational experience or attitudes), most researchers today would use event history, or hazards, models (Heaton and Call 1995; Landale 1994; Yamaguchi 1991). Using these techniques, one could model the transition to marriage as a dynamic process, also allowing covariates (predictors) to vary with time (Petersen 1991; Xie 1994; Yamaguchi 1991). For example, one could allow school enrollment to vary month to month in predicting the hazard of marriage (Thornton et al. 1995).

Using neighborhood event history calendar data, we can take the same dynamic approach in a multilevel model of marriage timing in which the neighborhood is the contextual level being examined. For example, in a discrete-time hazards model of the transition to marriage, we could code each of the increments of time with a characteristic of the neighborhood and allow those characteristics to change over time. So in some periods, a neighborhood might be characterized as having no school; in other periods, it might be characterized as having only an elementary school; and in still other periods, it might be characterized as having both an elementary and a high school. One could then estimate the impact of the different schooling opportunities on the transition to marriage through various periods. Using this time-varying covariates framework, we could also construct measures of the amount of time since any neighborhood change took place. For example, we could estimate the impact of years of exposure to the opportunity to attend high school on the hazard rate of marriage. Thus, the combination of detailed dynamic neighborhood history data and the flexibility of event history or hazards models will allow the construction of dynamic multilevel models.

Estimation of dynamic multilevel models with contextual-level time-varying covariates raises some technical obstacles. Although these estimation issues are beyond the scope of this chapter, recent advances in multilevel modeling of discrete dependent variables provide the means to overcome these obstacles (Barber et al. 2000; Goldstein 1995; Sastry 1997; Wong and Mason 1985). As a result, a number of recently published works use contextual-level time-varying covariates to operationalize fully dynamic multilevel models. These include analyses of the impact of community change on fertility limitation (Axinn and Yabiku 2001), analyses of the impact of mass education on fertility limitation (Axinn and Barber 2001), and analyses of the impact of community change on educational attainment (Beutel and Axinn 2002). Readers interested in more-detailed discussion of the use of contextual history data for dynamic multilevel models should consult these examples.

Evaluating Data Quality

Evaluation of data quality often depends on the availability of two or more independent sources of information about the same issue or event. Because the CVFS collected data from multiple sources about a number of topics, a good deal of information gathered during the course of the study speaks to the quality of the data. However, it is rare that researchers are in a position to know which of the two or more measures of the same event is, in fact, correct. In some circumstances, when errors are reasonably presumed to be in one direction only (such as underreporting), it is possible to interpret the difference between data collected by two different techniques as a reflection of data quality. Previous work in Nepal indicates that in these circumstances ethnographic interviewing generally provides higher-quality measures of individual behaviors than surveys (Axinn 1989; Stone and Campbell 1984).

Our design of the Neighborhood History Calendar instruments was based on ethnographic interviews and pretests that compared various techniques for collecting information on the timing and sequencing of changes in objective characteristics of community contexts. These comparisons led us to believe that multiple-respondent interviews were superior to single-respondent interviews because different respondents remembered different changes in the community and the conversation among respondents helped them remind each other of the sequences of changes. The comparisons also led us to believe that the calendar instrument provided a critical visual aid giving multiple respondents the means to pool their input. Finally, our comparisons also led us to believe that the structure and visual representation of data inherent in the calendar helped interviewers make fewer errors in recording complex sequences of community change over time.

Our ethnographic work also revealed the limits of the Neighborhood History Calendar method. Although neighborhood residents defined broad aspects of the context in which they lived, they were often unable to provide reliable information about specific characteristics of that context. For example, residents of the neighborhood could always identify the school or health service nearest to the neighborhood, but they often had difficulty knowing the date that that particular school or health service first opened. Neighborhood residents were generally even less knowledgeable about the timing of changes in more detailed characteristics of the school or health service, such as the number of teachers, classrooms, clinicians, or examining rooms. To measure many of these specific dimensions, we found it necessary to visit the school or health service in question and collect data with a calendar designed especially for the purpose.

We used our ethnographic interviews, archival data collection, and specific school (or health service, etc.) history information to create a composite measure of the time each school or other service first opened. This process involved comparison of several sources of information regarding the same event and a subjective evaluation of the quality of each source. Investigators made decisions regarding the likely accuracy of each source and then, using all the sources, created a final composite measure. We kept careful records of the information used to reach this subjective evaluation, and we applied the same criteria across the entire sample; the judgment regarding quality of source is nonetheless subjective. We argue that direct involvement of the investigators in the fieldwork and their participation in the processes of collecting the different reports gives the investigators the best possible chance of reaching a reasonable judgment about the quality of reports.[7]

Table 5.4 provides a comparison of our composite measures to the measures initially provided by neighborhood residents. As shown in the table, our final composite measure, based on multiple sources of information, matches the original report from neighborhood residents to within the same year in less than half of our neighborhoods. The corresponding figure dips to a mere 20% for health services.[8] In fact, in nearly one-third of the neighborhoods the neighborhood report of the opening date differed from the corresponding composite measure by more than 2 years (Table 5.4). Our initial ethnographic work led us to suspect the accuracy of residents' reports, and these comparisons support the notion that our composite measures (compiled from several sources) provide somewhat different information. Note that for some specific analyses researchers may feel that residents' perceptions of the timing of change is more relevant than the actual timing of change. Because of this possibility, we chose

Table 5.4. *Deviation between neighborhood respondents' report of school or health service opening date and composite measure of opening date (schools and health services within a 15-minute walk)*

Deviation (years)	Schools (%)	Health Services (%)
0	46	20
1–2	25	50
More than 2	29	30
Total	100	100

to preserve both the residents' reports and our composite measures in the final data.

We found residents' reports of more-specific aspects of change over time in local schools and other parts of the infrastructure even less reliable. We found official government reports at the regional and national levels equally suspect. Officials often had motivation to inflate change in their region. As a result, we turned to written records kept at the specific school, health service, etc. and interviews with staff at these services to gather accurate measurement of change over time. Below, we outline the techniques that we used to gather dynamic event histories of changes in schools, health services, and other contextual features. By applying our contextual history calendar methods to other contexts, we were able to both improve the accuracy of our event timing data and refine our measurement of contextual characteristics.

Key Advantages of the Neighborhood History Calendar Design

Before turning to extensions of the neighborhood history calendar method described above, we briefly review the key advantages of this hybrid mixed method approach.

Advantages of a Calendar Format

An important reason for using a neighborhood (or contextual) history calendar is that it improves respondent recall (Caspi et al. 1995; Freedman et al. 1988). This may be because a calendar instrument allows a respondent to see the sequence of events on paper. This visual inspection helps individuals recall the timing and sequencing of events. The calendar format also helps respondents use events that are more salient to help them remember the timing of less salient events

(Eisenhower et al. 1991). For example, as discussed in the previous chapter, a respondent might use his or her recall of graduation from college to help recall the timing of a change in living arrangements from a dorm to an apartment. Or, in recalling contextual history, a respondent might use her or his recall of an important national event, such as a national election, to recall an event in the neighborhood, such as the building of a school nearby.

Calendars also improve data quality by improving interviewing quality. Previous research on the quality of retrospective data collected using calendar instruments indicates no significant differences in data quality when the calendar was administered face-to-face versus a telephone interview (Freedman et al. 1988). This finding suggests that the *interviewer's* inspection of the calendar may be equally important in obtaining complete and accurate data. This may be particularly so in cases with detailed sequences of events, when the calendar technique makes sequences easy to record and overlaps quick to detect. Thus, interviewers use the visual calendar display to quickly review a respondent's recall for completeness and accuracy and then probe to improve data quality.

Given the multiple-interview approach used in the contextual history data collection we describe here, the impact of the calendar format on interviewing quality may be even more important to overall data quality. Although measurement errors due to the respondent are likely to occur (Groves 1987), by interviewing multiple respondents about the same events and cross-checking with archival sources, this method is designed to detect and correct such errors in the field. The calendar format becomes one of the interviewers' most important tools for detecting such errors. So although the calendar format is an aid to a particular respondent during one interview, it is also an aid to the interviewer across multiple interviews regarding the same subject.

Advantages of a Mixed Method Data Collection Approach

A mixed method contextual-level data collection approach has many advantages. First, by combining the structure of a calendar with multiple semi-structured interviews, we gathered a standardized set of contextual measures while also providing respondents with an opportunity to describe important contextual characteristics or changes that could not be known before visiting the neighborhood. This allowed us to counterbalance the weaknesses of a fully structured approach with that of a less structured approach. The approach constituted a useful technique for uncovering important, but localized, contextual changes and events that investigators could not know until the study was in the field, but also provided enough structure to ensure that the same dimensions of context were measured similarly in all the neighborhoods. Another benefit of having the investigators involved in the field was the local knowledge of the context they gained through ethnographic components of the study. With this background and rich, detailed information, we were also able to collect information on contextual characteristics that may have been difficult to interpret without ethnographic data. Examples include the aims and activities of local women's groups and government programs. Third, by implementing a high level of supervision and investigator involvement, we were able to maintain the flexibility that allows for the revision of instruments and data collection procedures in the field. We believe this iterative redesign led to the most complete data collection possible as well as to higher data quality. By collecting redundant data from multiple sources, including multiple respondents and available archival sources, we were able to discover discrepancies in the field and resolve them before the data collection was complete. This multiple-interview format also allowed us to seek out respondents who were most informed about each specific subject. For example, recent in-migrants to a neighborhood usually knew little of early events in the history of the neighborhood. In sum, although the methods described in this chapter focus on collecting contextual-level data, the approach still aims to improve data quality through counterbalancing the strengths and weaknesses of multiple methods, requiring high investigator involvement in the field and incorporating a flexibility that addresses issues as they arise.

Other Contextual History Calendars

The Neighborhood History Calendar data collection method can easily be adapted for other forms of contextual history data collection. Different substantive aims may lead researchers to apply this technique to a variety of social, economic, or cultural contextual features. As mentioned above, even in the CVFS we found important reasons for expanding our contextual history data collection beyond Neighborhood History Calendars alone. By applying our contextual history calendar methods to other contexts, we were able to both improve the accuracy of our event timing data and refine our measurement of contextual characteristics.

School History Calendars

We used regional government records and local interviews to make a list of every school in our study area. This included schools in the study area that were not mentioned in neighborhood interviews and those that were open previously but closed by the time of the data collection. So any school that had ever existed in our study area was included in the list. Our data collection at each of these schools was organized around a School History Calendar and an accompanying questionnaire designed using the same protocols as described above for Neighborhood History Calendars. Figure 5.2 provides an example

School ID : 07-06-195   Name of the School: Khaja Secondary School

Events 1–7 (Years 54–75)

Event	54	55	56	57	58	59	60	61	62	63	64	65	66	67	68	69	70	71	72	73	74	75
1. School Location		X			X1	X2																
2. Highest Grade			2	3	4	5	6	7	8	8	9	10										
3. Lowest Grade	1												6						4			
4. No. of Classrooms		1							1	7												
5. No. of Teachers		1	2	2	3		6	6	7	8	8	11	12	13	15	16	20	19	20	21	22	22
6. No. of Students					7	20	60	100	109	123	121	136	189	348	510	565	270	275	261	434	464	485
7. No. of Female Students			0	5	10	12	14	19	16	24	33	38	67	74	32	34	36	39	77	76	90	103

Events 1–7 (Years 76–96)

Event	76	77	78	79	80	81	82	83	84	85	86	87	88	89	90	91	92	93	94	95	96
1. School Location					*	*								*	*					X2	
2. Highest Grade																				10	
3. Lowest Grade																				1	
4. No. of Classrooms				7	18															8	
5. No. of Teachers	23	24			18								18	30					30	34	
6. No. of Students	503	579	617	672	695	783	838	679	769	925	974	756	667	708	637	715	1325	994	996	1064	
7. No. of Female Students	133	153	174	194	201	233	237	185	273	365	349	281	265	269	253	328	631	477	474	536	

Events 8–13 (Years 54–75)

Event	54	55	56	57	58	59	60	61	62	63	64	65	66	67	68	69	70	71	72	73	74	75
8. Tuition Grade 1		Inap		0																		
9. Tuition for Grade 10		Inap									10	10.3		10.3	10.5		10.5	11				
10. Other Fees Grade 1															Inap							
11. Other Fees Grade 10		Inap										5	2.5				2.5	22	22	35	25	25
12. General Curriculum																						
13. Curriculum Family Planning																						

Events 8–13 (Years 76–96)

Event	76	77	78	79	80	81	82	83	84	85	86	87	88	89	90	91	92	93	94	95	96
8. Tuition Grade 1																				0	
9. Tuition for Grade 10		13	13.8	16.3		16.3		20		20		26	26	40			Inap			40	
10. Other Fees Grade 1																	Inap				
11. Other Fees Grade 10		39	22	21.5	18	24	26	53	33	33			40	26	52	52	95	100	190	175	
12. General Curriculum																			X	X	
13. Curriculum Family Planning				X																X	

Year	54	55	56	57	58	59	60	61	62	63	64	65	66	67	68	69	70	71	72	73	74	75	76	77	78	79	80	81	82	83	84	85	86	87	88	89	90	91	92	93	94	95	96
Event																																											
14. No. Students in Hostel		0																																								0	
15. No. of Female Students in Hostel			Inap																													9	10									Inap	
16. No. of Graduate Teachers				0								1	4	4	5	5	7	8					8	9	8	9						9						1				0	
17. Medium																																											
18. No. of Female Teachers				0					0	1	0	1	2	2	0	0	0	1		1	2	2	2	3	3	3	1	0	1	2	1	0						0	2			2	
Year	54	55	56	57	58	59	60	61	62	63	64	65	66	67	68	69	70	71	72	73	74	75	76	77	78	79	80	81	82	83	84	85	86	87	88	89	90	91	92	93	94	95	96

Key:

*   National and regional events entered on calendars to aid respondent recall. Examples: elections, earthquakes, flooding.

X1, X2   (in Line 1 - School Location) X1 indicates the years the school was at its first location, X2 indicates the years the school was at its second location, and X3 indicates another location, etc.

Inap   Information not appropriate in this school (e.g., this school had no hostel, so the question about the number of girls in the hostel is inappropriate).

Numbers   (in Lines 8-11) Indicate the number of rupees for tuition or fees.

X   (in Line 12 - General Curriculum) Indicates that the standard, government curriculum was followed.

X   (in Line 13 - Curriculum Family Planning) Indicates that the curriculum included some family planning content.

Blanks   (in Lines 12 and 13) Indicate that the standard, government curriculum was not used, or that the curriculum did not include family planning content.

Note: Names and identifiers have been changed to protect the anonymity of the school. Nepali years were used in the data collection. Western year 1996 = Nepali year 2052/2053.

Figure 5.2. An example of a completed School History Calendar from the Chitwan Valley Family Study

of a completed School History Calendar from one of the oldest schools in the study area.

As shown in the figure, the design of the School History Calendar paralleled the design of our Neighborhood History Calendar. Time units run across the top marking the column headings, and substantive domains run down the side marking row headings. We began substantive domains with the location of the school, which was recorded on both the calendar and the questionnaire. As mentioned above, some schools changed location, such as the one depicted in Figure 5.2, so the timing of these changes was recorded on the first line of the calendar. Other lines of the calendar were used to record changes in a variety of important characteristics of schools in Chitwan, including highest grade offered; number of classrooms, teachers, and students; tuition and fees; and curriculum. This information dramatically improved our knowledge of the schooling opportunities available to the residents of each neighborhood, from simply knowing that a school existed to knowing how many grades, classrooms, and teachers were available, as well as other information. These procedures also allowed us to measure much more gradual changes over time in educational opportunities than the neighborhood calendars could alone.

At each school, we attempted to complete as much of the calendar as possible using data from the school's own records before turning to alternative means to gather missing information. Our first alternative was in-depth interviews with school administrators, and we followed this with in-depth interviews with teachers. In the older schools, we often encountered situations in which none of the current administrators or teachers was familiar with the early history of the school. To overcome this problem, we tracked retired administrators and teachers to their homes (usually in Chitwan but occasionally elsewhere) and interviewed them. We also tracked retired administrators and teachers in the few cases where a school existed previously but had closed by the time of our interview.

Health Service History Calendars

As we did with schools, we used regional government records and local interviews to make a listing of every health service outlet in our study area. These health services included hospitals, clinics, dispensaries, and pharmacies. We used a broad definition of health services because each of these outlets provides access to some types of contraceptive methods, and a central aim of the study was to estimate the impact of access to contraceptive methods on actual use of contraceptive methods. The type of health service was recorded in questionnaires accompanying the calendars.

Figure 5.3 provides an example of one of our completed Health Service History Calendars from a clinic in our study area. Again, years and events run across the top, forming column headings designed to provide cues to aid recall of the timing of service changes. Substantive domains run down the side, forming row headings. The first row of the calendar specifies the years in which the health service in question was open to the public. Exact dates were recorded in the accompanying questionnaire. The domains on the calendar include days and hours of operation, numbers of staff, aspects of the physical facility, types of contraceptive methods available, and the cost of each service (in rupees per unit). Blank lines indicate the service was not available, and "NA" indicates the interviewers were unable to ascertain whether the service was offered or its cost.[9]

As with schools, data collection was conducted by visiting each health service, gaining permission to consult the outlet's records and interviewing administrators and health workers to fill gaps in the records. Also similar to schools, a variety of recording techniques were used on the Health Service Calendars. The recording techniques are explained in Figure 5.3.

Other Extensions

The contextual history calendar method proved flexible enough to be used in a wide array of substantive applications. For example, we used the technique to gather histories of transportation changes in our study area. We designed a calendar to correspond to each road or bus route in the valley. The calendars were designed to record the types of vehicles used for public transportation on the route across time, such as tractors, jeeps, buses, and motorized rickshaws. The calendars were also designed to record the time to traverse the route and the cost of traveling the route in different periods. Data collection was conducted by going directly to the owners of vehicles used for public transportation on the route and to long-time residents who lived at important stops along each route.

In another example, we used the contextual history calendar method to collect data on changes in banking services. Bank records and bank administrators were consulted to provide a history of changes in loan programs, interest rates, savings levels, and special outreach programs. We used a similar strategy to apply the calendar technique to the collection of histories of government programs in the study area. By working with local program authorities and using their records, we collected histories of changes in program participation, activities, objectives, etc. These data provide rich measurement of the socioeconomic context within which our study population has spent their lives.

Overall, the history calendar techniques proved to be a useful method for piecing together data from multiple sources to collect a complete, dynamic record of changes over time in a wide range of infrastructure in our study area. The resulting data are quite flexible. The measures we gathered can be used to assemble a complete history of the many different types of services available or a

Health Service ID : 13-12-176   Name of the Health Service: Khaja Medical Hall

Year	54	55	56	57	58	59	60	61	62	63	64	65	66	67	68	69	70	71	72	73	74	75	76	77	78	79	80	81	82	83	84	85	86	87	88	89	90	91	92	93	94	95	96	Year
Event																																												Event
1. Open			*																*					*					*					*			*							1. Open
2. Service-days/week																														X	7				X	7								2. Service-days/week
3. Service-hours/day																														10			12										12	3. Service-hours/day
4. No. of Staff																														1		1	2					2						4. No. of Staff
5. Health Workers																														X			X											5. Health Workers
6. Patient Check-up																														X			X											6. Patient Check-up
7. No. of Rooms																														1		1	2			2								7. No. of Rooms

Year	54	55	56	57	58	59	60	61	62	63	64	65	66	67	68	69	70	71	72	73	74	75	76	77	78	79	80	81	82	83	84	85	86	87	88	89	90	91	92	93	94	95	96	Year
Event																																												Event
8. Pills			*																*					*					*				2				*				2.5	3	3	8. Pills
9. IUD & Loop																																					2							9. IUD & Loop
10. Depoprovera																																												10. Depoprovera
11. Condom																																		1.5						.5	2	2.5	2.5	11. Condom
12. Foam																																				3				3			6	12. Foam
13. Laproscopy																																												13. Laproscopy
14. Vasectomy																																												14. Vasectomy
15. Other																																												15. Other

Year	54	55	56	57	58	59	60	61	62	63	64	65	66	67	68	69	70	71	72	73	74	75	76	77	78	79	80	81	82	83	84	85	86	87	88	89	90	91	92	93	94	95	96
Event		*																	*					*				*					*			*							
16. Mobile Camp																																											
17. Motivation																																											
18. Birthing																														X					X								
19. Child Vaccination																																											
20. Diarrhea																														X					X								
21. Nutrition																														X				X	X								
22. Prenatal																					X									X					X								
Year	54	55	56	57	58	59	60	61	62	63	64	65	66	67	68	69	70	71	72	73	74	75	76	77	78	79	80	81	82	83	84	85	86	87	88	89	90	91	92	93	94	95	96

	Event
	16. Mobile Camp
	17. Motivation
	18. Birthing
	19. Child Vaccination
	20. Diarrhea
	21. Nutrition
	22. Prenatal

Key:

* National and regional events entered on calendars to aid respondent recall. Examples: elections, earthquakes, flooding.

X (in Line 1 - Open) Indicates that the facility was open in that year.

X (in Line 6 - Patient Check-Up) Indicates that the facility provided check-ups in that year.

Numbers (in Lines 8-15) Indicate the price (in rupees) for each service listed for each year. No number indicates that the service was not available during that year.

Blanks (in Lines 8-15) Indicate the service did not exist. (Interviewers were required to respond to opening questions about the existence of each service in the accompanying questionnaire.)

X (in Lines 16-22) Indicates that the service was provided in that year.

Note: Names and identifiers have been changed to protect the anonymity of the health service center. Nepali years were used in the data collection. Western year 1996 = Nepali year 2052/2053.

Figure 5.3. An example of a completed Health Services History calendar from the Chitwan Valley Family Study

history of the quality of the different services available. For example, one might create dynamic measures of change over time in teacher-to-student ratios or student-to-classroom ratios. Or one could create dynamic measures of the availability of contraceptive distribution outlets in the valley. In addition, by recording the location of each service, one can construct summary measures of the quality or availability of services within a particular radius of each neighborhood in the study area or, for that matter, each household in the study area. Techniques for accomplishing this are discussed in detail below. Once such summary measures are created, they can easily be incorporated in multilevel models of individual-level outcomes that quality of schooling opportunities are believed to affect, such as educational attainment.

Using Geographic Information System Technology to Enhance Contextual Data

Not only do neighborhood residents find it difficult to report on specific characteristics of services near their neighborhood, they also find it difficult to report on all the different services that shape their context. Residents of the 171 neighborhoods we sampled were able to tell us about the two or three schools nearest their neighborhood, or most salient to them, but reporting on all the different educational opportunities within a reasonable bicycling distance (say, 1 hour each way) proved too demanding a task. Yet Chitwan Valley is only 100 square miles, so the combination of all the schooling opportunities nearby constitutes an important element of the context within which these people live. The same is true for other services, such as health care services and government programs. The multiple calendar strategy, described above, gave us the means to collect detailed information about the changes over time in all the aspects of services and infrastructure in Chitwan. But in order to use the full breadth of this information to create measures of the context, these data must be linked to specific neighborhoods and a means must be devised to distinguish those services near each specific neighborhood from services that are further away.

Geographic Information System (GIS) technology provides the tools to solve this problem. GIS is a collection of computer software and hardware designed to create, enter, manage, and analyze data on spatial relationships (Burrough 1986; Maguire et al. 1991). The Global Positioning System (GPS) is a GIS tool specifically designed to measure the spatial location of points on the earth's surface in terms of their longitude, latitude, and altitude.[10] Other tools, such as digitizers, can be used to enter existing spatial data, such as maps, into a GIS. GIS software can then be used to organize multiple sources of spatial data and calculate distances between points. Although GIS technology is primarily used by geographers, it has many potential applications in the social sciences (Entwisle et al. 1996; Heywood 1990; Martin 1996). Our main interest here is the tremendous potential of these tools to contribute to the creation of contextual summary measures for use in models of individual behavior. For example, using these tools we can create measures of distance between each neighborhood and all the schools in Chitwan and summary measures of educational context within any particular distance of each specific neighborhood.

In the CVFS, GPS devices recorded the location of each of the neighborhoods in our study area. These devices were also used to measure the location of each of the contextual features of interest in the study, including schools, health service outlets, banks, and government programs. This location data can then be appended to the corresponding history calendar data. When the location data are entered into a GIS, the GIS can generate distance measures – for example, between a neighborhood and each of the schools in the study area. Using these distances, it is also possible to identify each of the schools within a certain distance of each neighborhood. Thus, we can construct measures of the distance to all the schooling opportunities in the study area or measures of all those schools within a specific distance. These measures can also be linked to measures of the characteristics of the schools to estimate the quality of schooling opportunities to which residents have access. Given the temporal dimension in our measures of quality of schooling opportunities, such measures can also be created for each specific point in time.

Data from other sources can also be input into the GIS in order to construct new access variables. For example, one can digitize maps of physical features or road networks into the GIS. In the CVFS, we used aerial photographs of the study area to make maps of the road network, which were digitized into the GIS. By linking specific roads with our bus service history calendar data, we developed measures of the location of various transportation services relative both to residents' households and to specific services. Because the bus service calendars include time to traverse the route and our neighborhood data include time to reach the nearest bus stop, we can use the GIS to create measures of the time or cost to travel from each neighborhood to any specific service (such as a health clinic) in the study area. In fact, GIS technology can use these variables to calculate the shortest route to nearby health clinics (e.g., Entwisle et al. 1996).

By using these GIS technologies to link our neighborhood history data together in space, we add an important new component to the array of measures possible from these data collection procedures. Now measures of historical change or of exposure to change can be ordered in space. From the perspective of each specific neighborhood, measures of exposure to change can be constructed to indicate whether the change is nearby, far away, or in between. These measures make it possible to test spatial hypotheses regarding the effects of context, such as the hypothesis that school opportunities near a family's household have more impact on that family's behavior than do schooling opportunities far from the family's household. Even in a multilevel hazards modeling framework, these spatial data allow researchers to add measures of distance to contextual-level time-varying covariates. This addition provides the means to test the impact of variations in distance to contextual changes on individual-level outcomes.

The spatial measures created with GIS have other uses as well. Residents' perceptions of access to contextual features are always likely to be an important aspect of evaluating the impact of context on individual behavior. However, independent information on spatial location provides an important advantage. Respondents' reports of distance and time to nearby services are known to be characterized by measurement error. Use of GIS technology to obtain an independent set of distance measures provides a means of correcting for this measurement error.

Conclusion

The Neighborhood History Calendar data collection method outlined here is designed to collect a record of community-level change over time for use in dynamic multilevel models. The method is based on Life History Calendar techniques that were designed to collect a dynamic event history of individual life courses (Caspi et al. 1995; Freedman et al. 1988). The Neighborhood History Calendar method integrates the structure of a calendar and accompanying questionnaires with a more flexible data collection strategy, including some reliance on archival data collection, so that the strengths of multiple methods could counterbalance their collective weaknesses. The result is a standardized technique for collecting measures of community change over time flexible enough to be adapted to many different settings and a wide range of substantive aims. In fact, we found that the technique worked equally well for measurement of changes over time in neighborhoods, schools, health services, transportation, banks, and government programs. Our success with the method across these many different contexts and among a multiethnic, multilingual study population is consistent with the conclusion that this history calendar technique provides a reliable means of gathering contextual event history data for many substantive purposes.

The method reported here generates data with three important advantages over contextual data from other sources that are commonly used in multilevel models. First, current multilevel modeling efforts tend to rely on static measures of context, taken at one or two points in time. Thus, individuals are assigned contextual characteristics that correspond only to the point in time at which they were measured. However, contexts are continually changing. For example, a neighborhood that had a school in 1990 may not have one by 1991. This issue is particularly problematic when comparing multiple contexts. Consider two neighborhoods (A and B) that both had health clinics in 1990 while neither had a clinic in 1980. Suppose the clinic in neighborhood A opened in 1981 while the clinic in neighborhood B opened in 1989. Contextual data from two points in time (1980 and 1990) will indicate the same health care contexts in these two neighborhoods even though individuals in neighborhood A have had a much different history of health care from those in neighborhood B. However, our complete neighborhood event history measurement will demonstrate that these two contexts are quite different. This continuous record of contextual dynamics is an important advantage over static measurement (Rossi et al. 1980).

Second, our method also allows examination of the sequence of contextual change, so that even when neighborhoods (or other contexts) have experienced multiple changes, we can decipher which came first. For instance, in neighborhoods with both bus service and a school, we can determine whether the neighborhood first had bus service and then a school was built or a school was built and then bus service began. This is an important advantage because community differences are often characterized by variations in more than one factor, and the order of changes allows researchers to differentiate among contexts (Casterline 1985). For instance, discovering that a respondent who lives in a neighborhood with both bus service and a school is more likely to use contraception than a respondent who lives in a neighborhood without either is difficult to interpret because it is unclear whether the effect is due to the presence of the bus service or the presence of the school.

Third, our approach provides direct measures of contextual features rather than secondary measures generated by aggregating individual-level measures. For example, using the Neighborhood History Calendar, we collected changes over time in the location of the nearest school and aspects of that school to measure the neighborhood's educational context rather than using the average level of individual educational attainment in the neighborhood. Many multilevel modeling efforts use contextual measures constructed by aggregating individual-level characteristics (Blalock 1985; Brewster 1994; Brooks-Gunn et al. 1993; Casterline 1985; Hirschman and Guest 1990). Using our method, the researcher collects data on contextual features rather than aggregating individual-level characteristics. This approach avoids some of the pitfalls involved with multilevel modeling using aggregated data (Blalock 1985) and instead focuses attention on contextual characteristics that cannot be disaggregated to the individual level.

Of course, as mentioned in the introduction, the Neighborhood History Calendar method does not solve all the problems involved in creating completely dynamic multilevel models. One problem facing all multilevel analysis is the mobility of individuals. When contextual data are linked to individual-level data, it is usually assumed that individuals have lived in that context for a long time, even their entire lives. When individuals move, this assumption is untenable. Those who have moved have been exposed to other contextual characteristics besides those measured in the analysis. Depending on the length of time lived in other contexts and the number of different contexts experienced, the mobile individual's cumulative contextual experience may be quite different than that of a lifetime resident. Unfortunately, the collection of dynamic contextual event histories is not a solution to this problem.

A variety of solutions to this problem may be possible. Migration histories administered at the individual level could be used to identify the location of previous residences. With this information, researchers could visit each previous residence of a respondent and gather contextual data from those neighborhoods. However, this strategy is likely to prove cumbersome in a highly mobile population. Both the number of moves and the distance between residences will dramatically increase data collection costs.

A second solution may be to ask respondents about their exposure to contextual characteristics of interest in an individual-level questionnaire. This strategy has the advantage of matching the contextual data collection directly to the individual's residence history. However, individuals may find it difficult to recall contextual characteristics from earlier in their lives. This problem may be exacerbated among individuals who have migrated often and have lived in many different contexts. This approach may also restrict the precision with which contextual characteristics can be measured. Individuals are unlikely to be able to recall many specific aspects of contextual features from their previous residences.

Though all solutions to this problem have limitations, individual-level mobility histories give researchers a tool to examine the plausibility of their assumptions about mobility. Life histories designed for use in multilevel models should always include mobility histories. By combining such life histories with dynamic histories of contextual change, researchers will be able to construct dynamic multilevel models that match dynamic reality. We turn to a detailed example of life history data collection, including mobility histories, in Chapter 6.

Given the broad interest in contextual effects across many substantive areas of social science inquiry, it is quite likely that multilevel modeling efforts will become more common in the future (Bryk and Raudenbush 1992; DiPrete and Forristal 1994; Goldstein 1995; Ringdal 1992). Furthermore, dynamic event history models have many advantages to offer in modeling the individual-level outcomes of interest to multilevel researchers (Petersen 1991; Yamaguchi 1991). Thus, it seems likely that future multilevel modeling efforts will take on an increasingly dynamic nature. Unfortunately, limitations of the contextual measurements currently available to researchers create an important obstacle to the development and application of truly dynamic multilevel models. The data collection method described here was designed to overcome that obstacle and provide the means to gather a complete event history record of contextual-level change.

Issues of Application

Throughout this chapter, we have argued that Neighborhood History Calendar methods can be used to measure contextual change over time across many different subjects and in many different settings. Nevertheless, some subjects may be less appropriate for this type of measurement. For example, the calendar methods described in this chapter are primarily designed to measure change over time in social and economic infrastructure, not the spread of ideational phenomena. If the spread of new ideas can be operationalized as change over time in an observable contextual characteristic – such as the spread of radios and televisions, changes in media programs, the creation of movie theaters, or the distribution of written media – then the calendar methods can be adapted for this purpose. When such changes are conceptualized as the spread of new ideas among individuals, then individual-level data collection strategies are more appropriate. Thus, some subject matter may not be well suited to Neighborhood History Calendar measurement.

Likewise, setting specific variation in the geographic spread of social relationships, social organizations, or social institutions may either render Neighborhood History Calendars an inappropriate method or force investigators to alter the method. In the Nepalese case described here, transportation and communication infrastructure are weak and most social relationships are organized on an extremely local level. This provides an important contrast to wealthy country contexts with more-complex transportation and communication infrastructures. Moreover, this setting contrast interacts with the subject being measured to render the Neighborhood History Calendar method differentially useful for the measurement of various subjects in these two types of settings.

For example, consider the measurement of marketplaces. In the rural Nepalese setting, most goods and services are purchased from nearby vendors – the Neighborhood History Calendar method works well for measures of access to markets. By contrast, in a rich country like the United States, if many products and services can be purchased by telephone or on the Internet, then the Neighborhood History Calendar method may not provide good measures of access to markets. Household or individual measures of access to telephone and Internet communication may be more appropriate measures of access to markets.

On the other hand, for some subjects the Neighborhood History Calendar method is likely to work equally well in both types of settings. Subject matter that refers to physical location of a service provides good examples of this. If attempting to measure change over time in the distance to the nearest bus stop, for example, this method is designed to work well in both Nepal and the United States. Thus, one must consider both the setting-specific context and the specific subject to be measured in reaching decisions about when and how to apply the Neighborhood History Calendar method.

Scaling the application of Neighborhood History Calendar data collection to larger or smaller projects may create important issues for researchers. The method requires field staff conducting the data collection to be more highly competent and well trained than most survey interviewers. This is because interviewers using these calendar tools must be able to capitalize on the flexibility introduced to facilitate recall. The interviewers must be conscientious and able to think quickly and creatively. The method works quite well when conducted by a single highly trained investigator familiar with the level of detail and flexibility necessary. On the other hand, when the number of institutions or places from which a history is being collected is too great for one interviewer, this method can be expanded to a larger number of highly trained data collection staff. In the application described in this chapter, we employed 10 highly trained interviewers to collect data from a large number of neighborhoods, schools, health services, bus routes, banks, and government projects over several years. To date, we have gathered more than one thousand contextual histories, and the time and training resources required have been substantial. With these investments, however, it is quite possible to use this method on a large scale.

Illustrations of Principles

The integration of mixed methods into a single hybrid tool such as the Neighborhood History Calendar provides illustrations of several of the mixed method data collection principles identified in Chapter 1. The illustrations include both principles closely tied to the theme of using strengths of some methods to counterbalance weaknesses of other methods and principles closely tied to the theme of comprehensive empirical documentation. As discussed above, the Neighborhood History Calendar method integrates the structure of a calendar and accompanying questionnaires with a more flexible data collection strategy, including some reliance on direct observation and archival data collection, so that the strengths of multiple methods can counterbalance the weaknesses of other methods. The method provides a standardized technique for collecting measures of contextual change over time that is quite flexible. This flexibility is advantageous both for adapting to new information learned during the course of the study and to applications across many different settings and a wide range of substantive aims.

Clearly, the Neighborhood History Calendar is also a hybrid method explicitly aimed at adding a new dimension to the comprehensive empirical documentation of a subject. The method both explicitly aims to measure dimensions of the social environment that are at a higher level of aggregation than the individual and aims to provide a high level of temporal order among measures. This information on temporal order is particularly powerful for establishing the order of changes at the contextual level of interest in an effort to document which changes may be responsible for causing other changes. By combining this contextual-level measurement with individual-level measurement that also includes a high degree of temporal order among measures, it is possible to establish the temporal order of changes potentially linking factors across levels. This characteristic can be extremely useful in both studies of the effects of context on individuals and studies of the effects of individuals on contexts.

Although the emphasis in the comprehensive empirical record created through Neighborhood History Calendars is clearly on temporal order, the flexibility of the method also makes it useful for the investigation of potential causal mechanisms. This is because the multiple-visit group interview, open-format techniques provide a great deal of opportunity for informants to explain what they believe has changed over time and how they believe these changes have taken place. This technique is explicitly aimed at discovering new contextual characteristics or changes that investigators did not know about before the field-work began. In some cases, this new information may point toward mechanisms or linking contextual changes over time or to individuals. Thus, these dimensions of the comprehensive empirical record generated by the Neighborhood History Calendar method are potentially quite useful in studies of cause and consequence that involve context.

6   Life History Calendars

Life History Calendars (LHCs) are designed to collect individual-level information on the timing of personal events and circumstances. As social scientists increasingly focus on cause and consequence and design complex dynamic models of individual behavior (Abbot and Hrycak 1990; Yamaguchi 1991), data collection designed to match these models and provide accurate information is in high demand. Life History Calendar methods attempt to strike a balance between structured and unstructured approaches for collecting retrospective reports. On the one hand, a series of highly structured survey questions may be detached or force less natural recall practices. On the other hand, less structured oral history methods that allow the respondent to report in an individually contextualized and meaningful way may run the risk of expending measurement effort on multiple topics irrelevant to the study aims. The Life History Calendar method explicitly combines elements of structured survey questioning with less structured oral history and adds a graphic reference to help informants provide accurate recall.

We describe the features of Life History Calendars below, as well as the particular application of Life History Calendar methods employed in the Chitwan Valley Family Study. The application we discuss provides examples of the flexibility of calendars and how they can be revised to work in a broad range of circumstances to study a wide variety of topics. It also demonstrates how less structured methods can be used to inform key features in the design of Life History Calendars.

Function and Design of Life History Calendars

Life History Calendars are typically designed in the form of a matrix in which the columns represent time units (weeks, months, years, etc.) and the rows contain the domains of life being studied.[1] They are most often collected in combination

Portions of this chapter are based on the following previously published article: Axinn, William G., Lisa D. Pearce, and Dirgha J. Ghimire 1999. "Innovations in Life History Calendar Applications." *Social Science Research* 28: 243–264.

with typical survey instruments and are used to collect precise data from a sizeable, representative sample of some population. Some calendars are paper-and-pencil versions where the interviewer and respondent sit together and use the visual cues and matrix format of the calendar to their advantage. Although this is the type of calendar we refer to most often in this chapter, there are also versions of LHCs designed for Computer Assisted Personal Interviewing (Belli, Shay, and Stafford 2001), that provide many of the same benefits of the paper-and-pencil calendars and streamline the data entry process.

As we have stated, the main objective of LHC methods is the collection of data on the timing and sequencing of personal events in the lives of individuals. Recall of the precise timing of various life events may present a cognitively challenging task for survey respondents (Eisenhower, Mathiowetz, and Morganstein 1991; Tourangeau 1984). LHC methods are designed to make this task easier by providing a matrix of visual cues respondents can use to help them recall the timing of those life events (Belli 1998; Caspi et al. 1995; Freedman et al. 1988; Petersen and Kerwin 1992). These timing cues include both a standardized set of cues, such as column headings marked with years and ages, and a variable set of cues, usually composed of respondents' reports of other life events. These reports are particularly important cues, because they allow respondents to use the timing of the most salient events in their lives to recall the timing of less salient events. Together, these visual cues may help respondents recall the precise timing of events and the sequencing of intertwined events.

LHC methods encourage recall at both thematic and temporal levels that may increase the power of respondents' autobiographical memory (Belli 1998). Although standard survey methods are known to facilitate "top-down retrieval," LHC methods should also encourage sequencing and parallel retrieval of common events (much like less structured interviews), promoting enhanced autobiographical recall (Belli 1998). Memory researchers have also found that individuals use spatial perceptions and metaphors to conceptualize time (Barsalou 1995; Neisser 1988). Therefore, the visual nature of the LHC, which allows respondents to see whether they have correctly reported the coincidence or ordering of various events, may improve temporal recall.

The calendar format also facilitates interviewers in collecting complex life history data (Caspi et al. 1995; Freedman et al. 1988). The same visual cues that are designed as an aid to respondent recall help structure the interviewers' questions. This structure helps to ensure that interviewers gather data with the required precision, in terms of both timing and sequencing. Visual aspects of the LHC method also help interviewers be sure they have collected complete data. Interviewers can easily detect gaps in the life history or unlikely sequences of events and probe to correct these problems. The flexible recording techniques usually associated with calendar methods also facilitate the recording of complex sequences of personal events. The flexibility of calendar methods, as well as the ability to visually cross-check, also aids interviewers. In fact, the benefits to interviewers are so important that LHC methods collect nearly as high-quality data over the phone as they do in face-to-face interviews (Freedman et al. 1988).

There are several important elements in the design of LHC methods. These include the choice of substantive domains, time units, and recording techniques. These basic design issues, along with many of the advantages of LHC techniques, are described in great detail elsewhere (Caspi et al. 1995; Freedman et al. 1988). Rather than repeat those discussions here, we focus on new design alternatives that make the LHC even more flexible. As a starting point, in order to provide comparisons, we begin by reproducing Figure 6.1 from Freedman et al.'s 1988 description of the LHC as Figure 6.1 in this chapter, which provides the basic LHC design features of substantive domain cues running down the left-hand margin and standardized timing cues running across the top of the calendar. Together, these cues define the LHC matrix. The LHC described by Freedman et al. (1988) is designed to gather monthly data on the timing and sequencing of personal events over a 9-year period from retrospective reports.

The new methods described in this chapter expand the range of applications for LHCs, facilitating their application in a broader range of studies. Below, we outline these new methods, beginning with techniques for applying the method to broad age range study populations.

Expanding the Age Range

As mentioned above, most of the early work to develop LHC methods applied these methods to narrow age range populations and covered only short periods of recall. For example, Freedman and colleagues designed an LHC to measure the timing and sequencing of events in the lives of a 1-month birth cohort of young adults, age 23. This particular application had two important advantages: (1) all the members of the study population were the same age, to the month, at the same time; and (2) the maximum period of recall for all respondents was relatively brief (9 years), limiting the cognitive task of recall. This path-breaking study was critical for describing the potential advantages of LHC methods, but many of the issues involved in applying these methods to broader age range study populations remained unsolved.

Designing LHC methods for narrow age range birth cohort studies is straightforward because all the respondents are the same age in the same year (or month). This allows ages to be printed in the matrix of standardized timing cues along with units of historical time. This is an important aid to recall, because many respondents recall the timing of personal events in terms of their own ages. As suggested by Freedman et al. (1988), for a broad age range population the obvious solution to the problem of varying ages in varying years is to treat age as a variable timing cue and write it on the matrix of timing cues during the interview, just under the presentation of historical time cues.

However, if the study requires full retrospective life history data and each respondent is a different age, each respondent must begin her or his LHC entries at a different point in historical time. In a narrow age range study population or in a study where the period of recall is constant regardless of respondents' ages, it is quite easy to begin all the respondents' calendars at the left-hand margin and print the matrix of substantive domain cues down the left margin (Figure 6.1). This technique has important advantages for guiding interviewers' questions and helping respondents provide their answers chronologically, beginning at the start of their lives and moving onward in time (Freedman et al. 1988). On the other hand, in a broad age range study population, only the oldest respondents will begin the calendar at the left-hand margin, with others forced to start the recording of life events somewhere in the center of the LHC.[2]

This variance in where respondents start their life history on the LHC creates problems for both interviewers and respondents for two reasons. First, older respondents will be forced to recall events over a longer period of time. This increases both the recording burden for interviewers and the recall burden for respondents. Second, younger respondents will start their histories in the center of the calendar, further from the substantive domain matrix usually located on the left side of the Life History Calendar. Along with adding to the complexity of the interviewers' recording tasks, to the extent that the LHC functions as a visual instrument to aid respondent recall, starting in the center also makes the LHC more confusing to respondents. We describe two types of solutions to these problems. The first standardizes the period of recall for all respondents, even though their ages vary. The second redesigns the entire LHC to accommodate this broader age range and to obtain rich, full-life recall from all respondents.

Standardized Recall Period

The first solution requires definition of a standard period of recall for all respondents and standardizes the LHC to accommodate this period of recall. For example, LHCs can be designed to collect detailed life history data for the 5 years directly preceding the study, regardless of the respondent's age. In this situation, all respondents begin the LHC at the left-hand margin, ages are entered into the matrix of timing cues as part of the interview process, and the period of recall is kept manageably brief. The main drawback inherent in this solution is that data are left censored, so detailed information on event timing is not available before the standardized period. This can be an especially crippling drawback for research focusing on the timing of first events, such as first marriage, the birth of the first child, or one's first job.

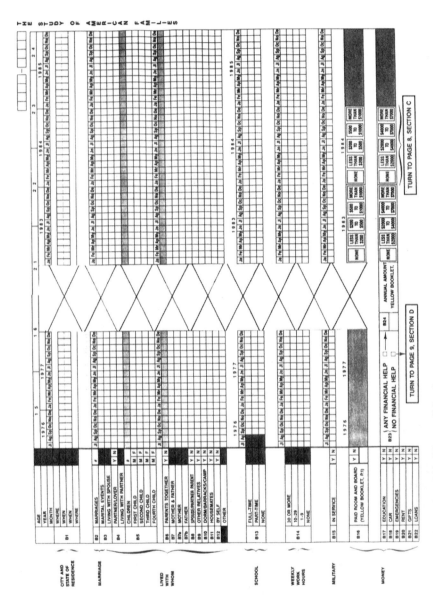

Figure 6.1. Life History Calendar

Figure 6.1(*continued*). An interviewer collecting data using the Life History Calendar

Redesigning the Life History Calendar

Another option is to redesign the Life History Calendar to help provide better timing cues for respondents of many ages, facilitate reports that begin in the center of the Life History Calendar, and allow ages to be entered as part of the interview. This solution is particularly useful in broad age range, cross-sectional studies that focus on the timing and sequencing of first events. The LHC width, from left margin to right margin, should accommodate as many units of time as the oldest respondent will need. So if the maximum age in the sample will be 59 years, the study plan is to begin recording events with the respondent's birth, and the unit of timing is the year, the LHC will need 59 vertical year columns from left to right. Figure 6.2 presents such a LHC.

The LHC presented in this figure comes from the Chitwan Valley Family Study, a survey of all residents, aged 15–59, residing in a sample of 171 neighborhoods in south central Nepal. This LHC was used to gather event history data from 5,271 men and women. The focus of this study is the timing and sequencing of first events, particularly first marriage, first childbearing, and first contraceptive use, so gathering complete life histories, beginning at birth, was a central aim of this study. The Life History Calendar in Figure 6.2, therefore, was designed to overcome problems associated with applying these techniques to broad age range populations without sacrificing coverage of any portion of the life course.

The CVFS also included a substantial ethnographic study component (integrated into the study as described in Axinn, Fricke, and Thornton 1991). One of the objectives of this ethnographic work was to evaluate the most appropriate method of gathering life history data from this respondent population. Throughout the remainder of the text, we draw on that ethnographic information (informal interviews and direct observations) to provide some assessments of the quality of data obtained using the LHC displayed in Figure 6.2.

Expanding the Timing Cues

Redesigning an LHC to include multiple timing cues may help limit the recall burden for older members of a broad age range population. To facilitate maximum recall and to ensure total flexibility, the timing cues included on the CVFS life history calendar were expanded to include important cognitive "landmarks" – noteworthy events that respondents may use as anchors to place the occurrence of other life events in time (Belli 1998; Loftus and Marburger 1983). To accomplish this, the matrix of timing cues included four types of information in addition to calendar years.

Years, the unit of historical time used in this study, mark the column headings for the main body of the LHC (Figure 6.2). In this case, the research was conducted in 1996 – or Nepali year 2053 – and 53 is the label at the top of the right-hand column. The second line of timing cues contained descriptions of important national event landmarks that were salient to many respondents. These were preprinted on the LHCs because the timing of these events is the same for everyone in the study population. We conducted unstructured group interviews with many different members of the study population in order to determine the list of national events used in this line. Because recall of important national events differs by cohort, it is useful to include respondents of many different ages in such discussions (Schuman and Scott 1989). The events we chose to include in this line were the most widely recognized events during pretesting. Two examples of salient national events that provided recall assistance to many respondents were the first democratic election held in Nepal, which occurred in Nepali year 2014, and the earthquake of 2045.

The third line of timing cues is blank in Figure 6.2. This line was reserved for salient local-level cognitive landmarks. The timing of those events was ascertained using the Neighborhood History Calendars described in the previous chapter. We chose the most salient events from the set of data gathered using those calendars to include in this LHC. Because the timing and occurrence of these local, neighborhood events differed across the focal neighborhoods in which respondents resided, this information had to be pre-edited onto individual calendars. The CVFS sample was clustered by neighborhood, so this task proved to be relatively straightforward. Information from Neighborhood History Calendars was pre-edited onto LHCs before cover sheets were released to interviewers, and then the pre-edited calendars were distributed with the associated cover sheets. These neighborhood events supplemented the other timing cues. Not only do they increase the density of timing cues, but they also serve as anchors for older respondents who often have a difficult recall task in this type of broad age range application. For example, events such as a new road or school being built in a neighborhood were often used by respondents to place life events into a time context.

The fourth line of timing cues contained the names of the animal year associated with each calendar year (Figure 6.2). Because a number of Nepalese ethnic groups use calendars with 12-year cycles of animal years to record the timing of personal events, these labels are a useful addition to the matrix of timing cues (Axinn, Fricke, and Thornton 1991; Fricke 1986). These animal year cues were preprinted on the calendar.

The final line of timing cues is blank in Figure 6.2 because it was reserved for entering respondents' ages during the interview. At the beginning of the Life History Calendar portion of the interview, after the LHC was introduced to respondents, they were asked the year of their birth. Interviewers entered 0 in the year of birth, edited ages into the remainder of the age line, and checked current age in the current year with the respondent making sure his or her age

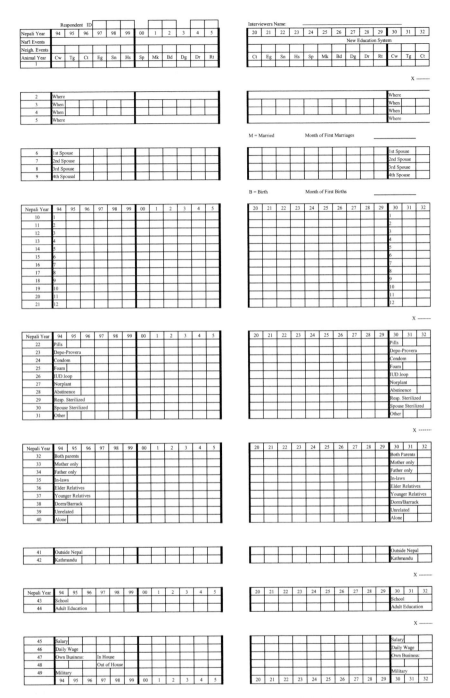

Figure 6.2. Summary of full CVFS Life History Calendar

146

Date of the Interview:

33	34	35	36	37	38	39	40	41	42	43	44	45	46	47	48	49	50	51	52	53			
		Referendum								Earthquake											Nepali Year		
																					National Events		
																					Neighborhood Events		
Eg	Sn	Hs	Sp	Mk	Bd	Dg	Dr	Rt	Cw	Tg	Ct	Eg	Sn	Hs	Sp	Mk	Bd	Dg	Dr	Rt	Animal Year		
																					Age		1

------------- X Time Living in Area

							Residence/Migration:		
							Where		2
							When		3
							When		4
							Where		5

S = Separated   A = Living Away from Spouse   D = Divorce   W = Widowed

			Marriage:	Yes	No
			1st Spouse		6
			2nd Spouse		7
			3rd Spouse		8
			4th Spouse		9

L = Living Together   S = School   Q = Quit School   X = Left Home   D = Death

33	34	35	36	37	38	39	40	41	42	43	44	45	46	47	48	49	50	51	52	53	Children: Name	Parent #	Son	Daugh	
																					1				10
																					2				11
																					3				12
																					4				13
																					5				14
																					6				15
																					7				16
																					8				17
																					9				18
																					10				19
																					11				20
																					12				21

------------- X Use of Contraceptive

33	34	35	36	37	38	39	40	41	42	43	44	45	46	47	48	49	50	51	52	53	Contraceptive Use: Method	Month	Yes	No	
																					Pills				22
																					Depo-Provera				23
																					Condom				24
																					Foam				25
																					IUD.loop				26
																					Norplant				27
																					Abstinence				28
																					Respondent Sterilized				29
																					Spouse Sterilized				30
																					Other				31

----------- X Living Together

33	34	35	36	37	38	39	40	41	42	43	44	45	46	47	48	49	50	51	52	53	Living Arrangements:	Yes	No	
																					Both parents			32
																					Mother only			33
																					Father only			34
																					In-laws			35
																					Elder Relatives			36
																					Younger Relatives			37
																					Dorm/Barrack			38
																					Unrelated			39
																					Alone			40

X = Visit

			Visit:	Yes	No	
			Outside Nepal			41
			Kathmandu			42

------------- X Time in School   Month First Attended School: _____

33	34	35	36	37	38	39	40	41	42	43	44	45	46	47	48	49	50	51	52	53	Education:	Yes	No	
																					School			43
																					Adult Education			44

----------- X Time in Work

			Occupation:	Yes	No	
			Salary			45
			Daily Wage			46
In House			Own Business: In House			47
Out of House			Out of House			48
			Military			49

33	34	35	36	37	38	39	40	41	42	43	44	45	46	47	48	49	50	51	52	53

147

was correctly recorded across the calendar. As mentioned above, age is usually one of the most important timing cues for respondents' recollection of personal events (Freedman et al. 1988).

Together, this more dense, complete set of timing cues goes beyond previous LHC efforts to provide respondents with aids for recall of the timing and sequencing of personal events. In our experience in Nepal, this additional effort to provide more timing cues gives older respondents more assistance as they grapple with the difficult cognitive task of recalling events from early in their lives. Eisenhower, Mathiowetz, and Morganstein (1991) report that respondent recall should be enhanced by encouraging the respondent to think about the environmental context surrounding a particular event. By placing the event to be recalled amidst other more easily recalled events, the LHC employs multiple pathways to recall in the respondent's memory. The more vivid a context or the more memory pathways engaged in an interview process, the easier it should be for the respondent to recall life events accurately (Belli 1998). Although a longer period of recall required in studies such as the one described here undoubtedly raises the risk of errors, especially among older respondents, the extra timing cues may compensate for some of that risk in important ways.[3]

Re-Arranging Domain Cues

Rows represent the substantive domains of the LHC. Figure 6.2 also presents all eight substantive domains on the far right of the calendar. To accommodate the broader age range population, we moved the row headings from the left-hand margin, as in previous LHCs (Freedman et al. 1988), to the right-hand margin. Only the oldest respondents begin the calendar at the left-hand margin, but all the respondents finish the calendar at the right-hand margin. Thus, the margin cues serve both to organize the interviewers' questions and to check that they have completed each of the substantive domains. The right-hand margin cues are used to organize the interview for all the respondents, but they also provide space to record additional information as required, such as the names and genders of the respondents' children.

Because different respondents begin the LHC at different locations, we reprinted substantive row headings in light blue at three different locations in each line of the LHC. The LHC runs from Nepali year 1994 to 2053. The first set of light blue row cues is printed in the extreme left margin, under year 1994. The second set is printed below year 2010. The third set is printed below year 2030. Because the right-hand margin cues are printed directly after year 2053, these light blue cues divide the LHC into roughly equal sections, with cues spread throughout. These cues must be printed in a light color, because those respondents who begin the calendar further to the left will require the interviewer to record over the top of these light-colored cues. The presence of these light cues, however, provides interviewers with row anchors at either margin of the calendar and assist with those respondents who begin in the center of the calendar.

Using Calendars Among Populations Who Don't Employ Time Records

The fact that many of the world's populations mark the timing of personal events with calendar time helps make the LHC an efficient method for collecting retrospective reports of the timing and sequencing of such events. However, some populations do not use standardized measures of historical time to mark personal events. Although one might assume that LHCs are difficult to apply among such populations, we argue that the LHC is in fact a necessary tool for gathering useful life history data from such a population. The CVFS includes some people who fit this description. Although most Indian-origin Hindus use the Nepali national calendar and most Tibetan-origin Buddhists use an animal year calendar, the Tharu of Chitwan Valley, one of the five major ethnic groups in our study population, do not use any standardized type of calendar to keep track of personal time. Many young Tharu attend schools run by the Nepalese government and have learned the Nepali national calendar. However, many older Tharu are unable to report the timing of personal events in terms of either historical time or age.

Three characteristics of the LHC make it appropriate for collecting retrospective life history data among such a population. The first is the possibility of a dense matrix of standardized timing cues. The broad set of timing cues used in the CVFS Life History Calendar, described above, proved to be an extremely valuable tool in this regard. Although Nepali calendar years and animal years were not useful in this population and many Tharu were unable to provide their date of birth or current age, these respondents often found that they could tell us about the timing of personal events relative to the timing of important national or local events. Our neighborhood event history timing cues were particularly important in this regard. Older Tharu respondents were often able to tell us about the timing of their own births, their marriages, the births of their children, and other important life events in terms of years before or after salient local events.

The second characteristic of the LHC that proved to be useful for this population is the flexibility of changing the order of questions within the LHC. Tourangeau (1984) points out that ordering questions in the most natural way for each respondent will increase his or her recall ability.[4] The CVFS calendar was designed to ask first about the respondent's migration history, second about his or her marital history, and third about her or his childbearing history. However, we found that many Tharu were best able to report their childbearing history. Beginning with the current age of one's youngest child, many were able to work backward in time, by piecing together the number of years between childbirths to eventually arrive at the timing of first marriage. Once this was accomplished, the vast majority were able to add their migration history in around these events, eventually arriving at a good estimate of their own birthdates. Then, armed with all of these timing cues, most Tharu were able to provide us with the timing and sequencing of other life events of interest.

The third important characteristic is the highly visual nature of the Life History Calendar. This proved to be quite helpful as respondents used the timing of the events they knew (either personal or neighborhood) to help them recall the timing of events that were more difficult to remember. In our experience, the written timing cues and visual representation of years before and after a particular event aided respondents as they attempted to piece together the sequence of events in their lives. Actually, the visual character of the LHC was just as much an aid for older respondents faced with the difficult task of recalling the timing of events from early in their lives as it was for respondents who knew neither historical time nor their own ages.

New Life History Calendar Recording Strategies

The Life History Calendar allows considerable flexibility in gathering detailed retrospective life history calendar data. Flexible recording alternatives provide the means to record complex sequences of personal events and assist interviewers in their efforts to gather complete life histories (Freedman et al. 1988). However, broader applications of the LHC method demand even greater recording flexibility. Below, we describe new recording strategies designed to facilitate three types of issues: (1) recording a broader range of culturally acceptable behaviors; (2) recording multiple interrelated events on the same calendar line; and (3) recording exact timing of events for broad age range calendars.

Recording a Broad Range of Culturally Acceptable Behaviors

LHC recording strategies generally feature a combination of symbols and lines connecting symbols designed to show when an event took place, when a new status began, how long that status continued, and when that status ended (Freedman et al. 1988). In combination with multiple substantive domain lines, the recording techniques are flexible enough to handle an extremely broad range of culturally acceptable behaviors. For example, though in the past it was common to expect cohabitation (coresidence of a sexually active heterosexual couple) to begin at the time of marriage, by employing multiple substantive domain lines it is quite straightforward to record the independence of these two statuses. Freedman et al. (1988) used one line to record marital events, another line to record living with or away from a spouse, and yet another line to record coresidence with an opposite-sex partner outside of marriage. This method provided the means to record premarital cohabitations that were subsequently transformed into marriage. In the Nepalese context, many spouses do not become coresident until a substantial amount of time *after* the marital event occurs. Once again, the same recording strategy easily accommodates this independence between the timing of marriage and the timing of cohabitation.

The Nepalese context, however, presented other recording obstacles. Prominent among these is the cultural acceptability of simultaneous multiple spouses. Both men and women may have more than one spouse at the same time, although it is more common among men. Using the symbols designed by Freedman et al. (1988), it would have been difficult to know which of the multiple simultaneous spouses entered and exited the household. However, by adding additional spouse lines to the Life History Calendar it became easy to record the independent movements of simultaneous multiple spouses. Figure 6.3 displays the right-hand side of the CVFS Life History Calendar showing the lines and symbols used to record the independent movements of simultaneous multiple spouses.

In Figure 6.3, this portion of the LHC has been completed with simultaneous multiple spouses to demonstrate the recording strategy. The "M" in the "1st spouse" line indicates the respondent first married in Nepalese year 2035, and the "S" indicates the respondent and his first spouse separated in 2037. The respondent then married a second spouse in 2038, but did not begin to live with the second spouse until 2040. The respondent began living away from the second spouse in 2043 and married a third spouse in 2044. The respondent lived with the third spouse the entire time from marriage until the time of the interview, and the second spouse rejoined the respondent in 2046. So this LHC shows the respondent lived with two spouses simultaneously from 2046 until the time of the interview.

Recording Multiple Interrelated Events on the Same LHC Line

Adding new substantive domain lines to the LHC allows researchers to record additional information on multiple independent life events. However, in some situations adding lines may be impractical or disadvantageous. The substantive aims of the CVFS required collection of data on the timing and sequencing of childbirths, child deaths, and children's schooling. Recording a child's birth, death, and living arrangements (with or away from the respondent) can be accommodated on the same Life History Calendar line (Freedman et al. 1988). Information on children's entrances into and exits from formal schooling might

Month of First Marriage: March   M = Married   S=Separated   L=Living together with spouse   A=Living away from spouse   D=Divorced   W=Widowed

Year	35	36	37	38	39	40	41	42	43	44	45	46	47	48	49	50	51	52	53	Marriage	Yes	No
6	1st Spouse		M		S															1st Spouse	X	
7		2nd Spouse					M		L		A									2nd Spouse	X	
8		3rd Spouse										M		L						3rd Spouse	X	
9	4th Spouse																			4th Spouse		X

Figure 6.3. Recording independent events of simultaneous spouse

be recorded on the LHC in an additional set of substantive lines, equal in number to the number of children. However, in a setting like Nepal, where a non-trivial fraction of the population has 10 or more children, adding lines for children's schooling becomes quite cumbersome. Furthermore, information on children's schooling is not independent of information on children's births and deaths. A child must have been born and survived past age 5 to be exposed to the risk of going to school.

Instead, we used more-complex symbols and recorded children's schooling on the same LHC line as other childbearing information. Figure 6.4 displays an example of a completed set of childbearing lines demonstrating this recording strategy. The symbol "B" is used for the live birth of a child, "D" for the death of a child, "X" for a move by the child to live away from the respondent, and "L" for a return by the child to live with the respondent. Horizontal lines are used to show the continuation of a state through time. The symbol "S" denotes the beginning of a spell of schooling, and the symbol "Q" denotes the end of such a spell. Spells of schooling are presumed to continue through time until either the end of the calendar or a "Q" is recorded, even when no horizontal line is present. This strategy allows recording of children's schooling experiences on the same line as children's living arrangements. Note that this strategy also occasionally leads to multiple symbols recorded within the same square of the calendar.

Drawbacks of this approach include a heightened possibility of recording errors. One remedy for this problem is the provision of extra training for both interviewers and data entry personnel. In general, LHC methods require additional training of both interviewers and data entry staff (Freedman et al. 1998), but recording multiple events on the same LHC line requires even more care in training. On the other hand, this strategy provides the means of recording an even greater density of information on the life history calendar without increasing the size of the instrument beyond reasonable limits.

Exact Timing of First Events

As mentioned above, in broad age range applications of LHC methods it is necessary to have enough time units on the calendar for the oldest respondents in the study. For studies that include older respondents, the length of the resulting calendar may prohibit the use of smaller time units, such as months. This was the case in the CVFS, and instead we used years as the unit of time in our LHC (Figure 6.2). However, in many substantive applications more-precise data on event timing are desirable. For example, the substantive aims of the CVFS made exact timing of first events (e.g., first marriage, first childbirth, first contraceptive use) highly desirable.

B = Birth   Month of first birth: April   D = Death   L = Living together   S = School   Q = Quit school   X = Left home

																			Daughter	Son	10
																			⨉		11
																			⨉		12
																				⨉	13
																				⨉	14
																			⨉		15

Children

35	36	37	38	39	40	41	42	43	44	45	46	47	48	49	50	51	52	53	Name	Parent #
1					B	D													1 ————	1
2								B				S					QX		2 Sita	2
3										B				S				Q	3 Nirmala	2
4											BD								4 ————	2
5													B				S		5 Ram	2
6															B	————	X	L	6 Chandra	3
7																			7	
8																			8	
9																			9	
10																			10	
11																			11	
12																			12	

Figure 6.4. Recording multiple events for each child

To accomplish this objective, we added space on the calendar to record the exact date of the first event in each of several substantive domains. Figure 6.5 provides an example from the contraceptive domain. Here, calendar lines and columns show the year in which the respondent's first contraceptive use took place, and a space in the domain heading column to the right of each method provides a place to record the month in which that first contraceptive use occurred. If respondents are able to recall this additional timing information, it can easily be recorded in the space provided, coded, and entered along with the other data from the LHC matrix.

For LHC applications that employ years as the unit of time but also require more-precise information about the beginning and ending of every spell, alternative recording strategies must be used. Rather than recording the beginning and ending of a spell with a neutral symbol, such as an "X," investigators may record the beginning and ending with a numeral denoting the month (i.e., 1 = January, 6 = June). Figure 6.6 provides an example of education and labor force participation lines recorded using this strategy. This approach has the advantage of providing monthly precision on the duration of spells. However, in a broad age range population respondents may not be able to supply this level of recall accurately. The accuracy of their responses may depend on other characteristics of the study population, such as their own use of calendar time to record personal events, their educational background, or the salience of the substantive domains of the study.

Overall, by adding substantive domain lines or increasing the range of symbols used to record events on the Life History Calendar, LHC recording techniques can be expanded to handle an extremely wide range of behavior in a wide array of settings. Increasing the range or density of symbols that are used to record events will increase the need for training among both interviewers and data entry staff. Increased complexity in the LHC is likely to reduce the quality of data, unless enhanced training is used to compensate for the increased complexity (Fowler 1991). Of course, the level of precision that can be recorded on the LHC also will depend on respondents' abilities to recall the required information.

Conclusion

In the preceding paragraphs, we have outlined a series of new ways to apply Life History Calendar data collection methods to a wider variety of studies. In order to apply LHC methods to broad age range populations, we advocate expanding the timing cues presented to respondents and re-arranging domain cues. Expanding the set of timing cues by adding salient national and local events to the LHC increases the density of cues in the LHC matrix and provides respondents with more memory landmarks (Belli 1998). These additional cues

Yea[r]	35	36	37	38	39	40	41	42	43	44	45	46	47	48	49	50	51	52	53
22 Pills																			
23 Depo-Provera																			
24 Condom													X						
25 Foam																			
26 IUD loop																			
27 Norplant																			
28 Abstinence																			
29 Respondent sterilized																X			
30 Spouse sterilized																			
31 Other																			

Contraceptive use				
Method	Month	Yes	No	
Pills			X	22
Depo-Provera			X	23
Condom	November	X		24
Foam			X	25
IUD loop			X	26
Norplant			X	27
Abstinence			X	28
Respondent sterilized	March	X		29
Spouse sterilized			X	30
Other			X	31

Figure 6.5. Recording exact month of first contraceptive use

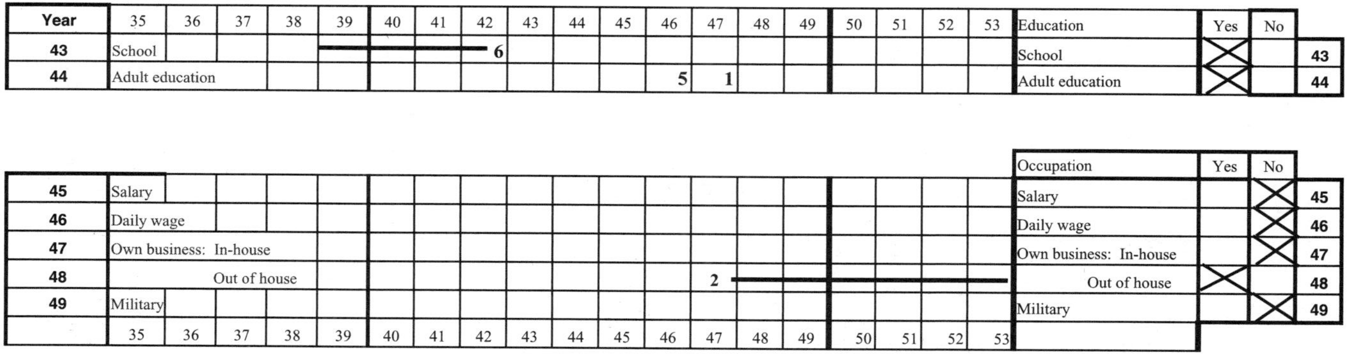

Year	35	36	37	38	39	40	41	42	43	44	45	46	47	48	49	50	51	52	53	Education		Yes	No
43	School							6												School		⊠		43
44	Adult education										5	1								Adult education			⊠	44

	35	36	37	38	39	40	41	42	43	44	45	46	47	48	49	50	51	52	53	Occupation		Yes	No
45	Salary																			Salary		⊠		45
46	Daily wage																			Daily wage		⊠		46
47	Own business: In-house																			Own business: In-house		⊠		47
48	Out of house												2							Out of house		⊠		48
49	Military																			Military			⊠	49

1=January; 2=February; 3=March; 4=April; 5=May; 6=June; 7=July; 8=August; 9=September; 10=October; 11=November; 12=December

Figure 6.6. Recording month of event to obtain more-precise timing data

157

provide useful assistance to respondents as they attempt to recall the timing and sequencing of personal events. The application of LHC methods to broader age range populations dramatically expands the range of studies that can use these methods.

The combination of this expanded set of timing cues, the flexibility of the LHC to incorporate different interviewing sequences, and the highly visible nature of the Life History Calendar also make LHC techniques instrumental for gathering personal history data from populations that do not employ standardized time records to track the passage of time. Thus, these features of the LHC method make it suitable for gathering life history data from an extremely broad range of settings.

Finally, the flexibility of LHC recording strategies makes it a useful tool for collecting data on an extremely diverse set of subjects. As shown above, LHC recording strategies can be reformulated to incorporate many different culturally relevant and substantively important behaviors and events. This makes the Life History Calendar a useful tool for collecting life history data on many different subjects and under a large variety of circumstances.

Of course, several issues related to the quality of data from Life History Calendar methods deserve further research. Having the highest priority among these are experimental studies that explicitly compare the quality of data obtained using Life History Calendar methods to the quality of data obtained using alternative retrospective methods. An experimental design would provide strong tests of the advantages of Life History Calendar methods, and such tests could be used to judge the relative merits of alternative Life History Calendar approaches. Another important issue for further research is a systematic evaluation of the impact of allowing interviewers some flexibility on the quality of data gathered using Life History Calendars. Interviewer characteristics and practices are known to affect data quality (Bradburn 1983; Sudman and Bradburn 1974), and allowing interviewers some flexibility may increase those effects. Finally, a critical emerging topic in the application of LHC methods is integration of the calendar with Computer-Assisted Personal-Interviewing (CAPI) methods. Although CAPI provides many important advantages for the administration of complex survey instruments, optimal techniques for integrating CAPI methods with calendar methods, so that the visual advantages of calendars are not compromised, remain to be developed. As more survey data collection efforts become computerized, the demand for research integrating special techniques such as the LHC into computerized modes of administration is likely to continue to grow.

Nevertheless, by increasing the breadth of populations and substantive topics that are accessible via LHC methods, the innovations discussed in this chapter give researchers additional means to collect data for sophisticated event timing analyses. As behavioral models of the timing and sequencing of life experiences and events have grown increasingly common in the social sciences (Lillard and Waite 1995; Massey and Espinosa 1997; Thornton 1991; Thornton, Axinn, and Teachman 1995; Waite and Lillard 1991; Wu 1996), we have seen a rapid expansion in analytic methods designed for estimating these models. Event history analysis has grown to become one of the dominant methodological approaches in the discipline (Petersen 1991; Teachman and Hayward 1993; Yamaguchi 1991). Innovative new methods, such as sequence analysis, continue to be developed (Abbott and Hrycak 1990). Unfortunately, the expansion in life history data collection methods has not kept pace with the expansion in life history data analysis methods. This prevents social scientists from using these powerful analytic tools to specify complex dynamic models of individual behavior in new settings and for different substantive applications. The innovations described in this chapter are designed to expand the flexibility of LHC methods, enabling these valuable methods to successfully collect data on a variety of substantive issues. The use of LHC data collection methods in a broader range of settings will give social scientists the means to estimate complex dynamic models of the timing and sequencing of life events across a wide range of study populations.

Issues of Application

Although we have argued that Life History Calendar methods can be used to measure many subjects in many different settings, some subjects may be less appropriate for this type of measurement. For example, the calendar methods described in this chapter are primarily designed to measure events and experiences, not attitudes, values, or beliefs. The nature of these ideational phenomena makes it unlikely that individuals can accurately describe them retrospectively, even with detailed memory cues. Thus, some subject matter may not be well suited to LHC measurement.

Scaling the application of Life History Calendar data collection to larger or smaller projects may create important issues for researchers. This method, like Neighborhood History Calendar collection, requires the interviewing staff to be very competent and well trained. Having a single highly trained interviewer to collect these histories is ideal; however, as in our application, there are often too many histories to conduct to make this feasible. Many studies successfully integrate Life History Calendars into surveys for interviews with large numbers of people. Although the inclusion of this data collection tool requires more training than generally associated with survey interviewer training, by adding days of training focused specifically on the calendar most survey interviewers can be trained to use a Life History Calendar. Thus, with these investments it is quite possible to use the LHC on a large scale.

Illustrations of Principles

The integration of mixed methods into a single hybrid tool, such as the Life History Calendar, provides illustrations of several of the mixed method data collection principles identified in Chapter 1 and illustrated in Chapter 5 about Neighborhood History Calendars. The illustrations include principles closely tied to the theme of using the strengths of some methods to counterbalance the weaknesses of other methods *and* principles closely tied to the theme of comprehensive empirical documentation. The Life History Calendar method integrates the structure of a calendar and accompanying questionnaires with a more flexible data collection strategy, so that the strengths of unstructured interviewing can counterbalance the weaknesses of highly structured interviewing. Particularly important is the flexibility in unstructured interviewing to follow the individual's biography in whatever order it is easiest for that specific individual to recall the information.

Clearly, the Life History Calendar is also a hybrid method explicitly aimed at adding temporal detail to the comprehensive empirical documentation of a subject. This information on temporal order is particularly powerful for establishing the order of events and experiences in an individual's life. This ordering, in turn, can become a powerful tool in analyses aimed at understanding which events or experiences are potential causes of other events or experiences. Note that by combining the contextual-level measurement described in Chapter 5 with individual-level measurement described in this chapter, it is possible to establish the temporal order of changes potentially linking factors across levels. As mentioned in Chapter 5, this can be extremely useful in both studies of the effects of context on individuals and studies of the effects of individuals on contexts. Thus, these dimensions of the comprehensive empirical record generated by the LHC method are potentially quite useful in studies of cause and consequence in the social world.

7   Longitudinal Data Collection

Over the last three decades of the 20th century, longitudinal research designs, in which the same people or other units of observation are measured repeatedly over time, have become social sciences' most powerful tools for studying cause and consequence. By measuring the same people over time, social scientists can better understand how conditions or characteristics at one time shape ideas, decisions, or outcomes at a later time. This approach also allows social scientists to ensure that the temporal order among measures matches the temporal order embedded in causal hypotheses themselves. In this sense, longitudinal measurement designs are similar to the calendar-type measurement designs described in Chapters 5 and 6. However, where calendar methods are explicitly retrospective, longitudinal designs are explicitly prospective, or intended to take measures forward over time. This gives longitudinal designs advantages for studying phenomena that are difficult to measure retrospectively, such as attitudes and values, mental health, relationship content and quality, or plans and expectations.

A key issue in the use of longitudinal data to answer questions of cause and consequence is that initial (time one) conditions or characteristics are rarely randomly assigned. Lack of random assignment violates a key aspect of experimental design and renders observed relationships open to the threat that they are the spurious product of some other unmeasured factor (Campbell and Stanley 1963; Winship and Morgan 1999). Although a small number of longitudinal studies do feature random assignment of a set of initial conditions, the vast majority do not, making them vulnerable to this weakness when used to make causal inferences.[1]

A number of approaches are used to address this problem, perhaps the most common of which is to attempt to measure all factors believed to produce initial characteristics or conditions in a non-random way. These measures can then be used in sophisticated statistical models to simulate random assignment of initial conditions (Barber, Murphy, and Verbitsky 2004). Although this approach reduces the risk of spurious results in causal research, it can never fully succeed because the potential number of unobserved factors is infinite, and even the most comprehensive measurement strategy will miss some factors and measure others with error.

Nevertheless, random assignment remains outside the bounds of most research in the social sciences, and this is not likely to change anytime soon. It is difficult to imagine a world in which social scientists are allowed to randomly assign conditions such as parental divorce, poverty, low education, criminal experience, or low birth weight. The opportunity to assign some conditions to special populations or self-selected populations in laboratory situations is always likely to be available. But the opportunity to randomly assign the full array of conditions social scientists study to the general population is never likely to exist, making longitudinal designs with comprehensive measurement the best tools available for the study of cause and consequence in the social sciences.

Two other approaches for addressing limitations produced by the non-random assignment of initial conditions deserve mention. One is the selection of study participants at very young ages, even sometimes at birth. Using very young study participants reduces the chance that non-random life experiences select individuals into the study. For example, if a longitudinal study is initiated by recruiting high school seniors, it will be selective of those who did not drop out or die before their senior year of high school. Of course, even selection of participants at birth does not remove the possibility that non-random selection occurred. For example, because birthrates vary among populations, individuals from high-birth rate groups are more likely to be selected into a longitudinal study that begins at birth. Nevertheless, selection of study participants at a very young age is a powerful tool for reducing the likelihood that unmeasured conditions or experiences produce observed relationships among measures.

The second strategy for addressing the limitations of non-random assignment is using very large samples in longitudinal studies. Natural experiments (see Chapter 1) capitalize on situations in which social conditions act to assign individuals to varying conditions virtually at random. In longitudinal studies, researchers often sample large numbers of individuals in the hope that groups of individuals who otherwise are very similar will be exposed to different conditions or experiences virtually at random. Using large numbers of study participants increases the chances that such serendipitous randomization will occur. Longitudinal studies that focus on units at higher levels of aggregation – such as schools, businesses, communities, or countries – also increase the chances of serendipitous randomization by studying larger numbers of units.

In this chapter, we begin by discussing longitudinal studies of individuals. We identify some key elements of this strategy, provide examples, and discuss its strengths and weaknesses. Next, we briefly discuss longitudinal studies that use units of analysis other than individuals. Then we describe approaches for creating continuous longitudinal measurement, such as those that use household registries or population-monitoring tools. Finally, we examine options for integrating multiple data collection methods into longitudinal research designs, explicitly drawing on the approaches described in Chapters 3, 4, 5, and 6.

Longitudinal Studies of Individuals

As described above, the defining characteristic of a longitudinal study of individuals is that the same people are studied repeatedly over time. Measures are taken for a specific person at one time, and then measures are taken again for that person at a later time. Longitudinal studies often use survey interviews to collect these measures, but nothing about the longitudinal design requires a survey interview. Unstructured or semi-structured interviews – or even observations – may be used to collect measures over the course of a longitudinal study. The key is repeated measurement of the same individuals over time, regardless of the methods used.[2] When obtaining repeated measurements from individuals across time, there is a range of design decisions to be made, careful effort must be made to avoid attrition, and a balance between new and repeated measurement must be cast.

Design

Several components of longitudinal study design differ across applications. We mentioned that the method of measurement might vary from study to study. Also, the number of times individuals are measured varies. A study must interview the same people at least twice to be considered longitudinal, but some studies measure the same individuals three or four times and others repeat measures dozens of times. Also, the time period between measurements varies across studies, ranging from days to years.

Each approach has its own strengths and weaknesses. For example, frequently repeated measurements may produce more continuous data, but this strategy can sometimes introduce testing effects (Campbell and Stanley 1963). Testing effects imply that the measurement process itself affects the behavior and attitudes of those being studied. On the other hand, although longer intervals between measurements will reduce testing effects, it will be more difficult for participants to accurately recall events or experiences that occurred between interviews. Researchers must weigh the strengths and weaknesses of alternative designs and choose a strategy that best fits the research question they plan to investigate.

Attrition

A fundamental threat to the reliability and validity of all longitudinal studies is attrition out of the study (Campbell and Stanley 1963). Failure to measure the initial participants in later rounds of a longitudinal study reduces its total inferential power and, in general, creates bias. Inferential power is reduced by attrition because the number of observations is decreased. Bias is created because study attrition is almost never random. Processes producing attrition include death, failure to contact because of geographic mobility, and refusal to continue participating. Deaths are selective of those more frail and those who engage in behaviors most likely to cause death (Pampel 2002; Salomon and Murray 2002; Schofield and Reher 1991). Failure to contact because of geographic mobility is selective of those who are most mobile or who have experiences likely to promote migration, such as job loss or divorce (Brockerhoff 2000; Guilmoto and Sandron 2001; Massey 1990). Refusal to participate in follow-up rounds is selective of those with characteristics that, in general, increase the likelihood of refusing to participate in any study, such as having a high income, long work days, or involvement in illegal activities (Groves and Couper 1998). Because attrition through any of these processes is non-random – that is, it tends to select out individuals with certain characteristics – it increases the possibility that observed correlations may be partially attributed to the selected-in characteristics (e.g., healthier, lower income) of the participants who remain in the study. Thus, attrition increases bias and reduces the generalizability of analytic results based on longitudinal data. A number of careful analyses of attrition from longitudinal studies demonstrate the types of substantive bias that may occur as the result of this selective attrition (Burkam and Lee 1998; Falaris and Peters 1998; Fitzgerald, Gottschalk, and Moffit 1998; Lillard and Panis 1998; Thomas, Frankenberg, and Smith 2001).

Several strategies have proven to be useful for reducing attrition from longitudinal studies. One group of strategies focuses on reducing the likelihood that individuals will refuse to participate. All the strategies used to reduce the chances of refusal to participate in the initial rounds of a study are also useful for reducing refusals to participate in following rounds of a study (Groves, Cialdini, and Couper 1992; Groves and Couper 1998). These include advance letters, incentives, and carefully tailored refusal conversion protocols. (For a more detailed description of techniques for reducing refusals and non-response, see Groves and Couper 1998). But in longitudinal studies, other techniques are also important. Efforts to keep the initial interview experience as pleasant as possible increase the likelihood that individuals will continue to participate in the study. These efforts include keeping initial interviews short, making questions simple, and maintaining a low cognitive burden on respondents. Of course, these practices are principles of sound questionnaire design in any situation (Presser and Converse 1986), but in longitudinal studies they may also help maintain high participation rates in future rounds of the study. Another technique commonly used to reduce refusals is the distribution of tokens of appreciation to study participants between rounds of a longitudinal study. Though relatively little research has been conducted on this subject, a type of token believed to be particularly useful in this regard is sending reports to respondents summarizing study findings and describing key uses of the data. These reports can help motivate future participation in the study by conveying to the respondents the importance of their time and effort (Freedman, Thornton, and Camburn 1980; Thornton, Freedman, and Camburn 1982). Also, it is common for investigators to provide tokens of appreciation in the form of cash payments to participants in exchange for their continued involvement in the study.

It is important to acknowledge that longitudinal studies place a particularly high burden on participants in terms of both cognitive effort and time requirements. Respondent burden is a concern in the design of all survey data collection efforts, and in longitudinal studies the concern is magnified by the increased burden of repeated data collection. If data collection is by interview: The greater the number of these interviews or the total length of time covered by the study, the higher the burden. Thus, researchers might attempt to reduce respondent burden by keeping the length, frequency, or total number of the interviews low or by balancing these factors. So if interviews must be lengthy, investigators might keep the total number of them low. Or if the interviews must be frequent, they might be kept brief.

Another set of attrition reduction techniques focuses on maintaining contact with those who are geographically mobile. The most important of these techniques is collecting detailed recontact information from participants during the initial round of the study. In addition to names, addresses, and phone numbers, this recontact information might include social security numbers, names, and phone numbers of close friends or relatives or other identifying information that can be used to track down study participants who move between rounds of a longitudinal study. In fact, in the United States, tracking respondents for longitudinal studies has become something of a field of its own. Various automated locating databases are available from private vendors and can be used to help track study participants. Of course, the efficiency of these tracking efforts depends a great deal on the quality of the recontact information available. However, even in settings without many of these tracking aids, such as low-income settings, effort devoted to tracking can yield important reductions in attrition and produce significant improvements in the information obtained (Thomas, Frankenberg, and Smith 2001).

Measurement

Other fundamental issues in the design and implementation of longitudinal studies of individuals revolve around repeated measurement. Here the tension is between maintaining close comparability of measures over time and changing measures over time to adapt to life course differences among those being studied, new historical conditions, or new subjects of interest to the investigators. Because we know that question sequence and wording influence responses (Sudman and Bradburn 1974; Tourangeau et al. 1989; Tourangeau and Rasinski 1988; Tourangeau and Smith 1996), changing either of these across rounds of a longitudinal study reduces the comparability of responses to altered questions. This is a serious threat to longitudinal studies because it is the comparability of responses across rounds that provides the means to draw reliable conclusions regarding change over time among the same individuals – a key motivation for conducting any longitudinal study.

At the same time, however, participants generally change over the course of a longitudinal study, sometimes making it necessary to alter, add, or delete study questions. The longer the duration of the study, the greater is this necessity. For example, a longitudinal study that follows individuals from early childhood into adulthood may begin with questions for parents, followed in later years by questions for participants during later childhood (5–10 years of age), adolescence, and adulthood. Questions about family-of-origin income, size of allowance, enjoyment of school, romantic relationships, contraception, or child rearing would be included as appropriate to the participant's age. Strict repetition of questions merely for the sake of comparability over the course of the study would, in this case, produce ridiculous comparisons across ages.

Two other common features of long-term longitudinal studies – changes in the social context or the subject matter of interest to investigators – also produce a natural pressure to modify questions over time. During the study period, events may stimulate new questions or render old questions strange or out of date. Sudden or dramatic social events, such as economic crises, natural disasters, or political upheavals, often motivate investigators to design new questions for longitudinal studies. Changes that evolve over long periods of time, such as increasing equality for women, greater freedom of sexual expression, or widespread reductions in smoking may render previous questions obsolete. Also, because investigators tend to turn over and/or research agendas tend to evolve over the course of long-term studies (Phelps, Furstenberg, and Colby 2002), measures are likely to be added, altered, or eliminated to conform to changing investigator interests. Thus, both a changing social context and new research interests contribute to the tension inherent in the need to repeat questions for the sake of measurement comparability and the need to modify questions for measurement relevancy.

Many studies address this measurement tension by doing both – that is, given a sufficient length of time to conduct interviews, a longitudinal study can both repeat all previous questions and add new questions to each round. Eventually, however, the cumulated number of questions will exert pressure to limit either the repetition of old questions or the introduction of new ones. Although this accumulation of old and new questions is a problem specific to longitudinal studies, efforts to limit the length of questioning are common to all interview-based research.

Intergenerational Panel Study

The Intergenerational Panel Study (IPS) is an example of a longitudinal study that faced the attrition and measurement challenges inherent to long-term longitudinal investigations (Thornton, Axinn, and Xie 2002; Thornton, Freedman, and Axinn 2002). The IPS followed a group of young people born in 1961 to age 31 and followed the mothers of these young people as well. The mothers were interviewed twice in 1962, when their children were infants, and then in 1963, 1966, 1977, 1980, 1985, and 1993 – years that roughly correspond to the associated children's ages of 0, 1, 5, 15, 18, 23, and 31. The children were interviewed in 1980, 1985, and 1993, at ages 18, 23, and 31. Although the IPS focused on intergenerational relationships and family formation processes, it illustrates many of the fundamental issues facing all longitudinal studies.

In response to the threat of attrition, IPS investigators used standard strategies for maintaining high levels of recontact and cooperation and custom strategies that were tailored to the study's design. The standard strategies included several components. First was the collection of detailed recontact information from both the study participants and a close friend, relative, or neighbor who was likely to know the study participant's address in case she or he moved. A second strategy was the use of interviewers who worked in previous rounds of the study to help track participants who may have moved between rounds of the study. A third tactic was the distribution of a "Report to Respondents" providing some analyses of previous rounds of data, examples of data uses, and appeals from the investigators to continue participating in the study. A fourth strategy was the use of various tracking measures for participants who may have moved, including postal requests for updated address information and automated searches of address databases. A fifth tactic was a series of refusal conversion efforts for reluctant participants, culminating in a personal call from the principal investigator in an attempt to convey the long-term importance of each person's participation.

The tailored approaches used in the IPS to reduce attrition also focused on both tracking and refusal conversion. In particular, efforts were made to capitalize on the two-generation design of the study. Contact efforts – which began shortly after the winter holiday season, when family members were likely to be in touch – used information from mothers to help locate children and information from children to help locate mothers. Because the younger generation was more mobile than the older generation, contacts began with the older generation. The same interviewer was initially assigned to both mother and child, which allowed tracking efforts to proceed in either generational direction and allowed interviewers to learn information from one generation that might assist in convincing reluctant members of the other generation to participate. Such tailored refusal conversion efforts are believed to be highly effective in reducing study attrition (Groves and Couper 1998). The result of combining both these standardized and study-specific approaches to tracking and refusal conversion was very low attrition between rounds of the Intergenerational Panel Study. For example, from 1980 to 1985 and again from 1985 to 1993, the study succeeded in re-interviewing greater than 98% of those who had participated in the previous round of the study – an extremely high rate for interviews spanning so many years. More-detailed discussions of the specific methods used to minimize attrition are described in a pair of articles by the investigator team (Freedman, Thornton, and Camburn 1980; Thornton, Freedman, and Camburn 1982).

In addition to dealing with attrition, the IPS also dealt with the problem of tension between the desires to repeat measures and to add new measures. Because the children in this study were extremely young at the outset, questions initially were directed solely to the mothers, and this continued until the children reached age 18. However, even among the cohort of mothers, pressures for and against changing measures were an issue over those 18 years. For example, at the baseline interview in 1962 mothers were asked to say whether they agreed or disagreed with a variety of statements about appropriate roles for men and women. To document trends in the attitudes toward gender roles, these questions were repeated in subsequent rounds in exactly the same form and sequence. However, by 1980 (and even more so by 1993) questions that measured substantial variation in the general population in 1962 began to sound dated and thus measured little variation in the general population.[3] Nevertheless, these items continued to be repeated word for word to maintain the extremely valuable comparability over time. On the other hand, the changing and increasingly complex lives of this cohort of mothers motivated IPS investigators to add new measures to the study in the same period. By the 1977 round of interviews, 15 years after the baseline, many of the mothers were now divorced and some had remarried. Also, many who had been out of the labor force with their small children had now entered or returned to the labor force. As a result, the 1977 round of the IPS interviews included new measures for divorce, remarriage, and labor force participation.

The 1980 launch of the second-generation interviews of the 18-year-olds, which set the baseline measurement for this group, introduced even more of these tensions. On one hand, investigators were strongly motivated to repeat many of the measures collected from the mothers to maintain response comparability across generations. This motivation was the highest in subjective domains, such as measurement of attitudes, beliefs, and preferences, because of strong evidence that question wording and order alter responses in these domains (Sudman and Bradburn 1974; Tourangeau et al. 1989; Tourangeau and Rasinski 1988; Tourangeau and Smith 1996). On the other hand, the life course position of the younger participants was much different than that of their mothers – who were parents of infants at the inception of the study – making many questions salient for them that would not have been appropriate for their mothers. Examples include first dating and first sexual experiences, high school experiences, and future expectations regarding education, work, career, and family. And as subsequent rounds of interviews with these young people ensued, other measurement tensions grew. For example, although questions regarding marriage preferences and intentions were valuable at age 18 and precise question repetition is desirable in these subjective domains, by age 31 questions regarding the content, nature, and quality of existing marital relationships were much more appropriate.

Investigators involved in the Intergenerational Panel Study faced many other measurement tensions during the course of this highly successful 31-year study (Thornton, Axinn, and Xie 2002; Thornton, Freedman, and Axinn 2002). In most cases, they resolved these tensions as illustrated by the examples presented here: They combined continuation of repeated measures with some modest addition of new measures. These issues were faced by other long-term longitudinal studies as well. For a detailed discussion of the implementation and evolution of several longitudinal studies across a broad range of substantive applications, see Phelps, Furstenberg, and Colby (2002).

Longitudinal Studies of Other Units of Observation

Longitudinal studies are not always focused on individuals. Sometimes they investigate units made up of individuals, such as households, communities, schools, businesses, governments, or nation-states. Repeated measurements over time of the same unit or group of individuals is the fundamental design feature of these studies – one that raises the issue of maintaining a common definition of the group over time. Consider, for example, a longitudinal study of households. Each household is composed of multiple individuals, and that composition changes over time. Although it may be relatively easy to add new individuals to households as they enter through birth, marriage, or some sort of boarding arrangement, other decisions must be made as individuals exit households. When individuals leave their original household to form a new household, for example, should they be ignored in subsequent rounds of the study? Or should the new household be added to the study? Or should the exiting individuals be considered continuing members of the original household?

Longitudinal studies of households have handled these decisions in different ways. Most attempt resolutions that are consistent with the study's substantive aims. So, for example, a study of migration or remittance from migrant household members might choose to designate an individual who moves from the home as a household member who is temporarily away if a representative of the original household views the individual this way (Massey et al. 1987). But this type of decision introduces a new source of dynamics in household membership. In the example given, the household representative may change or the representative may decide that the "temporarily-away" individual is no longer a household member if the individual's circumstances change.

Other types of exits from households create different complexities. Exit through divorce often results in a redefinition of the individual as no longer a family member, even if the individual has strong family ties to one or more members of the household, as, for example, a parent would. Exits may include multiple family members, which makes decisions regarding which part of the original group to follow extremely complex. For example, imagine a four-member household in which three members decide to leave. Should the longitudinal study follow the three who leave or continue to interview the one who remains in the original dwelling? If a democratic tendency leads investigators to follow the majority, the dilemma is unresolved when a household of four splits into two households of two members. In any case, studies of households over time will present challenges to maintaining comparable definitions across dynamic membership processes.

The same membership dynamics will challenge studies of other units of observation, such as communities, schools, businesses, governments, or nation-states. For units of observation defined by geography, such as communities or nation-states, a potential variation of the membership dynamics problem is changing boundary definitions. If a geographic unit's boundaries shift over time, the criteria for who is or is not included in the unit must be redefined. In addition, if geographical features are important to the investigation, shifting boundaries may alter other study definitions.

These potential dynamics in the definition of the unit to be studied are problematic for two reasons. First, they may destroy the comparability of measurements over time and thus much of the value of a longitudinal study. Second, these dynamics may create bias in the comparison of units across time. Most processes that create group membership dynamics are not distributed randomly. For example, the processes governing household membership dynamics – including marriage, divorce, migration, and household fission – have known predictors (Fricke 1986; Massey et al. 1987; Morgan and Rindfuss 1985; Thornton, Axinn, and Xie 2002). Therefore, households that experience membership changes tend to be systematically different from those that do not, and these systematic differences will produce bias in comparisons across households over time.

Although investigators cannot eliminate these inherent problems in long-term longitudinal studies of entities, they should formulate firm protocols for addressing unit dynamics before the study is launched and stick with these throughout the study period. These include definitions of entity membership and protocols for following its members over time.

Tools for Continuous Measurement

Periodic measurement is not the only method for creating information that documents change over time. Some research designs attempt continuous measurement. In practice, of course, continuous measurement simply means shrinking the interval between rounds of measurement to as brief a period as possible. In interview-based studies, for example, interviewing participants daily, weekly, or even monthly creates a small enough interval to refer to such measurement as continuous. Population registries, household registries, or population monitoring systems are designed to gather extremely frequent interview- or observation-based data on a population. Interested readers can learn more about these and other continuous measurement approaches, including their operational parameters, by investigating specific applications of these methods (Binka et al. 1999; D'Souza 1984; Menken and Phillips 1990; Shrestha, Shrestha, and Biddlecom 2002; Smith et al. 1997).

Most continuous monitoring systems feature very frequent interviews with a well-defined population. By focusing a large interviewer staff on a small geographic area or a small population, it is possible to increase the frequency of interviews enough to mimic a continuous interviewing situation. Because extremely frequent interviews substantially increase the level of participant burden, such systems often feature very brief interviews that collect a small amount of information. Thus, continuous measurement often involves a trade-off of frequency of measurement with breadth and depth of measurement.

Some governments operate registry systems that require the general population to report events when they occur. Most vital registration systems, which record and certify births, marriages, divorces, and deaths, are an example of this type of design. For example, a birth registration system generally requires the completion of some type of standardized form in exchange for an official birth certificate (Shryock and Siegel 1976). By making such certificates a legal requirement, governments can motivate high levels of participation in such systems and create nearly a continuous record of events across a population. In many ways, the household registry or monitoring systems described above attempt to mimic such vital registration systems on a smaller scale, usually by focusing on information not available from vital registration data.

As it is for all longitudinal data collection efforts, attrition is a fundamental issue for population monitoring or registration systems. Failure to follow migrants or high levels of refusal to participate create important sources of bias in data coming from these systems. Failure to follow migrants is a common flaw, particularly when the population to be monitored is defined by a geographic area rather than some other criteria, and those who leave the geographic area are, by definition, lost to follow-up. The longitudinal measures of change over time resulting from such data will be biased by the omission of migrants, because, as with other processes that create group membership, migration is not randomly distributed and has known predictors (Brockerhoff 2000; Guilmoto and Sandron 2001; Massey 1990). Systematically omitting to follow up a subset of the population that behaves in ways that are different from the larger population will cause the resulting data to misrepresent the total population.

Some studies make great efforts to avoid the introduction of migration-related bias. One example is the household registry system conducted in Nepal as part of the Chitwan Valley Family Study (CVFS). This study began with a baseline census of all individuals (approximately 10,000) living in the 151 neighborhoods selected for the study.[4] Neighborhoods were defined by geographic boundaries, and these were recorded and maintained throughout the study. The registry was conducted by sending an interviewer to each household every month to update records of births, deaths, marriages, divorces, and migrations in or out of the household for each household member. New households established within the geographic boundaries of the neighborhood were added to the registry system. These in-migration additions created some dynamics in the registry, but they were clearly the easier migration consequence to address. Individuals or sets of individuals who left their households, either temporarily or permanently,[5] were tracked through the remaining household members. That is, every month the remaining household members were asked to provide information about all those currently residing within the household *and* all of those who had resided in the household at the time of the census but subsequently left. This procedure was also used to track those who joined the household after the census and later left. Also, individuals who left their households of origin were visited by interviewers at their new locations every 3 months to confirm the registry records. These visits were crucial to tracking efforts because under some migration circumstances, such as when couples divorced or entire households moved outside the study area, the household of origin could not serve as a source of ongoing information on migrants. In these cases, investigators were dependent on the 3-month visits for all follow-up data. Although it was not feasible to conduct 3-month interviews with individuals who migrated outside of the country, the vast majority of them returned periodically to Nepal, allowing for follow-up interviews.

These tracking efforts, which required the availability of interviewers who could follow up with migrants anywhere in the country, kept study attrition to less than 2%. The high level of success was due in part to the detailed contact information for migrants obtained from the household of origin – sometimes from migrants themselves before their departure. Another reason for its success was the frequency of recontact with migrants. Because many of those who migrate once will migrate again, the visits every 3 months helped investigators maintain contact information for migrants' subsequent destinations. For more details about the design of this migrant tracking effort and the CVFS household registry system, see Shrestha, Shrestha, and Biddlecom (2002).

Although studying migration was not the main aim of this household registry system, analyses of migrant data confirmed that migrants were systematically different from non-migrants in other domains of interest to the study. That is, migrants exhibited significantly different marital and childbearing behavior than non-migrants. These differences demonstrate the potential bias of omitting migrants from follow-up, which is of course part of a more general problem with attrition in longitudinal studies (Thomas, Frankenberg, and Smith 2001). When comparisons over time are the objective, efforts to track migrants and avoid losses to follow up in general are just as important in registry or population monitoring systems as they are in other longitudinal data collection efforts.

Mixing Methods in Longitudinal Designs

Up to this point, we have cataloged various techniques for implementing longitudinal designs and identified important issues in their implementation. Now we turn our attention to the integration of multiple methods within a single longitudinal design. Keeping with the general themes of this book, the objectives in integrating multiple methods are to use the strengths of some methods to compensate for the weaknesses of others, to use triangulation across multiple sources of information for providing new insights into cause and consequence, and to promote the high level of investigator involvement that can make introspection a tool rather than a liability.

Integrating Calendar Methods in a Longitudinal Design

Longitudinal studies have included life history calendar (LHC) methods, such as those described in Chapter 6, in their designs for a long time. In fact, some of the key breakthroughs in LHC design took place within the framework of the Intergenerational Panel Study described earlier in this chapter (Freedman et al. 1988). Longitudinal studies that leave substantial time gaps between rounds of measurement often require tools for measuring behavior or events that take place between rounds. The LHC is a natural tool to use in this situation because it can provide detailed retrospective measurements of the timing and sequencing of events and behaviors over the course of many months or even years. The advantages may be most obvious when the interval between rounds of a longitudinal study are relatively long, as they were in the Intergenerational Panel Study (Thornton, Freedman, and Axinn 2002). But even when the intervals are relatively short, calendar techniques out-perform alternative approaches in terms of accuracy and precision of respondent reports (Axinn et al. 2002; Belli, Shay, and Stafford 2001).

The LHC can be integrated into a longitudinal design by administering it as a discrete part of a more highly structured survey interview. A key trade-off is that adding this retrospective measurement tool may curtail either the collection of survey-based prospective measurements or extend the overall length of the interview. Another important consequence is the necessity for additional interviewer training. Because of their more open-ended nature, life history calendars require significant interviewer training that is different from training necessary for more-structured surveys.

One of the first choices to be made in designing an LHC for use in a longitudinal study is how far back in time the calendar should go or, in other words, how far back respondents will be asked to recall. A calendar might be designed to cover the interval beginning immediately after the most recent interview up to the current interview, to overlap with the most recent interview, or to cover an entire lifetime in a way that would complement or confirm data from previous interviews. As with any measurement method that relies on recall, the greater the period of retrospective time covered, the higher the risk of measurement error. However, designing calendars to overlap a period from the previous round of a longitudinal study affords special advantages for the evaluation of calendar data quality. Overlapping measures from two consecutive rounds can be compared to assess the level of discrepancy between two reports of the same characteristic, and these discrepancies can be used to estimate overall variance in calendar data quality across substantive domains (Belli, Shay, and Stafford 2001; Freedman et al. 1988). These analyses can prove quite useful in interpreting the results from calendar-based measures embedded within longitudinal studies.

A key feature of longitudinal studies is repeated measurement over time. Integrating an LHC into a study provides repeated date-based measurement over time; but when sequential calendars are spliced together to form a continuous time series of LHC measures, data quality will suffer if mismatches occur at the connecting time points. To improve the likelihood of a smooth transition from one calendar to the next, interviewers should begin new rounds of interviews by helping respondents recall the circumstances reported at the end of the previous interview. That is, interviewers should use the study's records to remind respondents of their situation and context at the time the previous calendar was completed. These memory anchors can help respondents pick up their reporting where they left off, creating a more accurate splice between two sequential LHC measures.[6] Because some recall errors will always occur, data analysts should take special note of events reported near the time of the splice. In fact, many such events may reflect recall error that is simply recorded on the more recent calendar. Of course, the more frequent the longitudinal measurement, the shorter the period of recall across calendars and the lower the likelihood of splicing errors.

Although the linking of *static* contextual measurement to data from longitudinal studies had become relatively common by the end of the 20th century, using neighborhood history calendars or other similar contextual history measures in longitudinal studies is a much more recent and infrequent practice. Linking static contextual data to longitudinal measurement at multiple points in time has allowed investigators to create some dynamics in the measurement of context (Leventhal and Brooks-Gunn 2001). However, integrating a method such as the Neighborhood History Calendar (see Chapter 5) into a longitudinal study offers the possibility of linking fully dynamic contextual history measurement to fully dynamic, prospective, individual-level measurement. This potential is likely to grow in importance for at least two reasons – first, because most multi-level social science theories and models include dynamics at multiple analytic levels; and second, because such dynamic measurements reveal the temporal sequencing of contextual and individual changes and thereby help establish whether contextual effects on individuals or individual effects on contexts are a more likely explanation for observed multilevel associations.

In addition to the data collection issues outlined for the NHC in Chapter 5, another challenge in using this method in a longitudinal study is the splicing problem described above for the LHC. That is, if NHC data are collected in sequential rounds of a longitudinal study, care must be taken to help respondents pick up where they left off in their reporting, without duplicating or omitting information at the connecting points. Whether the NHC is conducted along with or separate from the individual-level data collection operation, the key is creating links between the individual and the context across space and time, with the added complication that following individuals over time increases the chances they will be exposed to multiple contexts through mobility. As discussed in Chapter 5, when the context to be measured has a physical location, such as a neighborhood, Geographic Information System (GIS) tools can prove quite useful for making links across spaces. When the context to be measured is a social group, such as a club, individual-level measures of participation may be required to make the appropriate links across space and time. For some other social organizations, such as educational institutions or employers, both GIS measurement and individual-level measures of participation in or exposure to these entities may be needed to create dynamic links between individuals and the social contexts they experience. Adding these individual-level measurements requires more time and effort from respondents, however, and may conflict with other individual-level measurement aims in a longitudinal study. This issue is merely another example of the trade-off that all longitudinal data collection efforts must make between gathering rich and salient data and keeping respondent burden, and thus study attrition, low.

The use of LHC- and NHC-type data collection in longitudinal studies is quite likely to increase in the coming years given social sciences' high demand for fully dynamic measurement at multiple analytic levels and the existence of appropriate implementation tools. The ability to combine prospective longitudinal measurement and retrospective dynamic measurement of individual and social contexts through tools like the LHC and the NHC is likely to unleash unprecedented measurement of dynamic interrelated social processes in the first half of the 21st century.

Combining Structured and Unstructured Methods

Another approach to mixing data collection methods in a longitudinal study is to execute multiple methods simultaneously. For example, as described in Chapter 3, investigators could combine structured methods such as surveys with unstructured methods such as observations and unstructured interviews and repeat this combination in each round of the study. This approach enhances the kinds of insights produced by using the mixed method approaches while providing the dynamic, prospective, temporally ordered measurement characteristics of longitudinal studies.

Just as with the methods described in Chapter 3, geographic proximity is likely to play a key role in the success of using multiple data collection methods simultaneously in a community-based longitudinal study. Attempts to achieve this sort of integration at multiple sites, over great distances, or among large study populations are likely to prove extremely difficult. By contrast, in a single community among a well-defined and limited population, it is quite possible to combine multiple methods into a single data collection strategy that is repeated at multiple points in time. The techniques described in Chapter 3 are applicable, and the repetition of them over time focused on the same unit(s) of observation will produce a longitudinal design.

Of course, longitudinal community studies suffer from the same design constraints as any longitudinal study of a unit of aggregated individuals. Change over time in group membership – or in community residents – will reduce the comparability of multiple sequential measures. Thus, as individuals move in and out of the community, the community-level measures gathered at different points reflect the circumstances of different sets of people. When such studies integrate individual-level measurement, as described in Chapter 3, this problem is exacerbated. Failure to follow individuals as they move will create bias in the results of longitudinal measurement of individuals, as discussed elsewhere in this chapter. Effort to avoid such bias will create a natural tension in a longitudinal study of a community.

Using a combination of data collection methods, however, offers opportunities to reduce bias created by the attrition of individuals out of the study. As discussed in Chapter 3, using unstructured interviews and observational methods can reduce coverage errors in longitudinal studies because it increases investigators' familiarity with households in the community, which allows investigators to track movers to new areas for follow-up interviews or to recontact them when they visit the community.

Also, investigators who use an integrated multimethod approach have greater opportunity for insight into the processes creating attrition in longitudinal studies. As discussed in Chapter 2, an integrated multimethod design increases investigators' involvement in the production of the measures and knowledge of methodological limitations. The impact of attrition on results from a longitudinal study depends greatly on the subject matter being examined (Thomas, Frankenberg, and Smith 2001). In part, this is because the selection processes driving attrition, including respondent mobility and reluctance to participate, differ in their relationships to various substantive outcomes. Having multiple sources of insight into the processes producing study attrition increases investigators' ability to understand the processes and accommodate that attrition in analyzing the longitudinal data. Thus, in addition to enhancing insight into the substantive phenomena being studied, multiple methods of data collection simultaneously can promote greater insight into methodological issues and other limitations associated with longitudinal studies.

Sequential Integration of Multiple Methods

Another approach to mixing data collection methods in a longitudinal study framework is to add them sequentially. Chapter 4 discussed methods for using existing highly structured survey measures to guide the purposive collection of new, unstructured interview and observational measures on specific topics of interest. The explicit aim of this sequential technique is to improve models of cause and consequence by allowing researchers to refine hypotheses, research strategies, and measures.

To the extent that this approach features unstructured interviews and observations of individuals and families previously interviewed using survey methods, it is longitudinal in design, even if it generally covers a relatively brief period of time. However, the sequential multimethod approach described in Chapter 4 could be readily adapted into a longer-term, multiple phase longitudinal design. In the latter half of the 20th century, researchers often used unstructured interviews, observations, and focus groups to design subsequent survey measurements (Dressler 1991; Knodel 1995; Morgan 1997; O'Brien 1993; Zeller 1993). In a variation on this practice, a round of survey measurement could be used to guide a round of less structured measurement (as described in Chapter 4), which in turn could be used to guide the design of a second round of survey measurement. In fact, investigators could use this sequence of mixed method measurements over several rounds of a longitudinal study to refine measures, focus on topics of interest, and deepen understanding of the study population. The result would be an integrated series of measures and measurement techniques, all designed to improve models of cause and consequence.

This sequential approach to data collection has many advantages. First, as with a simultaneously integrated approach, insights created from one method can be used to enhance what is learned from another method. As discussed in Chapter 1, less structured methods such as unstructured interviewing, observational methods, and focus groups have special advantages for deepening understanding of respondents' views on the issues being studied, revealing new information, and stimulating new hypotheses. On the other hand, highly structured methods, such as surveys, have special advantages for documenting the extent of a behavior, attitude, or other phenomena and for testing hypotheses. The sequential application of structured and unstructured methods gives researchers an ideal tool for the investigation of cause and consequence, enhancing their ability to alternatively formulate and test hypotheses in an iterative fashion.

Second, information gleaned from methods used at one point can be used to guide implementation of the next round of alternative methods. For example, researchers may use insights gained from observations conducted between rounds of survey data collection to formulate new survey questions and prioritize among them for inclusion. Because researchers conducting longitudinal studies must balance the need to repeat measures for comparability against the need to introduce new measures for saliency, information arising from unstructured methods is valuable in helping them gauge which new measures are most important to integrate into the structured parts of an ongoing study. In a similar fashion, ongoing analysis of longitudinal survey data can be used to help target the collection of less structured measurements. The methods involved are analogous to those described in Chapter 4, but in this framework they acquire the special analytic advantages of a longitudinal design.

A third advantage is that, although the simultaneous integration described in Chapter 3 is probably easiest to use in a single-site, community-based longitudinal study, the sequential integration of multiple methods can be easily used in a larger-scale, multiple site longitudinal study. Researchers can use analyses of early rounds of survey data from a large-scale, multisite study to guide the subsequent execution of less structured measurement techniques at a small number of analytically selected sites. The key is that use of analyses of survey data to guide unstructured measurement substitutes for the serendipity likely to occur in a community study application of unstructured methods (see Chapter 3).

It allows researchers to target their investments in time-intensive unstructured measurement methods at the locations and with the people likely to prove most informative for a specific subject matter. This targeting helps make it possible to effectively integrate highly intensive unstructured measurement techniques into a large scale, multisite longitudinal study.

Although most of the longitudinal studies conducted in the latter part of the 20th century were based on repetition of highly structured survey interviews, this was not always the case. Some longitudinal studies also employed less structured methodology (Phelps, Furstenberg, and Colby 2002). As the use of multiple methods in a single study design becomes more common in the social sciences, the integration of multiple methods into longitudinal study designs will also become more common. The sequential integration of these multiple methods affords special opportunities to use the results from one type of measurement to guide the implementation of another – an attractive potential for longitudinal research. And in general, mixed method measurement strategies comprise an effective counterpart to the sophisticated statistical analyses of longitudinal survey data used in social science investigations of cause and consequence.

Integrating Self-Report Measures in a Longitudinal Design

As measurement technology improves, new opportunities arise to integrate dynamic self-reporting into longitudinal studies. Self-reported measurement in general and diary-keeping in particular both have a long history of use in the social sciences (Bates, Viken, and Alexander 2002; Bolger, Davis, and Rafaeli 2003; Fals-Stewart 2003; Gieseman and Rogers 1986; Gijsbers et al. 1999; McKenzie 1983; Rook 2003; Terry 1988; Tidwell, Reis, and Shaver 1996). Diary-keeping by study participants allows investigators to collect a dynamic record of events and experiences at a high level of temporal and substantive detail. New electronic alternatives for social science data collection (Couper 1998, 2000; Couper and Rowe 1996; Couper, Traugott, and Lamias 2001), including various forms of computer-assisted interviewing and Web-based surveys conducted via PCs, PDAs, and wireless communication devices, are reshaping the science of self-reported measurement methods.

Integrated into longitudinal study designs, such methods have vast potential to revolutionize the measures available to study cause and consequence in the social sciences. For example, distributing PDAs with wireless Internet connectivity to a set of study participants allows them to keep a continuous electronic record of diary-type information. These dynamic self-reported records of experiences and events afford study participants maximal privacy at minimal effort for those collecting the data. Integrating such dynamic self-reporting into longitudinal studies can introduce previously unknown levels of temporal and substantive detail in the measurement of events, experiences, or attitudes between rounds of other types of longitudinal measurement. For the study of cause and consequence, such detailed records of changes over time provide the essential means to learn which actions, experiences, or beliefs precede which outcomes of interest.

The use of computers and other electronic devices to collect social science data, including measurements in longitudinal studies, was common by the close of the 20th century. Although using such technologies to integrate dynamic self-reporting into longitudinal studies is not yet widespread, continued improvements in electronic information-gathering technology and the extremely high analytic value of such measurements are likely to dramatically increase the use of these kinds of integrated design methods in the near future.

Conclusion

Longitudinal studies, which follow the same individuals or other units of observation over time, are one of the social sciences' most promising tools for the study of cause and consequence. Given social scientists' inability to randomly assign individuals to conditions of interest, this is likely to remain true for many years to come. In this chapter, we discuss some of the fundamental issues in the implementation of longitudinal studies and associated methodological limitations. Key among these are the threats to comparability over time introduced by both study attrition and measurement changes. Although there are techniques to mitigate these threats and to improve the quality of longitudinal studies, both those who conduct longitudinal studies and those who use data from such studies must be wary of these threats.

The social sciences stand at the brink of a revolution in the integration of mixed methods of data collection into longitudinal study designs. Although several longitudinal studies have integrated Life History Calendar measurement already, this is likely to become more pervasive and creative. Longitudinal studies of individuals are beginning to include contextual-level measurement, but the integration of Neighborhood History Calendar – type methods into longitudinal studies is just beginning. Combining structured and unstructured methods – either simultaneously or sequentially – holds the promise of substantially advancing our understanding of cause and consequence. Both approaches offer multiple advantages for gathering broader information on the substantive subject under investigation and for addressing some of the key methodological issues in the implementation of longitudinal studies. Finally, new technologies are creating opportunities to integrate dynamic self-reporting into longitudinal studies, which has the potential to create unprecedented levels of temporal and substantive measurement detail.

Neither longitudinal studies or mixed method data collection strategies resolve the problem of causal inference in the social sciences; however, their approaches provide the means for social scientists to study the empirical world from multiple vantage points and in ways consistent with the temporal ordering embedded in our causal hypotheses. Integrating calendar methods and dynamic self-reporting into longitudinal data gathering is the best opportunity available to create measurement that matches the temporal order of our hypotheses. Integrating less structured data collection methods with highly structured survey designs is the best opportunity available for producing new information with which to stimulate new hypotheses, while maintaining comparable measures with which to test existing hypotheses. The tools described here are designed to both advance and test theories of cause and consequence in the social world against the empirical reality.

Issues of Application

Even more so than micro-demographic community studies, most longitudinal studies are intensive, multi-investigator endeavors that require many resources. Because longitudinal studies require ongoing investigation with the same people (or other units of observation) over time, they usually rely on the work and energy of several different investigators and a substantial set of resources. Therefore, we highly recommend working in a collaborative team to conduct such a study. As discussed elsewhere, having collaborators who each bring their own perspectives and skills provides another useful set of contrasts to the research process. Multidisciplinary teams can provide especially fruitful collaborations. In longitudinal studies having strong specialists in all design, data collection, analytical, and substantive domains involved in the project will help to ensure high quality in every phase. Also as discussed elsewhere, the challenge to a multidisciplinary team approach is that team members often have different standards, languages, or strategies for dealing with the issues at hand. Multidisciplinary team members must work harder than other teams to communicate and resolve disagreements or misunderstandings. Nevertheless, the payoffs from this variation in perspective are likely to outweigh the costs.

Both the setting and subject matter of the study will shape any particular longitudinal data collection. Throughout this chapter, we have addressed issues of formulating and implementing a successful longitudinal study. In fact, there are many successful examples of longitudinal studies – examples that include success across many different subjects, in many different settings, at many different scales (Lillard and Panis 1998; Phelps, Furstenberg, and Colby 2002; Thomas, Frankenberg, and Smith 2001). We urge readers to study these successful examples closely in preparation for the design and implementation of a new longitudinal study.

Illustrations of Principles

The integration of mixed methods into a longitudinal design provides illustrations of several of the mixed method data collection principles identified in Chapter 1. The illustrations include both principles closely tied to the theme of using strengths of some methods to counterbalance weaknesses of other methods and principles closely tied to the theme of comprehensive empirical documentation. Just as with cross-sectional application of the micro-demographic community study approach, longitudinal applications of this approach use highly structured surveys in simultaneous combination with less structured interviewing and direct observation – combining methods to counterbalance strengths and weaknesses. Sequential integration of unstructured methods into a highly structured longitudinal study offers many of the same counterbalancing opportunities. Through this counterbalancing, mixed method longitudinal data collection also provides greater flexibility, allowing the measures to adapt to the local setting and change midstream to document key beliefs or behaviors discovered through the data collection process. The counterbalancing elements of these strategies also encourage a high level of investigator involvement with the study population.

Integration of calendar methods into a longitudinal study design clearly has the capability to provide extremely comprehensive empirical documentation. The combination of prospective longitudinal measurement with retrospective calendar measures for the intervals between data collections offers an extremely high level of temporal order among measures. By combining quite different measurement strategies simultaneously or sequentially in a longitudinal design, investigators can also gather redundant measures to check results from data collected in different ways. This comprehensive measurement also provides substantial opportunities to document mechanisms that may be responsible for producing causal relationships. Use of all of these strategies within the framework of a single longitudinal data collection greatly facilitates this discovery and documentation process. The creation of a comprehensive empirical record is certainly one of the greatest advantages of a mixed method longitudinal strategy.

8   Conclusion

The objective of this book is the practical. To that end, the methods described here are predicated on a specific philosophy of science. This philosophy argues that causal relationships and social processes are a property of the social world, *not* a property of data we collect about the social world, and thus data can never be used to *prove* a causal theory. Instead, this philosophy argues that theory can be used to construct hypotheses about cause and that data about the empirical world can be used as evidence to support or fail to support these hypotheses. Based on this philosophy, we argue that new data collection techniques that maximize our ability to test causal hypotheses and provide us with new insights into social cause and consequence are of paramount importance in the social sciences.

The methods we describe are also motivated by our conviction that causal inference based on observational data will *always* be part of social science research. This may be especially the case for key public policy issues. We argue that because random assignment to important social conditions will continue to be a rare circumstance, we must devise other means of documenting causal relationships. From time to time, a new program or public policy may provide the opportunity to randomly assign some people and not others to a specific new condition. This is most likely when the costs of a new program are high, making it difficult to provide the service to all, and random access to the service is considered the fairest way to launch such a program. But the vast majority of important social conditions that social scientists hope to study will never be possible to randomly assign. They will never have the opportunity to randomly assign, for example, divorce, incarceration, depression, pregnancy, college education, crime, illness, or marriage. Acceptance of this fact forces us to invest in further advancing the science of making causal inferences from observational designs.

In the endeavor to advance understanding of cause and consequence in the social world, we believe social scientists should exploit every possible approach. This includes the use of "natural" experiments, special population studies (such as twin studies or studies of adoptees), and statistical techniques for improving our modeling of causal relationships (such as selection corrections, use of strong statistical instruments, or statistical matching approaches). Social science should make use of every design alternative, measurement strategy, approach to summarizing data, and analytic method. We should take time and care to select approaches that are appropriate to the specific subject we intend to study, but we should always be prepared to use multiple approaches to study any specific topic. The use of multiple approaches is more important than merely providing complementary views of the same causal relationships. The use of multiple approaches that systematically vary the potential biases characterizing each method constitutes our most powerful tool for creating convincing empirical evidence of causal relationships in the social world (Moffit 2005; Rosenbaum 1999, 2001).

In this book, we focus on data collection strategies for the observational study of cause and consequence in the social sciences. Until now, the vast majority of methodological efforts devoted to improving the study of causal inference has been devoted to analytic techniques. There are numerous reviews of the general parameters of the causal-inference problem, the various analytic techniques for addressing these problems using existing data, and both the prospects and limitations of those solutions (Bachrach and McNicol 2003; Snijders and Hagenaars 2001). Careful consideration of the issues involved in any potential analytic solution to the problem of causal inference leads to the conclusion that all analytic approaches are characterized by important flaws and limitations (Moffitt 2003). Data collection strategies for addressing causal inference from observational designs do not solve these problems either, but they do offer two critical points of assistance. First, new data collection techniques can improve the measurement necessary to optimize the application of available analytic approaches. Second, innovative multiple method strategies can provide a coordinated set of alternative empirical insights into a single issue of causal inference (Moffit 2005).

In this book, we focus on data collection and measurement strategies that involve both the simultaneous and the sequential use of multiple approaches to measurement. We highlight integration of multiple methods that vary in the level of structure involved in the measurement – that is, highly structured survey methods integrated simultaneously or sequentially with less structured interviewing and observational methods. Use of multiple approaches that vary in level of structure combines the hypothesis-testing power of highly standardized measurement with the hypothesis-discovering power of extremely open-ended measurement (Chapters 3 and 4). We also highlight measurement strategies closely tied to research designs organized around the study of cause and consequence in the social world. Most important here are measurement strategies that focus on temporal ordering among measures (Chapters 5, 6, and 7). These methods can be used to create measures that match the temporal ordering embedded in causal hypothesis – that cause precedes consequence.

The specific applications of mixed method research we describe in this book are intended to illustrate general principles in the integration of multiple methods. Although each application focuses on a specific topic in a specific setting, all of the applications share a general set of principles useful in the effort to forge new data collection methods that will advance the social sciences. We begin this concluding chapter by reviewing those principles. Then we turn to another fundamental reason for integrating structured and unstructured methods: the role of introspection in causal reasoning about the social world. To follow that, we review a few key issues involved in the application of mixed method approaches to specific research problems. Finally, we close by identifying some of the key frontiers in mixed method data collection and measurement strategies.

Principles of Mixed Method Data Collection

As we have discussed throughout the book, systematic consideration of mixed method data collection strategies reveals two key themes. The first theme is that mixing multiple methods affords opportunities to use the strengths of some methods to counterbalance the weaknesses of other methods. Because all methods have strengths and weaknesses, combinations of multiple methods that achieve this counterbalancing aim are particularly valuable. The second theme is that mixing multiple methods is a valuable strategy for producing a comprehensive empirical record about a topic. Empirical documentation that combines redundant measurement using radically different approaches has special strengths for reducing errors, discovering new hypotheses, and testing hypotheses. These themes of counterbalancing strengths and weaknesses and comprehensive empirical documentation illuminate a set of common principles in the design of mixed method data collection. We summarize those principles below.

Method Balance

The first theme of mixed method data collection – that using different types of research methods allows one to counterbalance the weaknesses of one method with the strengths of another – overarches three specific principles. The first principle is that method balance is best achieved using a combination of more and less structured methods. The structured nature of survey methods and the flexibility of observational or less structured interviewing methods combine to provide, respectively, data useful for testing hypotheses and data useful for discovering new hypotheses (Sieber 1973). Less structured methods are also useful for discovering and documenting key causal mechanisms that are responsible for producing the overall causal relationships documented using more highly structured methods. This combined approach is similar to the "triangulation" method as proposed by Denzin (1970; 1978). Chapter 3 of this book focuses on integration of multiple research methods to simultaneously provide data for hypothesis generation and hypothesis testing. Chapter 4 is devoted to approaches for integrating methods in ways that provide a more systematic application of less structured methods while adding flexibility to the development of models for survey data. Chapters 5 and 6 focus on hybrid methods that mix and match the strengths of multiple methods into one tool: event history calendars. Chapter 7 discusses longitudinal studies using multiple methods. Though every approach described in this book aims to use the strengths of some methods to help compensate for the weaknesses of others, the approaches described here are merely examples of this principle. The principle itself has much to offer social scientific study of cause and consequence. It is a fundamental element in the creation of new data collection approaches and methods not yet imagined.

The second key principle underlying the benefits of method balance is that by incorporating methods into the mix that *require* heavy investigator involvement, this increases the investigators' involvement and familiarity with the overall research project. Increasing investigator involvement in all phases of the research process helps ensure that introspection serves as a beneficial tool rather than a liability. Certainly, methods such as unstructured interviewing and participant observation tend to involve the investigator with the people being studied and the methods being used. But investigator involvement can be enhanced as well in other more structured methods, such as surveys, focus groups, and archival research, promoting more comprehensive understanding of the study population and more comprehensive insight into the strengths and weaknesses of the specific methods being used. Integrated use of multiple methods is an important way to increase investigator involvement and firsthand knowledge in studies making use of more highly structured methods. Introspection is unavoidable in the social sciences. Misused, it is a dangerous liability; used carefully, it provides social scientists with a tool for studying cause and consequence that is not available in most other sciences.

The third key principle underlying the advantages of method balance is that mixed method research brings flexibility to the design and application of data collection methods, allowing new methods and integrative designs to unfold and be tailored specifically to the research question at hand. Such flexibility is a common feature of every data collection approach described in this volume, and the examples provided demonstrate how that flexibility has been employed to advance the substantive aims of specific studies of cause and consequence. The methods described here can be used to study many different social science topics in a range of settings, but they are not designed to be applied wholesale to new topics and new settings without careful consideration of the match between methods and substantive aims. The methods described here are tools. As when using any collection of tools, the user is expected to understand each tool's purpose and appropriate application before choosing which combination to use for the task. Careful consideration of the substantive aims of a particular study is necessary for the assembly of an appropriate combination of data collection tools. The flexibility embedded in the mixed method strategies described in this book makes it possible for others to tailor these approaches to meet the specific aims of new studies.

Comprehensive Empirical Documentation

The second theme of benefits associated with mixed method research focuses on the production of a comprehensive empirical record about a topic. Comprehensive empirical documentation that combines redundant measurement using radically different approaches is a particularly valuable tool in the effort to investigate causal relationships using observational research designs (Moffit 2005). Three principles regarding the advantages of comprehensive measurement are particularly important in the design of mixed method approaches for the investigation of causal questions.

First, comprehensiveness of measurement is especially useful because redundant measurement of an association using different methods is useful for assessing the role of method-specific bias in producing that association. To the extent we can produce consistent evidence of the same association using radically different data collection tools that are likely to be characterized by different forms of bias, confidence in that association is greatly increased (Moffit 2005; Rosenbaum 2001). Just as mixed methods can be used for counterbalancing weaknesses of one method with strengths of another to reduce measurement errors, from a causal reasoning perspective varying data collection method-specific biases produces stronger empirical evidence. All data collection methods can be characterized by biases. Varying the method-specific bias by integrating multiple methods reduces the chance that such bias is responsible for observed associations.

Second, from a causal reasoning perspective comprehensive measurement is also useful for discovering potential mechanisms responsible for producing an association (Moffit 2005). Reasoning that a particular empirical association corresponds to a causal relationship requires reasoning about the mechanisms that produce that causal relationship. Empirical documentation of those mechanisms is, therefore, another important element in producing empirical evidence of a causal relationship. Highly structured methods, such as surveys, have advantages for documenting overall associations, but less structured methods, such as unstructured interviewing and observation, have advantages for discovering the mechanisms responsible for overall associations (Groves et al. 2004). By using mixed method approaches that integrate these different types of data collection methods, investigators have greater opportunity to both discover and document the mechanisms responsible for causal relationships.

Third, the causal-reasoning perspective highlights the need for comprehensive measures that include the temporal ordering of measurement. The temporal-ordering issue is in no way specific to mixed methods. It is equally important in the application of any one data collection method, if that method is being used to gather measures to test causal hypotheses. Measures of causes are expected to precede measures of consequences. Use of mixed method approaches to study causal relationships also requires attention to these temporal-ordering issues. Because this issue is fundamental to data collection for causal analysis, a substantial portion of the mixed method strategies we describe are devoted to issues of temporal ordering. These issues are the main focus of Chapters 5, 6, and 7. Together, these three causal-reasoning dimensions of a comprehensive empirical record form one of our strongest motivations for the mixed methods data collection techniques described in this book.

Role of Introspection

For too long, the social scientific study of cause and consequence has been organized around an effort to mimic the physical sciences. Physical scientists study phenomena by randomly assigning chemicals to test tubes, particles to acceleration, or enzymes to petri dishes. If social scientists believe this is the only route to understanding cause and consequence, we will find ourselves wrestling with increasingly complex statistical solutions to a problem that is ultimately intractable – we cannot randomly assign people to most of the conditions we study. The methods described in this book are designed to provide pragmatic alternatives: observational studies designed to advance our understanding of cause and consequence in the social world. We reject the efforts designed to mimic the physical sciences in favor of constructing new methods suited to the problems of social science.

In particular, we reject the goal of eliminating introspection from social science research. Physicists, chemists, and biologists cannot use introspection to advance the study of cause and consequence in their fields. In the social sciences, however, ignoring the role of introspection can be disastrous. With no information about the day-to-day lives of those we study, we tend to impute the missing connections in the lives of others with what we know about our own life. This process looms as a key threat to the reliability and validity of conclusions drawn by social scientists. But rather than attempt to eliminate introspection, an effort we believe will ultimately fail, we advocate careful attempts to harness it for the advancement of the social scientific study of cause and consequence.

Firsthand experience and detailed knowledge of the day-to-day lives of the people we study can provide the means to gain a more accurate and comprehensive understanding of their lives, their social interactions, and the choices they make. Greater insight into the lives of those we study facilitates investigators' abilities to make informed guesses about cause and consequence in the lives of others. These guesses are not hypothesis tests, but they can help us formulate stronger hypotheses and better identify the mechanisms responsible for creating causal connections (Babbie 2004). Methods that promote direct interaction with and observation of the people we study facilitate the accumulation of these insights. This is one of the main reasons we advocate the integration of hypothesis-generating methods, such as less structured interviewing and observation, with more standardized hypothesis-testing methods, such as survey interviews.

The Application of New Mixed Method Research

A small number of general issues arise in the design and implementation of virtually all mixed method research projects. We discuss three of them here: language, redundancy, and scale.

Language

Common language is an essential ingredient in a successful mixed method data collection. Language creates the meaning that accompanies social interactions and frames behavior; language creates the building blocks of ideas that guide all aspects of social interaction and behavior. To attempt to observe or interview others without knowing their language – and then to draw meaningful conclusions about their ideas, behavior, or social interaction – is to engage in social research at great peril. At best, the outcome is likely to be characterized by moderate levels of measurement error that generate misleading conclusions. At worst, the level of such error may be so high that the researcher's insights into social cause and consequence will bear no resemblance to the actual social world being studied. To the extent that researchers purposefully engage in introspection to help derive insight into cause and consequence, lack of a common language will exacerbate these problems.

Language is of fundamental importance when social scientists from one country attempt to study those in another. As discussed in Chapter 2, methodologists have designed techniques for reliably translating measures across languages. These techniques can be used to construct measures in one language that parallel measures from another language, and these techniques have had some success in survey research (Groves et al. 2004). However, lack of a common language remains a substantial obstacle to implementation of mixed method data collection, particularly that aimed at investigation of causal relationships.

This issue is most obvious when social scientists engage in unstructured interviewing or observation among a group speaking a different language. Without a common language, the social scientist cannot directly interpret interview responses or observations. But the issue is just as problematic when applying highly structured methods. It is possible for social scientists in one country to collect data using highly structured methods, translate the measures they collect into numbers, and share those numeric summaries for secondary analysis with social scientists in other countries who speak other languages. However, secondary analyses of numeric data without direct knowledge of what the measures actually ask, how respondents might interpret those measures, and how specific social processes might link multiple measures is more likely to generate misleading conclusions than accurate conclusions.

As social scientists become increasingly engaged in the study of cause and consequence, merely coding responses in an unfamiliar language into numbers and then statistically analyzing those numbers will not substitute for a more direct understanding of responses achieved through common language. Beyond the potential issues of measurement errors and insufficient involvement in the process to be aware of those errors, misunderstanding the social processes linking multiple measures looms as an overwhelming threat to causal interpretation. Here introspection can become an enemy rather than an ally. Without benefit of a common language, the investigator may have no direct idea of how the people being studied think about, or even talk about, the subject of the investigation and no direct knowledge of the meanings attached to specific behaviors, interactions, or ideas. The social mechanisms that link cause and consequence must be derived from somewhere else. Previous studies and descriptive accounts of the people and place(s) under study offer some assistance; however, ultimately, social scientists in this situation must resort to their own experience – to some form of introspection – to fill in the gaps for a people with whom they cannot speak. The resulting hypotheses will not emanate from context-specific mechanisms grounded in the day-to-day meanings ascribed by respondents to the dimensions of their lives. Instead, it will arise from the context, language, and meanings attached to the investigator and applied to the people being studied. The simultaneous or sequential integration of less structured data collection methods into the research process that we advocate in this book is designed to help overcome this threat to causal interpretation, but the approach we suggest cannot be implemented successfully without a common language.

Consider an example from social demography to illustrate this point. When the descriptive task of social demographers was simply to count numbers of people in other countries, lack of a common language seemed merely an inconvenience. Even when this task was expanded to include counting the events that influence numbers of people, such as births, deaths, and migrations, lack of a common language was not considered an overwhelming obstacle. But as this field has progressed toward causal analysis of *why* people give birth, migrate, or engage in behaviors that increase their risk of death, the terms of investigation have changed. These causal questions demand direct, detailed knowledge of the meanings associated with behaviors and the measurements we use to learn about those behaviors. Common language is no longer a convenience; it is a necessity for accurate insight into the context-specific causal processes shaping fertility, mortality, and migration in other countries. Common language is certainly necessary to use any of the semi- or unstructured methods described in this book. But even when using measures from highly structured data collections, attempts to draw inferences regarding causal connections will be undermined by lack of familiarity with respondents' language. As a result, the rules of evidence and associated terms of international demographic research are making a transition. It is no longer acceptable to engage in research on causal issues in other countries without speaking the language of the people being studied. This transition is nearly complete, and it is not likely to reverse.

The issue of common language is most obvious in international research, but it deserves equal attention in research within an investigator's own country. Important subgroup variations within a society are often associated with important language differences, without knowledge of which an investigator is likely to make errors in causal inference. For example, in the United States a well-paid white researcher attempting to investigate causal processes among a group of poor African Americans may encounter subtle yet important language differences that, unrecognized, result in misleading conclusions regarding the causal connections among various dimensions of the social life of those being studied. The same problem may disadvantage a middle-aged investigator studying the behavior of teenagers or a native studying the behavior of recent immigrants.

Investigators using mixed method approaches must learn the language of those they intend to study, whether it's a completely new language spoken by people from another country or a variation on their own language spoken by a group within their society. Grounding in the language is necessary to establish a common framework of meaning that allows investigators to use introspection in beneficial ways and make causal inferences that reflect reality.

Redundancy

As discussed often in this book, an important aim of mixed method approaches is redundant measurement, varying the method of the measurement. This form of redundancy has advantages for both reducing measurement errors and strengthening our confidence that observed associations reflect causal processes rather than method-specific biases. However, redundancy of measurement can create conflicting empirical results.

In fact, one advantage of the simultaneous use of multiple methods is that use of different methods heightens the opportunity to create conflicting results. Although the discovery of congruent results using different data collection methods can strengthen conviction in those results, often different methods will produce different results. We argue that this conflict among empirical results, and therefore conflict with the theoretical framework guiding the data collection, is the essence of the scientific process these methods are designed to achieve. When multiple methods each produce results consistent with a theoretical framework or hypothesis, it may increase confidence in that element of theory, but it certainly does not produce new theoretical insights. By contrast, when we arrive at conflicting empirical results we are forced to carefully re-examine either our methods, our theory, or both. Conflicting results that stimulate reconsideration of each of the methods used, the specific theory or hypothesis being investigated, and the operationalization of theory in each specific method are the results most likely to stimulate new theoretical reasoning. In this sense, the redundancy embedded in mixed method approaches is designed in anticipation of conflicting empirical results. This design encourages discovery and innovation and makes the documentation of consistent results all the more remarkable.

Scale

The scale of new data collection methods should always be designed to match the substantive aims of the research. In the latter half of the 20th century, many social scientific resources were invested in the creation of data designed to represent countries. Such national studies are the raw materials used to create facts about national populations, and many serve important administrative functions for national governments. However, there is little connection between the social scientific study of cause and consequence and national administrative boundaries. Meaningful social boundaries and social scientific categories rarely correspond to national or international borders. This issue is increasingly important given the immense costs of creating data to represent national populations. Such representation requires a tremendous investment of scientific resources – investments that could be made in more effective means of advancing our understanding of cause and consequence.

As mixed method approaches for advancing the study of cause and consequence become a common part of social science data collection, the strain on investments in the creation of new data will increase. This is because mixed method approaches require a level of effort and funding that usually exceeds that of implementing a single method of data collection. Increased competition for investments in social science data collection will force greater optimization of scale.

As discussed in Chapter 7, studies that use mixed method data collection embedded within longitudinal designs hold a great deal of promise for the advancement of social science research on cause and consequence. But the investment required to conduct such intensive studies must be balanced against the scale of the research design. Intensive longitudinal studies need not be designed to represent national populations. The aim of advancing our understanding of cause and consequence is not the same as the aim of creating facts that represent national populations. Sometimes, these two aims overlap, but when they do not it is unnecessarily resource intensive to attempt to accomplish both aims through a single study. Instead, regional, local, or other subpopulation longitudinal designs may be sufficient for the study of cause and consequence.

Reduced geographic scope not only decreases the resources needed to implement a study, it may also facilitate the integration of multiple methods into a single design. This is true when geographic overlap is used as one of the ways to create integration across multiple methods – for example, conducting observations, unstructured interviewing, and survey interviewing in the same neighborhood. Because spatial integration is likely to be a desirable element of mixed method approaches and because smaller geographic scale can help control the effort needed to complete data collection, smaller-scale intensive studies will be an important complement to large-scale national studies.

Although small scale has many advantages for the implementation of mixed method data collection, many studies have successfully expanded the scale of their multimethod investigations. In this book, we contrast the simultaneous implementation of multiple methods in a pair of communities (Chapter 3) with the sequential implementation of multiple methods in 171 communities (Chapter 4). An increase in scale involves trade-offs: greater variance and external validity at the expense of reduced overlap in multimethod data collection and increased effort. But such trade-offs characterize every decision in research design, with investigators choosing the design characteristics that maximize their research aims and topics.

The study of 171 neighborhoods in Nepal described throughout this book is one example of a recent large-scale mixed method study. The project "Welfare, Children, and Families: A Three-City Study" is another (Burton, Hurt, and Avenilla 2002). In this study, an ethnographic research team of 210 scientists conducted both structured survey data collection in 2,400 households and less structured ethnographic data collection in 215 households in Boston, Chicago, and San Antonio. The National Study of Youth and Religion (NSYR) is another example. Again, this study is an explicitly mixed method, beginning with a national survey of 3,290 American youth and parents, followed by semi-structured, in-person interviews of 267 of the young people nationwide (Denton 2003; Smith 2003). A second wave of the phone survey and semi-structured interviews is being fielded as we write this book.

As mixed method approaches are applied to more and more topics, we will continue to see more experimentation with expanding the scale of mixed method data collection. This, as mentioned above, will produce trade-offs. The creation of unstructured data on large numbers of individuals or communities will provide information about greater variance among those being studied and make inference to larger populations more robust. On the other hand, when a principal investigator must train a dozen or a hundred assistants to collect unstructured measurement, the process itself limits the investigator's involvement in the data collection. This, in turn, limits the investigator's ability to use insights gained from such involvement to harness introspection constructively.

Also important, as we scale up unstructured data collection methods, such as unstructured interviewing, they are beginning to look remarkably like structured methods, such as survey interviewing. As researchers train a large number of interviewers or observers, they almost always resort to some form of standardization to ensure comparability across measurements. Often this standardization involves a prespecified series of questions that, although not in the form of a questionnaire, begin to resemble survey interview questions. When a dozen or a hundred assistants are trained to collect "unstructured" interviews following a common set of practices, these interviews will become either less comparable or more structured. To the extent that such large-scale "unstructured" data collection begins to resemble highly structured survey data collection, many of the benefits of mixing extremely different methods of data collection will be lost. As the quantity of data increases, the methods to analyze them also become increasingly standardized. Standard codes are developed, multiple coders employed, and themes quantified.

Ironically, these consequences of scaling up unstructured methods are taking place at the same time that computer-assisted personal interviewing (CAPI) is adding more flexibility to survey interviewing. The use of CAPI technology to tailor specific questions to specific respondents dramatically reduces the standardization characterizing survey interviewing. As a result, many of the large-scale surveys conducted at the turn of the century feature much less standardization than those conducted two decades earlier.

This blurring of the lines between large-scale unstructured interviewing and large-scale structured interviewing is neither good nor bad. It simply imposes certain characteristics on the data generated from these methods. But these characteristics do deserve careful attention. In this book, we have focused on the benefits of simultaneously or sequentially applying multiple methods that vary greatly in the level of structure. A single large-scale study featuring semi-structured interviewing by either a large group of trained ethnographers or a sophisticated computer-assisted protocol does not provide variation in the method of data collection. As a single source of data, it may have useful characteristics, but it does not provide multiple points of insight, the counterbalancing of methodological strengths and weaknesses, or the high levels of investigator involvement that applications of multiple *different* methods can provide. In this sense, such studies have the characteristics of a single hybrid method, not the characteristics of multiple methods applied simultaneously or sequentially.

Of course, such hybrid methods may offer an extremely constructive element to a multimethod mix. Medium-scale, unstructured interviewing with some level of standardization may be a useful complement to small-scale, unstructured interviewing with no standardization and large-scale structured interviewing with high levels of standardization. There is no single correct scale or level of structure. Decisions about the scale and standardization of specific designs must be matched to the specific aims of each study. The variance in scale of mixed method approaches, however, is likely to fuel continued innovation in the specific nature of multimethod integrated designs.

New Frontiers in Mixed Method Approaches

As we discussed in detail in Chapter 7, mixed method longitudinal research designs hold tremendous promise for the future of social research on cause and consequence. Longitudinal designs, which follow the same study participants over time, provide opportunities for both simultaneous and sequential integration of multiple methods. Periodic contact with study participants can be supplemented with calendar methods, as described in Chapter 6, to provide a continuous record of changes between interviews. When integrated with dynamic contextual measurement, as described in Chapter 5, such data collection can yield a multilevel continuous record of change over time in both individuals' lives and the social contexts within which they live their day-to-day lives. The combination of this dynamic measurement and a mixture of structured measurement for hypothesis testing and unstructured measurement for hypothesis discovery yields a set of tools for the study of cause and consequence that social scientists will likely exploit for decades to come.

But other combinations of methods will also be used to advance the study of cause and consequence. One combination with tremendous potential involves mixing experimental designs with observational designs. Structured survey interviewing, unstructured interviewing, and observation can be combined with many different designs. Experimental designs in which some of the study participants are randomly assigned to a key condition and other participants are not will always be one of our most powerful tools for the study of cause and consequence. Randomization helps to eliminate the possibility that unobserved factors produce the empirical relationships we observe (Campbell and Stanley

1963; Cook and Campbell 1979). Social scientists rarely have the opportunity to randomly assign key conditions; but when we do, we must exploit such opportunities to their fullest potential.

Although experimental designs are rare in the social sciences, they do exist. As discussed in Chapter 1, the most common circumstance is the implementation of a new government program or service that is sufficiently costly that it is difficult to provide to everyone eligible at the same time. Sometimes, these circumstances lead officials to distribute the new program or service randomly in the interest of fairness. In other cases, new government programs or services are distributed randomly, with the specific aim of evaluating the causal impact of that program or service. Under other circumstances, it may be possible to randomly assign some portion of a key condition, like new information. Social scientists must be vigilant for such opportunities and build random sources of variation into their study designs whenever possible. Such random sources of variation give us an uncommonly powerful set of tools for identifying causal elements of the associations we observe.

Even small random elements may become particularly powerful when combined with a longitudinal, mixed method research design. The possibility of embedding a randomized element within an ongoing longitudinal study affords a unique opportunity to evaluate change in ideas or behavior before and after that element. Mixed method approaches provide both the unstandardized measurement to learn about study participants' awareness of and reactions to the randomized element and the standardized measurements to enhance comparability of observations before and after randomized elements. The opportunities to introduce randomized elements into longitudinal mixed method studies may be beyond our imagination at this moment, but such multimethod designs are likely to offer unparalleled new insights into cause and consequence in the social world.

Another mixed method approach likely to hold great potential is the combination of existing data, often in archival sources, with new data collection. In many settings around the world, researchers, governments, local communities, and nongovernment organizations have already accumulated a great deal of information. As the technology for preserving, cataloging, and linking such existing information continues to improve, new opportunities to study important social issues with existing data resources are quite likely to arise. In some cases, existing measures may be sufficient to answer important research questions, but in many cases new data collection that can be directly linked to existing data resources will be needed to realize the full potential of such research opportunities. The rising costs of new data collection provide motivation to use existing measures to their fullest potential. Those same costs motivate careful consideration of investment in only those new data collection efforts that yield the maximum possible additional value to existing data resources. The creation of new mixed method approaches that link existing archival measures with new data collection will be essential to maximize the scientific value of such work.

As emphasized in Chapter 5, recent revolutions in geographic data collection and geographic information systems (GIS) have produced many new opportunities to link multiple sources of measurement. These tools are likely to foster mixed method integration of multiple data sources with explicit geographic connection. Once again, the opportunities to link existing data resources in mixed method studies may be beyond our imagination at this moment, but multimethod designs utilizing existing measures are likely to offer efficient opportunities to gain new insights into cause and consequence in the social world.

In fact, we hope very much that the full array of mixed methods approaches to social scientific studies of cause and consequence is beyond our imagination at this moment, that the years to come will see social scientists devising creative new approaches. In fact, our greatest ambition for this book is that a technique, an idea, or even an error you find in the book will inspire you to invent a new approach to collecting data that will improve our ability to investigate and understand the social world around us.

Notes

ACKNOWLEDGMENTS

1. Axinn, William G., Tom Fricke, and Arland Thornton. 1991. "The Microdemographic Community-Study Approach: Improving Survey Data by Integrating the Ethnographic Method." *Sociological Methods and Research* 20(2): 187–217.
2. Axinn, William G., Jennifer S. Barber, and Dirgha J. Ghimire. 1997. "The Neighborhood History Calendar: A Data Collection Method Designed for Dynamic Multilevel Modeling." *Sociological Methodology* 27: 355–92.
3. Axinn, William G., Lisa D. Pearce, and D. Ghimire. 1999. "Innovations in Life History Calendar Applications." *Social Science Research* 28: 243–64.
4. Pearce, Lisa D. 2002. "Integrating Survey and Ethnographic Methods for Systematic Anomalous Case Analysis." *Sociological Methodology* 32(1): 103–132.

CHAPTER 1

1. A large literature exists debating definitions of qualitative and quantitative research (e.g., Abbott 1998; Guba and Lincoln 1994; Richardt and Rallis 1994). Given our focus on data collection methods, we believe that other method-specific distinctions are more useful and so focus on those in this chapter.
2. The number of demographers who believe that Caldwell is correct may exceed the number of demographers who know exactly what he means.
3. Numerous books on anthropological methods do this. In fact, one text, called *Research Methods in Cultural Anthropology*, by H. Russell Bernard (1988), lists all the same research methods one might expect to see in virtually any other social science data collection text, including surveys, unstructured or semi-structured interviewing, and observational techniques.

CHAPTER 2

1. Using this approach, investigators who fail to find the relationship they expect often have the opportunity to argue that they did not have enough cases to detect the relationship in question.

CHAPTER 3

1. Earlier research had been conducted in 1981–2 by one of the study's principal investigators in the more remote of our two settings (Fricke 1986).

2. By village context, we mean the overall environment – economic, educational, social, and ecological – in which individual and family processes are carried out.
3. Raniban Village. See Kathmandu Valley map (Figure 3.3).
4. These visits were begun earlier, even before the interviewer training. The impending data collection was explained throughout the study area, and permission to conduct research, once government clearance was given, had been obtained from community leaders, older clan members, and representatives of each household. The total period of presurvey rapport building in the first community was approximately 3 weeks. The presurvey rapport building in the second community was shorter, but one of the investigators had previously spent 8 months in that village, which contributed significantly to the project's rapport.
5. Of course, the issue of sampling error is relevant at a higher level of aggregation, that is, when one is concerned with the choice of communities. This study chose two Tamang communities representing opposite ends of a Tamang spectrum: access to wage labor and schooling opportunities. Although the choice was not arrived at systematically, it would certainly be possible to employ systematic sampling procedures to choose the communities to be studied (See Chapter 3).
6. The analysis is presented in multiple classification format. See Andrews et al. (1973) for details. Eta-squared is comparable to R-squared in standard regression models.

CHAPTER 4

1. All personal names have been changed to protect the identity of the informants.
2. Measures of mothers' religiosity and the religiosity of the oldest female in the household were also created. The measures of average household religiosity had stronger effects, so those were used in the analyses. In addition, this allowed for respondents who had no elder female relatives living in the household to remain in the analyses.
3. One informant could not be located, and one repeatedly refused to give answers to the Coombs Scale questions.
4. Four informants were uncomfortable answering the Coombs Scale questions; their interviews provided insight on the cognitive challenges these questions can pose.
5. When using the statistical package SAS for data analysis, the DFBETA test statistics will identify cases that are having undue influence on the model due to a particular independent variable value.

CHAPTER 5

1. As discussed in Chapter 1, social scientists sometimes argue that a third factor (Z), which is the anticipation of X, actually causes Y when X follows Y in time. If this is the case, we argue measurement strategies for testing such hypotheses should focus on direct measurement of Z. We discuss such strategies in Chapter 6.
2. These groups typically mark time in terms of personal events, such as marriage, childbirth, or direct experience with disasters (e.g., floods) or rare events (e.g., animal attacks).
3. Examples of these discrepancies are provided in the section titled "Other Contextual History Calendars."
4. These clusters are called "*tols*" or "*chowks*" in Nepalese, and each of the clusters in our sample has a unique name, used by the residents to identify their place of residence.

5. Although not a problem in this part of Nepal, neighborhoods in other settings that are characterized by extremely high levels of migration among residents may prove to be extremely difficult for this type of data collection.

6. The diversity of informants was designed to produce disagreements as interviewers worked toward a consensus report from residents. We recorded the consensus value; and when there were substantial discrepancies, we recorded the discrepancies as well.

7. This is similar to the argument many ethnographers might make about the quality of individual-level data (Caldwell 1985; Hammel 1990; Stone and Campbell 1984; Weiss 1994).

8. Because respondents' knowledge of these events is probably higher for nearby schools or health services, these comparisons are limited to schools and health services within a 15-minute walk of the neighborhood.

9. Note that for each domain on the calendar, interviewers were required to check off the response to an opening question in order to indicate that questions about each domain had been asked and answered.

10. GPS handheld roving units use satellite readings to provide location measures.

CHAPTER 6

1. For examples of different designs of life history calendars, refer to Freedman et al. 1988, Belli 1998, and Figure 6.1.

2. Another possible solution is to use a different LHC instrument for each age group (e.g., one for ages 15–24, another for ages 25–34, etc.). Note, however, that even the variance within these ages will force some respondents to begin the calendar in different positions than other respondents.

3. Note, again, that this LHC is designed to collect data on an annual basis rather than a monthly basis as in some previous calendars (Freedman et al. 1988). Although gathering annual data sacrifices some precision on event timing, we supplemented the LHC matrix by asking for the month in which each first event occurred (among events most central to the study's aims). This month data provides more-precise information on the timing and sequencing of first events. Because first events were the main focus of this study, the month timing of these events was an important addition to the data.

4. A substantial body of research demonstrates that changes in question order can produce significant variations in responses (Schuman and Presser 1996). However, there is also reason to expect that these ordering effects will be much smaller when respondents are reporting on their previous behavior and experience than when they are reporting their attitudes and beliefs.

CHAPTER 7

1. Of course, all retrospective designs are vulnerable to this same threat. Lack of random assignment of initial conditions is a central weakness of all non-experimental research designs (Campbell and Stanley 1963).

2. In general, though, it is desirable to maintain some consistency over time in the method of measurement. We discuss this issue in greater detail in the subsection titled "Measurement."

3. For example, respondents were asked whether they strongly agree, agree, disagree, or strongly disagree that "It's perfectly all right for women to be very active in clubs, politics, and other outside activities before the children are grown up."

4. For more details regarding the original sample selection process, see Barber et al. 1997.

5. In fact, it is difficult for all involved, including the migrant, to know whether a move will actually be temporary or permanent at the time of the move itself.

6. Axinn et al. 2002 and Thornton, Axinn, and Xie 2002 describe data created from such splicing of multiple sequential calendars in the Intergenerational Panel Study.

Bibliography

Abbott, Andrew. 1998. "The Causal Devolution." *Sociological Methods and Research* 27: 148–181.

Abbott, Andrew, and Alexandra Hrycak. 1990. "Measuring Resemblance in Sequence Data: An Optimal Matching Analysis of Musicians' Careers." *American Journal of Sociology* 96(1): 144–185.

Agar, Michael H. 1996. *The Professional Stranger.* San Diego, CA: Academic Press.

Agar, Michael H., and James MacDonald. 1995. "Focus Groups and Ethnography." *Human Organization* 54: 78–86.

Alexander, Jeffrey C. 1988. *Action and Its Environments: Toward a New Synthesis.* New York: Columbia University Press.

Allison, Paul D. 1984. *Event History Analysis.* Newbury Park, CA: Sage Publications.

Anderson, R., J. Kasper, and M. R. Frankel. 1979. *Total Survey Error.* San Francisco: Jossey-Bass.

Andrews, Frank, James N. Morgan, John A. Sonquist, and Laura Klem. 1973. *Multiple Classification Analysis.* Ann Arbor, MI: Institute for Social Research.

Anspach, Renee. 1997. *Deciding Who Lives: Fateful Choices in the Intensive Care Nursery.* Berkeley: University of California Press.

Aquilino, William S., and Leonard A. Lo Sciuto. 1990. "Effects of Interview Mode on Self Reported Drug Use." *Public Opinion Quarterly* 54: 362–395.

Atkinson, Paul, and Martyn Hammersley. 2003. "Ethnography and Participant Observation." In Norman K. Denzin and Yvonna S. Lincoln (eds.), *Strategies of Qualitative Inquiry*, 2nd ed., pp. 110–136. Thousand Oaks, CA: Sage Publications.

Axinn, William G. 1989. "Interviewers and Data Quality in a Less Developed Setting." *Journal of Official Statistics* 5(3): 265–280.

Axinn, William G. 1991. "The Influence of Interviewer Sex on Responses to Sensitive Questions In Nepal." *Social Science Research* 20: 303–318.

Axinn, William G. 1992. "Rural Income-Generating Programs and Fertility Limitation: Evidence from a Microdemographic Study in Nepal." *Rural Sociology* 57(3): 396–413.

Axinn, William G., and Jennifer S. Barber. 2001. "Mass Education and Fertility Transition." *American Sociological Review* 66(4): 481–505.

Axinn, William G., and Scott T. Yabiku. 2001. "Social Change, the Social Organization of Families, and Fertility Limitation." *American Journal of Sociology* 106(5): 1219–1261.

Axinn, William G., Arland Thornton, Lishou Yang, Linda Young-DeMarco, and Yu Xie. 2002. "A Mother's Reports of Children's Family Formation Behavior." *Social Science Research* 31(2): 257–283.

Axinn, William G., Jennifer S. Barber, and Dirgha J. Ghimire. 1997. "The Neighborhood History Calendar: A Data Collection Method Designed for Dynamic Multilevel Modeling." *Sociological Methodology* 27: 355–392.

Axinn, William G., Linda Young-DeMarco, and Mee-So Caponi. 2003. "The Gender Double Standard and Parents' Attitudes Toward Family Formation." Paper presented at the annual meetings of the National Council on Family Relations, November, Vancouver, BC.

Axinn, William G., Lisa D. Pearce, and Dirgha J. Ghimire. 1999. "Innovations in Life History Calendar Applications." *Social Science Research* 28: 243–264.

Axinn, William G., Thomas E. Fricke, and Arland Thornton. 1991. "The Microdemographic Community-Study Approach: Improving Survey Data by Integrating the Ethnographic Method." *Sociological Methods and Research* 20(2): 187–217.

Babbie, Earl. 2004. *The Practice of Social Research*, 10th ed. Belmont, CA: Wadsworth.

Bachrach, Christine, and Geoffrey McNicoll. 2003. "Causal Analysis in the Population Sciences: A Symposium." *Population and Development Review* 29(3): 443–447.

Back, Kurt W., and J. Mayone Stycos. 1967. *The Survey Under Unusual Conditions: Methodological Facets of the Jamaica Human Fertility Investigation*, 2nd ed. Ithaca, NY: Cornell University Press.

Baker, R. P., N. M. Bradburn, and R. A. Johnson. 1994. "Computer-Assisted Interviewing: An Experimental Evaluation of Data Quality Costs." Chicago: NORC (unpublished paper).

Barber, Jennifer S., Ganesh Shivakoti, William G. Axinn, and Kishore Gajurel. 1997. "Sampling Strategies for Rural Settings: A Detailed Example from the Chitwan Valley Family Study, Nepal." *Population Journal of Nepal* 6(5): 193–203.

Barber, Jennifer S., Lisa D. Pearce, Indra Chaudhury, and Susan Gurung. 2002. "Voluntary Associations and Fertility Limitation." *Social Forces* 80(4): 1269–1301.

Barber, Jennifer S., Susan A. Murphy, and Natalya Verbitsky. 2004. "Adjusting for Time-Varying Confounding in Survival Analysis." *Sociological Methodology* 34(1): 163–192.

Barber, Jennifer S., Susan A. Murphy, William G. Axinn, and Jerry Maples. 2000. "Discrete-Time Multilevel Hazard Analysis." *Sociological Methodology* 30(1): 201–235.

Barsalou, Lawrence W. 1995. "The Content and Organization of Autobiographical Memories." In Ulric Neisser and Eugene Winograd (eds.), *Remembering Reconsidered: Ecological and Traditional Approaches to the Study of Memory*, pp. 193–243. New York: Cambridge University Press.

Bates, John E., Viken, Richard J., and Douglas B. Alexander. 2002. "Sleep and Adjustment in Preschool Children: Sleep Diary Reports by Mothers Relate to Behavior Reports by Teachers." *Child Development* 73(1): 62–74.

Bazeley, Pat. 2003. "Computerized Data Analysis for Mixed Methods Research." In Abbas Tashakkori and Charles Teddie (eds.), *Handbook of Mixed Methods in Social and Behavioral Research*, pp. 385–422. Thousand Oaks, CA: Sage Publications.

Beath, Kenneth J., and Annette J. Dobson. 1991. "Regression to the Mean for Nonnormal Populations." *Biometrika* 78(2): 431–435.

Becker, Howard S. 1996. "The Epistemology of Qualitative Research." In Richard Jessor, Anne Colby, and Richard A. Shweder (eds.), *Ethnography and Human Development: Context and Meaning in Social Inquiry*, pp. 53–72. Chicago: University of Chicago Press.

Becker, Howard S., B. Geer, E. C. Hughes, and A. L. Strauss. 1961. *Boys in White: Student Culture in Medical School*. Chicago: University of Chicago Press.

Belli, Robert F. 1998. "The Structure of Autobiographical Memory and the Event History Calendar: Potential Improvements in the Quality of Retrospective Reports in Surveys." *Memory* 6: 383–406.

Belli, Robert F., Michael W. Traugott, Margaret Young, and Katherine A. McGonagle. 1999. "Reducing Vote Overreporting in Surveys: Social Desirability, Memory Failure, and Source Monitoring." *Public Opinion Quarterly* 63: 90–108.

Belli, Robert F., William L. Shay, and Frank P. Stafford. 2001. "Event History Calendars and Question List Surveys: A Direct Comparison of Interviewing Methods." *Public Opinion Quarterly* 65(1): 45–74.

Benedict, Ruth. 1989 (1934). *Patterns of Culture*. Boston: Houghton Mifflin.

Bernard, H. Russell. 1988. *Research Methods in Cultural Anthropology*. Newbury Park, CA: Sage Publications.

Beutel, Ann M., and William G. Axinn. 2002. "Social Change, Gender, and Educational Attainment." *Economic Development and Cultural Change* 51(1): 109–134.

Biemer, Paul P., Robert M. Groves, Lars E. Lyberg, Nancy A. Mathiowetz, and Seymour Sudman (eds.). 1991. *Measurement Errors in Surveys*. New York: Wiley-Interscience.

Binka, Fred K., Pierre Ngom, James F. Phillips, Kubaje Adazu, and Bruce B. MacLeod. 1999. "Assessing Population Dynamics in a Rural African Society: The Navrongo Demographic Surveillance System." *Journal of Biosocial Science* 31(3): 375–391.

Bishop, George S., Alfred J. Tuchfarber, and Robert W. Oldendick. 1986. "Opinions on Fictitious Issues: The Pressure to Answer Survey Questions." *Public Opinion Quarterly* 50(2): 240–250.

Bista, Dor B. 1994. *Fatalism and Development*. Calcutta, India: Orient Longman.

Blalock, Hubert M. 1985. "Cross-Level Analysis." In John B. Casterline, (ed.), *The Collection and Analysis of Community Data,* pp. 187–206. Voorburg, Netherlands: International Statistical Institute.

Blumberg, Stephen J., Julian V. Luke, and Marcie L. Cynamon. 2004. "Has Cord-Cutting Cut into Random-Digit-Dialed Health Surveys? The Prevalence and Impact of Mobile Phone Substitution." In C. B. Cohen and J. M. Lepkowski (eds.), *Eighth Conference on Health Survey Research Methods*, pp. 137–142. Hyattsville, MD: National Center for Health Statistics.

Blumer, Herbert. 1969. *Symbolic Interactionism*. Englewood Cliffs, NJ: Prentice-Hall.

Bolger, Niall, Angelina Davis, and Eshkol Rafaeli. 2003. "Diary Methods: Capturing Life as It Is Lived." *Annual Review of Psychology* 54: 579–616.

Bonnell, V. 1980. "The Uses of Theory, Concepts and Comparison in Historical Sociology." *Comparative Studies in Society and History* 22(2): 156–173.

Bound, J., and G. Solon. 1999. "Double Trouble: On the Value of Twins-Based Estimation of the Return to Schooling." *Economics of Education Review* 8(2): 169–182.

Bracher, Michael, Gigi Santow, and Susan Cotts Watkins. 2004. "Assessing the Potential for Condoms to Prevent the Spread of HIV: A Case Study from Rural Malawi." *Studies in Family Planning* 35(1): 48–64.

Bradburn, Norman M. 1983. "Response Effects." In Peter H. Rossi, James D. Wright, and Andy B. Anderson (eds.), *Handbook of Survey Research*, pp. 289–328. New York: Academic Press.

Brannen, Julia, (ed.). 1992. *Mixing Methods: Qualitative and Quantitative Research.* Aldershot, England: Avebury.

Brewster, Karin. 1994. "Race Differences in Sexual Activity Among Adolescent Women: The Role of Neighborhood Characteristics." *American Sociological Review* 59: 408–424.

Briggs, Charles L. 1986. *Learning How to Ask: A Sociolinguistic Appraisal of the Role of the Interview in Social Science Research.* New York: Cambridge University Press.

Brockerhoff, Martin. 2000. "An Urbanizing World." *Population Bulletin* 55(3): 3–18.

Brooks-Gunn, Jeanne, Greg J. Duncan, Pamela Kato Klebanov, and Naomi Sealand. 1993. "Do Neighborhoods Influence Child and Adolescent Development?" *American Journal of Sociology* 99(2): 353–395.

Brooks-Gunn, Jeanne, Greg J. Duncan, and J. Lawrence Aber. 1997a. *Neighborhood Poverty: Vol. I: Context and Consequences for Children.* New York: Russell Sage Foundation.

Brooks-Gunn, Jeanne, Greg J. Duncan, and J. Lawrence Aber. 1997b. *Neighborhood Poverty: Vol. II: Policy Implications in Studying Neighborhoods.* New York: Russell Sage Foundation.

Bryk, Anthony S., and Stephen W. Raudenbush. 1992. *Hierarchical Linear Models: Applications and Data Analysis Methods.* Newbury Park, CA: Sage Publications.

Burawoy, Michael, (ed.). 1991. *Ethnography Unbound: Power and Resistance in the Modern Metropolis.* Berkeley: University of California Press.

Burgess, R. G., (ed.). 1982. *Field Research: A Sourcebook and Field Manual.* London: Allen & Unwin.

Burkam, David T., and Valerie Lee. 1998. "Effects of Monotone and Nonmonotone Attrition on Parameter Estimates in Regression Models with Educational Data." *Journal of Human Resources* 33(2): 555–574.

Burrough, P. 1986. *Principles of Geographical Information Systems for Land Resource Assessment.* Oxford: Clarendon Press.

Burton, Linda M., Tera R. Hurt, and Frank R. Avenilla. 2002. "The Three-City Ethnography: An Overview." Paper presented at the annual meetings of the American Sociological Association of America, August 16–19, Chicago.

Burton, Linda M., R. Jarrett, L. Lein, S. Matthews, J. Quane, D. Skinner, C. Williams, W. J. Wilson, and T. Hurt. 2001. "Structured Discovery: Ethnography, Welfare Reform, and the Assessment of Neighborhoods, Families, and Children." Paper presented at the biennial meeting of the Society for Research in Child Development, Minneapolis.

Caldwell, John C. 1982. *Theory of Fertility Decline.* London: Academic Press.

Caldwell, John C. 1985. "Strengths and Limitations of the Survey Approach for Measuring and Understanding Fertility Change." In J. Cleland and J. Hobcraft (eds.), *Reproductive Change in Developing Countries, Insights from the World Fertility Survey*, pp. 45–63. London: Oxford University Press.

Caldwell, John C. 1986. "Routes to Low Mortality in Poor Countries." *Population and Development Review* 12(2): 171–220.

Caldwell, John C., Allan G. Hill, and Valerie J. Hull (eds.). 1988. *Micro-approaches to Demographic Research*. London: Kegan Paul International.

Caldwell, John C., P. H. Reddy, and Pat Caldwell. 1983. "The Social Component of Mortality Decline: An Investigation in South India Employing Alternative Methodologies." *Population Studies* 37(2): 185–205.

Caldwell, John C., P. H. Reddy, and Pat Caldwell. 1988a. "Investigating the Nature of Population Change in South India: Experimenting with a Micro-approach." In J. C. Caldwell, A. G. Hill, and V. J. Hull (eds.), *Micro-approaches to Demographic Research*, pp. 25–38. London: Kegan Paul International.

Caldwell, John C., P. H. Reddy, and Pat Caldwell. 1988b. *The Causes of Demographic Change: Experimental Research in South India*. Madison: University of Wisconsin Press.

Caldwell, John C., Pat Caldwell, and Bruce Caldwell. 1987. "Anthropology and Demography: The Mutual Reinforcement of Speculation and Research." *Current Anthropology* 28(1): 25–43.

Campbell, Donald T., and Julian C. Stanley. 1963. *Experimental and Quasi-experimental Designs for Research*. Boston: Houghton Mifflin.

Cantril, H. 1967. *The Human Dimension: Experiences in Policy Research*. New Brunswick, NJ: Rutgers University Press.

Card, D. E., and A. B. Krueger. 1995. *Myth and Measurement: The New Economics of the Minimum Wage*. Princeton: Princeton University Press.

Carlson, Marcia, Sara McLanahan, and Paula England. 2004. "Union Formation in Fragile Families." *Demography* 41(2): 237–262.

Carmines, Edward G., and Richard A. Zeller. 1979. *Reliability and Validity Assessment*. Newbury Park, CA: Sage Publications.

Caspi, Avshalom, Terrie E. Moffitt, Arland Thornton, Deborah Freedman, James W. Ameli, Honalee Harrington, Judith Smeijers, and Phil A. Silva. 1995. "The Life History Calendar: A Research and Clinical Assessment Method for Collecting Retrospective Event-History Data." *International Journal of Methods in Psychiatric Research* 6: 101–114.

Casterline, John B. (ed.). 1985. *The Collection and Analysis of Community Data*. Voorburg, Netherlands: International Statistical Institute.

Chambers, Robert. 1983. *Rural Development: Putting the Last First*. Harlow, England: Longmans.

Chambers, Robert. 1985. "Rapid Rural Appraisal: Rationale and Repertoire." In M. M. Cernea (ed.), *Putting People First: Sociological Variables in Rural Development*, pp. 399–415. London: Oxford University Press.

Chambers, Robert. 1997. *Whose Reality Counts? Putting the First Last*. London: Intermediate Technology Publications.

Chambers, Robert. 2002. *Participatory Workshops: A Sourcebook of 21 Sets of Ideas and Actions*. London: Earthscan.

Chambers, Robert, Arnold Pacey, and Lori Ann Thrupp. 1989. *Farmer First: Farmer Innovation and Agricultural Research*. London: Intermediate Technology Publications.

Cherlin, A. J., L. M. Burton, T. Hurt, and D. Purvin. 2004. "The Influence of Physical and Sexual Abuse on Marriage and Cohabitation." *American Sociological Review* 69(6): 768–789.

Cherlin, A. J., P. Fomby, and R. Moffitt. 2002. *Weight Construction and Usage in the Three-City Study*. Available at www.jhu.edu/~welfare/release.html.

Coleman, James S. 1990. *Foundations of Social Theory.* Cambridge, MA: Harvard University Press.

Converse, J. M., and S. Presser. 1986. *Survey Questions.* Beverly Hills, CA: Sage Publications.

Cook, T., and D. Campbell. 1979. *Quasi-experimentation: Design and Analysis Issues for Field Settings.* Boston: Houghton-Mifflin.

Coombs, Lolagene C. 1974. "The Measurement of Family Size Preferences and Subsequent Fertility." *Demography* 11(4): 587–611.

Couper, Mick P. 1996. "Changes in Interview Setting Under CAPI." *Journal of Official Statistics* 12(3): 301–316.

Couper, Mick P., (ed.). 1998. *Computer Assisted Survey Information Collection.* New York: Wiley.

Couper, Mick P. 2000. "Web Surveys: A Review of Issues and Approaches." *Public Opinion Quarterly* 64(4): 464–494.

Couper, Mick P. 2001. "The Promises and Perils of Web Surveys." In A. Westlake et al. (eds.), *The Challenge of the Internet,* pp. 35–56. London: Association for Survey Computing.

Couper, Mick P. 2002. "New Technologies and Survey Data Collection: Challenges and Opportunities." Invited plenary presentation at the International Conference on Improving Surveys, August, Copenhagen.

Couper, Mick P., and Robert M. Groves. 1992. "The Role of the Interviewer in Survey Participation." *Survey Methodology* 18(2): 263–271.

Couper, Mick P., and Benjamin Rowe. 1996. "Evaluation of a Computer-Assisted Self-Interview Component in a Computer-Assisted Personal Interview Survey." *Public Opinion Quarterly* 60(1): 89–105.

Couper, Mick P., Michael W. Traugott, and Mark J. Lamias. 2001. "Web Survey Design and Administration." *Public Opinion Quarterly* 65(2): 230–253.

Crowne, Douglas P., and David Marlowe. 1964. *The Approval Motive; Studies in Evaluative Dependence.* New York: Wiley.

DeMaio, T. J. 1984. "Social Desirability and Survey Measurement: A Review." In C. F. Turner and E. Martin (eds.), *Surveying Subjective Phenomena,* pp. 257–282. New York: Russell Sage Foundation.

Denton, Melinda Lundquist. 2003. "Survey and Interviews Research Methodology of the NSYR." Paper presented at the annual meeting of the Society for the Scientific Study of Religion, October 23–26, Norfolk, VA.

Denzin, Norman K. 1970. *The Research Act in Sociology.* London: Butterworth.

Denzin, Norman K. 1978. *The Research Act: A Theoretical Introduction to Sociological Methods,* 2nd ed. New York: McGraw-Hill.

DiPrete, Thomas A., and Jerry D. Forristal. 1994. "Multilevel Models: Methods and Substance." *Annual Review of Sociology* 20: 331–357.

Drake, St. Clair, and Horace R. Cayton. 1993. *Black Metropolis: A Study of Negro Life in a Northern City,* rev. ed. Chicago: University of Chicago Press.

Dressler, W. W. 1991. *Stress and Adaptation in the Context of Culture: Depression in a Southern Black Community.* Albany: State University of New York Press.

D'Souza, Stanislas. 1984. "Population Laboratories for Studying Disease Processes and Mortality: The Demographic Surveillance System, Matlab." In J. Vallin, J. H. Pollard, and L. Heligman (eds.), *Methodologies for the Collection and Analysis of Mortality Data,* pp. 65–88. Liege, Belgium: Ordina Editions.

Durkheim, Emile. 1984 (1933). *The Division of Labor in Society*. New York: Free Press.

Edin, Kathryn. 1998. "What Qualitative Research Can Do for Quantitative Researchers." Paper presented at the MacArthur Foundation Conference, Network on Family Economics, April, Chicago.

Edin, Kathryn. 1999. "The Qualitative/Quantitative Blend." Paper presented at the Conference on Blending Qualitative and Quantitative Approaches to Studying Welfare Reform, Chicago.

Edin, Kathryn, and Laura Lein. 1997. "Work, Welfare, and Single Mothers' Economic Survival Strategies." *American Sociological Review* 62: 253–266.

Eisenhower, Donna, Nancy A. Mathiowetz, and David Morganstein. 1991. "Recall Error: Sources and Bias Reduction Techniques." In Paul P. Biemer, Robert M. Groves, Lars E. Lyberg, Nancy A. Mathiowetz, and Seymour Sudman (eds.), *Measurement Errors in Surveys*, pp. 128–144. New York: Wiley.

Emerson, Robert M., Rachel I. Fretz, and Linda L. Shaw. 1995. *Writing Ethnographic Fieldnotes*. Chicago: University of Chicago Press.

Entwisle, Barbara, and William Mason. 1985. "The Multilevel Effects of Socioeconomic Development and Family Planning Programs on Children Ever Born." *American Journal of Sociology* 91(3): 616–649.

Entwisle, Barbara, Ronald R. Rindfuss, David K. Guilkey, Aphichat Chamratrithirong, Sara R. Curran, and Yothin Sawangdee. 1996. "Community and Contraceptive Choice in Rural Thailand: A Case Study of Nang Rong." *Demography* 33(1): 1–11.

Falaris, Evangelos M., and Elizabeth H. Peters. 1998. "Survey Attrition and Schooling Choices." *Journal of Human Resources* 33(2): 531–554.

Fals-Stewart, William. 2003. "The Occurence of Partner Physical Aggression on Days of Alcohol Consumption: A Longitudinal Diary Study." *Journal of Consulting and Clinical Psychology* 71(1): 41–52.

Fine, Michelle. 1992. "Passions, Politics, and Powers: Feminist Research Possibilities." In Michelle Fine (ed.), *Disruptive Voices: The Possibilities of Feminist Research*. Ann Arbor: University of Michigan Press.

Finkel, Steven E., Thomas M. Guterbock, and Marian J. Borg. 1991. "Race-of-Interviewer Effects in a Pre-election Poll: Virginia 1989." *Public Opinion Quarterly* 55: 313–330.

Firebaugh, Glenn. 2001. "Ecological Fallacy – Statistics of." In Neil J. Smelser and Paul B. Baltes (eds.), *International Encyclopedia of the Social and Behavioral Sciences*, pp. 4023–4026. Oxford: Elsevier.

Fitzgerald, John, Peter Gottschalk, and Robert Moffitt. 1998. "An Analysis of Sample Attrition in Panel Data: The Michigan Panel Study of Income Dynamics." *Journal of Human Resources* 33(2): 251–299.

Fowler, Floyd J., Jr. 1991. "Reducing Interviewer-Related Error Through Interviewer Training, Supervision, and Other Means." In Paul P. Biemer, Robert M. Groves, Lars E. Lyberg, Nancy A Mathiowetz, and Seymour Sudman (eds.), *Measurement Errors in Surveys*, pp. 259–278. New York: Wiley.

Fowler, Floyd J., Jr. 2004. *Survey Research Methods*. Thousand Oaks, CA: Sage Publications.

Fowler, Floyd J., Jr., and Charles F. Cannell. 1996. "Using Behavioral Coding to Identify Cognitive Problems with Survey Questions." In Norbert Schwarz and Seymour Sudman (eds.), *Answering Questions*, pp. 15–36. San Francisco: Jossey-Bass.

Fowler, Floyd J., Jr., and T. Mangione. 1990. *Standardized Survey Interviewing: Minimizing Interviewer-Related Error*. Newbury Park, CA: Sage Publications.

Freedman, David. A. 1991. "Statistical Models and Shoe Leather." *Sociological Methodology* 21: 291–313.

Freedman, Deborah, Arland Thornton, and Donald Camburn. 1980. "Maintaining Response Rates in Longitudinal Studies." *Sociological Methods and Research* 9(1): 87–98.

Freedman, Deborah, Arland Thornton, Donald Camburn, Duane Alwin, and Linda Young-DeMarco. 1988. "The Life History Calendar: A Technique for Collecting Retrospective Data." In Clifford C. Clogg (ed.), *Sociological Methodology*, pp. 37–68. Washington, DC: American Sociological Association.

Fricke, Thomas E. 1986. *Himalayan Households: Tamang Demography and Domestic Processes*. Ann Arbor: University of Michigan Research Press.

Fricke, Thomas E. 1990. "Elementary Structures in the Nepal Himalaya: Reciprocity and the Politics of Hierarchy in Ghale-Tamang Marriage." *Ethnology* 29(2): 135–158.

Fricke, Tom. 1997. "Culture Theory and Demographic Process: Toward a Thicker Demography." In David I. Kertzer and Tom Fricke (eds.), *Anthropological Demography: Toward a New Synthesis*, pp. 248–278. Chicago: University of Chicago Press.

Fricke, Thomas E., and Arland Thornton. 1989. "Family, Economy, and Changing Life Course Transitions: Evidence from the Agricultural to Wage Labor Transition in Nepal." Paper presented at the annual meetings of the Population Association of America, March, 29–April 1, Baltimore.

Fu, Haishan, Jacqueline E. Darroch, Stanley K. Henshaw, and Elizabeth Kolb. 1998. "Measuring the Extent of Abortion Underreporting in the 1995 National Survey of Family Growth." *Family Planning Perspectives* 30(3): 128–138.

Garfinkel, Irwin, and Sara McLanahan. 2003. "Strengthening Fragile Families." In Isabel V. Sawhill (ed.), *One Percent for the Kids*, pp. 76–92. Washington, DC: Brookings Institution Press.

Geertz, Clifford. 1973. *The Interpretation of Cultures*. New York: Basic Books.

Gerson, Kahleen. 1985. *Hard Choices: How Women Decide About Work, Career and Motherhood*. Berkeley: University of California Press.

Gieseman, Raymond, and John M. Rogers. 1986. "Consumer Expenditures: Results from the Diary and Interview Surveys." *Monthly Labor Review* 109: 14–19.

Gijsbers, Wijk van, M. T. Cecile, Henk Huisman, and Annemarie M. Kolk. 1999. "Gender Differences in Physical Symptoms and Illness Behavior: A Health Diary Study." *Social Science and Medicine* 49(8): 1061–1074.

Godsell, Gillian. 2000. "Religious and Familial Networks as Entrepreneurial Resources in South Africa." In Sharon K. Houseknecht and Jerry G. Pankhurst (eds.), *Family, Religion, and Social Change in Diverse Societies*. New York: Oxford University Press.

Goldstein, Harvey. 1995. *Multilevel Statistical Models*. New York: Halsted Press.

Gould, Roger V. 1991. "Multiple Networks and Mobilization in the Paris Commune, 1871." *American Sociological Review* 56(6): 716–729.

Gould, Roger V. 1993. "Trade Cohesion, Class Unity, and Urban Insurrection: Artisanal Activism in the Paris Commune." *American Journal of Sociology* 98: 721–754.

Gould, Roger V. 1995. *Insurgent Identities: Class, Community, and Protest in Paris from 1848 to the Commune*. Chicago: University of Chicago Press.

Gould, Roger V. 1999. "Collective Violence and Group Solidarity in Corsica." *American Sociological Review* 64(3): 356–380.

Graesser, Arthur C., Sailaja Bommareddy, Shane Swamer, and Jonathan M. Golding. 1996. "Integrating Questionnaire Design with a Cognitive Computational Model of Human Question Answering." In Norbert Schwarz and Seymour Sudman (eds.), *Answering Questions*, pp. 143–175. San Francisco: Jossey-Bass.

Greenhalgh, Susan. 1990. "Towards a Political Economy of Fertility: Anthropological Contributions." *Population and Development Review* 16(1): 85–106.

Groves, Robert M. 1987. "Research on Survey Data Quality." *Public Opinion Quarterly* 51(4): S156–S172.

Groves, Robert, M., and Mick P. Couper. 1998. *Nonresponse in Household Interview Surveys*. New York: Wiley-Interscience.

Groves, Robert M., Floyd J. Fowler, Jr., Mick P. Couper, James M. Lepkowski, Eleanor Singer, and Roger Tourangeau. 2004. *Survey Methodology*. Wiley.

Groves, Robert M., Robert B. Cialdini, and Mick P. Couper. 1992. "Understanding the Decision to Participate in a Survey." *Public Opinion Quarterly* 56(4): 475–495.

Guba, E. G., and Y. S. Lincoln. 1994. "Competing Paradigms in Qualitative Research." In N. K. Denzin and Y. S. Lincoln (eds.), *Handbook of Qualitative Research* 1st ed., pp. 105–117. Thousand Oaks, CA: Sage Publications.

Guilmoto, C., and F. Sandron. 2001. "Internal Dynamics of Migration Networks in Developing Countries." *Population: An English Selection* 13(2): 135–164.

Hall, J. R. 1992. "Where History and Sociology Meet: Forms of Discourse and Socio-historical Inquiry." *Sociological Theory* 10(2): 164–193.

Hammel, Eugene. 1990. "A Theory of Culture for Demography." *Population and Development Review* 16(3): 455–485.

Hammer, Dean, and Aaron Wildavsky. 1993. "The Open-Ended, Semi-structured Interview: An (Almost) Operational Guide." In Aaron Wildavsky (ed.), *Craftways: On the Organization of Scholarly Work*, 2nd ed., pp. 57–101. New Brunswick, NJ: Transaction Publishers.

Hansen, Morris, William Hurwitz, and William Madow. 1953. *Sample Survey Methods and Theory*, Vols. 1 and 2. New York: Wiley.

Harkness, Janet A., and Alicia Schoua-Glusberg. 1998. "Questionnaires in Translation." *ZUMA-Nachrichten Spezial: Cross Cultural Survey Equivalence* 3: 87–128.

Harkness, Janet A., J. R. Van de Vijver, and Timothy P. Johnson. 2003. "Questionnaire Design in Comparative Research." In Janet Harkness, Fons J. R. Vande Vijver, and Peter Ph. Mohler (eds.), *Cross-Cultural Survey Methods*, pp. 19–34. Hoboken, NJ: John Wiley and Sons.

Harknett, Kristen, and Sara McLanahan. 2004. "Explaining Racial and Ethnic Differences in Marriage Among New, Unwed Parents." *American Sociological Review* 69(6): 790–811.

Heaton, Tim B., and Vaughn R. Call. 1995. "Modeling Family Dynamics with Event History Techniques." *Journal of Marriage and the Family* 57(4): 1078–1090.

Heckman, James J. 1978. "Dummy Endogenous Variables in a Simultaneous Equation System." *Econometrica* 46(4): 931–960.

Heckman, James J. 2000. "Causal Parameters and Policy Analysis in Economics: A Twentieth Century Retrospective." *Quarterly Journal of Economics* 115(1): 45–97.

Heckman, James J., and Jeffrey A. Smith. 1995. "Assessing the Case for Social Experiments." *Journal of Economic Perspectives* 9(2): 85–110.

Helitzer, Allen D., M. Makhambeld, and A. M. Wangel. 1994. "Obtaining Sensitive Information: The Need for More than Focus Groups." *Reproductive Health Matters* 3: 75–82.

Heywood, I. 1990. "Geographic Information Systems in the Social Sciences." *Environment and Planning A* 22(1): 849–854.

Hirschman, Charles, and Philip Guest. 1990. "Multilevel Models of Fertility Determination in Four Southeast Asian Countries: 1970 and 1980." *Demography* 27(3): 369–396.

Hochschild, Arlie. 1989. *The Second Shift*. New York: Avon Books.

Hogan, Dennis P., and David I. Kertzer. 1985. "Migration Patterns During Italian Urbanization, 1865–1921." *Demography* 22(3): 309–325.

Horst, Paul. 1955. "The Prediction of Personal Adjustment and Individual Cases." In Paul F. Lazarsfeld and Moris Rosenberg (eds.), *The Language of Social Research*, pp. 173–174. Glencoe, IL: Free Press.

Huber, Joan (ed.) 1991. *Macro-micro Linkages in Sociology*. Newbury Park, CA: Sage Publications.

Hughes, D., and K. DuMont. 1993. "Using Focus Groups to Facilitate Culturally Anchored Research." *American Journal of Community Psychology* 21(6): 775–806.

Huston, A. C., C. Miller, L. Richburg-Hayes, G. J. Duncan, C. A. Eldred, T. S. Weisner, E. Lowe, V. O. McLoyd, D. A. Crosby, M. N. Ripke, and C. Redcross. 2003. "New Hope for Families and Children: Five-Year Results of a Program to Reduce Poverty and Reform Welfare." Available at www.mdrc.org/publications/345/overview.html.

Jick, Todd D. 1979. "Mixing Qualitative and Quantitative Methods: Triangulation in Action." *Administrative Science Quarterly* 24(4): 602–611.

Jones, Elise F., and Jacqueline D. Forrest. 1992. "Underreporting of Abortion in Surveys of U. S. Women: 1976 to 1988." *Demography* 29(1): 113–126.

Kahn, Robert L., and C. F. Cannell. 1957. *The Dynamics of Interviewing*. New York: Wiley.

Kaler, Amy, and Susan Cotts Watkins. 2001. "Disobedient Distributors: Street-Level Bureaucrats and Would-Be Patrons in Community-Based Family Planning Programs in Rural Kenya." *Studies in Family Planning* 32(3): 254–269.

Kalton, Graham. 1983. *Introduction to Survey Sampling*. Beverly Hills, CA: Sage Publications.

Kendall, Patricia L., and Katherine M. Wolf. 1949. "The Analysis of Deviant Cases in Communications Research." In Paul F. Lazarsfeld and Frank W. Stanton (eds.), *Communications Research, 1948–1949*, pp. 152–179. New York: Harper.

Kertzer, David I. 1984. "Anthropology and Family History." *Journal of Family History* 9(3): 201–216.

Kertzer, David I. 1995. "Political Economic and Cultural Explanations of Demographic Behavior." In Susan Greenhalgh (ed.), *Situating Fertility: Anthropology and Demographic Inquiry*, pp. 29–52. Cambridge: Cambridge University Press.

Kertzer, David I. 1997. "Qualitative and Quantitative Approaches to Historical Demography." *Population and Development Review* 23(4): 839–846.

Kertzer, David I., and Dennis P. Hogan. 1989. *Family, Political Economy, and Demographic Change: The Transformation of Life in Casalecchio, Italy, 1861–1921.* Madison: University of Wisconsin Press.

Kertzer, David I., and Dennis P. Hogan. 1991. "Reflections on the European Marriage Pattern: Sharecropping and Proletarianization in Casalecchio, Italy, 1861–1921." *Journal of Family History* 16(1): 31–45.

Kertzer, David I., and Tom Fricke. 1997. *Anthropological Demography: Toward a New Synthesis.* Chicago: University of Chicago Press.

Kish, Leslie. 1965. *Survey Sampling.* New York: John Wiley & Sons.

Kleinman, S., and M. A. Copp. 1993. *Emotions and Fieldwork.* Newbury Park, CA: Sage Publications.

Kmenta, Jan. 1986. *Elements of Econometrics*, 2nd ed. New York: Macmillan.

Knodel, John. 1993. "The Design and Analysis of Focus Group Studies: A Practical Approach." In David L. Morgan (ed.), *Successful Focus Groups: Advancing the State of the Art*, pp. 35–50. Thousand Oaks, CA: Sage Publications.

Knodel, John. 1995. "Focus Groups as a Method for Cross-Cultural Research in Social Gerontology." *Journal of Cross-Cultural Gerontology* 10(1/2): 7–20.

Knodel, John. 1997. "A Case for Nonanthropological Qualitative Methods for Demographers." *Population Development Review* 23(4): 847–853.

Knodel, John. 1998. "Using Qualitative Data for Understanding Old Age Security and Fertility." In A. Basu and A. Aaby (eds.), *The Methods and Uses of Anthropological Demography*, pp. 57–80. Oxford: Clarendon Press.

Knodel, John, and Wassana Im-em. 2004. "The Economic Consequences of Parents of Losing an Adult Child to AIDS: Evidence from Thailand." *Social Science and Medicine* 59(5): 987–1001.

Knodel, John, Aphichat Chamratrithirong, and Nibhon Debavalya. 1987. *Thailand's Reproductive Revolution: Rapid Fertility Decline in a Third World Setting.* Madison: University of Wisconsin Press.

Knodel, John, Chanpen Saengtienchai, Wassana Im-Em, and Mark Van Landingham. 2001. "The Impact of AIDS on Parents and Families in Thailand." *Research on Aging* 23(6): 633–670.

Knodel, John, Napaporn Havanon, and Anthony Pramualratana. 1984. "Fertility Transition in Thailand: A Qualitative Analysis." *Population and Development Review* 10(2): 297–328.

Kohler, Hans-Peter, Jere R. Behrman, and Susan C. Watkins. 2001. "The Density of Social Networks and Fertility Decisions: Evidence from South Nyanza District, Kenya." *Demography* 38(1): 43–58.

Krieger, S. 1991. *Social Science and the Self: Personal Essays on an Art Form.* New Brunswick, NJ: Rutgers University Press.

Krueger, Richard A. 1994. *"Focus Groups: A Practical Guide for Applied Research*, 2nd ed. Thousand Oaks, CA: Sage Publications.

Krueger, Richard and Mary Anne Casey. 2000. *Focus Groups: A Practical Guide for Applied Research*, 3rd ed. Newbury Park, CA: Sage Publications.

Krysan, Maria. 1998. "Privacy and the Expression of White Racial Attitudes: A Comparison Across Three Contexts." *Public Opinion Quarterly* 62(4): 506–544.

Krysan, Maria, Howard Schuman, Lesli Jo Scott, and Paul Beatty. 1994. "Response Rates and Response Content in Mail Versus Face-to-Face Surveys." *Public Opinion Quarterly* 58(3): 381–399.

Landale, Nancy. 1994. "Migration and the Latino Family: The Union Formation Behavior of Puerto Rican Women." *Demography* 31(1): 133–157.

Lazarsfeld, Paul F., and Morris Rosenberg. 1949–1950. "The Contribution of the Regional Poll to Political Understanding." *Public Opinion Quarterly* 13(4): 569–586.

Lee, Raymond M., and Nigel Fielding. 1991. "Computing for Qualitative Research: Options, Problems and Potential." In N. Fielding and R. M. Lee (eds.), *Using Computers in Qualitative Research*. London: Sage.

Leventhal, Tama, and Jeanne Brooks-Gunn. 2001. "Changing Neighborhoods and Child Well-Being: Understanding How Children May Be Affected in the Coming Century." In Sandra L. Hofferth and Timothy J. Owens (eds.), *Advances in Life Course Research*, Vol. 6: *Children at the Millenium: Where Have We Come From, Where Are We Going?* Amsterdam: Elsevier Science.

Lieberson, Stanley. 1985. *Making It Count: The Improvement of Social Research and Theory*. Berkeley: University of California Press.

Lieberson, Stanley. 1992. "Einstein, Renoir, and Greeley: Some Thoughts About Evidence in Sociology." *American Sociological Review* 57(1): 1–15.

Lillard, Lee A., and Constantijn W. A. Panis. 1998. "Panel Attrition from the Panel Study of Income Dynamics: Household Income, Marital Status, and Mortality." *Journal of Human Resources* 33(2): 437–457.

Lillard, Lee A., and L. J. Waite. 1995. "Til Death Do Us Part: Marital Disruption and Mortality." *American Journal of Sociology* 100(5), 1131–1156.

Lipset, Seymour Martin, Martin A. Trow, and James S. Coleman. 1956. *Union Democracy*. Glencoe, IL: Free Press.

Lofland, John, and Lyn H. Lofland. 1994. *Analyzing Social Settings*. Belmont, CA: Wadsworth.

Loftus, Elizabeth F., and W. Marburger. 1983. "Since the Eruption of Mt. St. Helens, Has Anyone Beaten You Up? Improving the Accuracy of Retrospective Reports with Landmark Events." *Memory and Cognition* 11(2): 114–120.

Lyberg, Lars, and Daniel Kasprzyk. 1991. "Data Collection Methods and Measurement Error: An Overview." In Paul Biemer, Robert M. Groves, Lars E. Lyberg, Nancy A. Mathiowetz, and Seymour Sudman (eds.), *Measurement Errors in Surveys*, pp. 237–258. New York: Wiley.

MacCorquodale, Patricia, and John DeLamater. 1979. "Self-Image and Premarital Sexuality." *Journal of Marriage and Family* 41(May): 327–339.

Maguire, D. J., Michael F. Goodchild, and David Rhind. 1991. *Geographical Information Systems*, Vol. 1: *Principles*; Vol. 2: *Applications*. London: Longmans.

Mahoney, James. 1999. "Nominal, Ordinal, and Narrative Appraisal in Macrocausal Analysis." *American Journal of Sociology* 104(4): 1154–1196.

Maples, Jerry J., Susan A. Murphy, and William G. Axinn. 2002. "Two Level Proportional Hazards Models." *Biometrics* 58(4): 180–188.

Marini, Margaret Mooney, and Burton Singer. 1988. "Causality in the Social Sciences." *Sociological Methodology* 18: 347–409.

Marsden, Peter V. 1992. *Sociological Methodology*, Vol. 21. Oxford: Blackwell.

Martin, David. 1996. *Geographic Information Systems and Their Socioeconomic Applications*. London: Routledge.

Martin, Elizabeth. 2004. "Vignettes and Respondent Debriefing for Questionnaire Design and Evaluation." In Stanley Presser, Jennifer M. Rothgeb, Mick. P. Couper, Judith T. Lessler, Elizabeth Martin, Jean Martin, and Eleanor Singer (eds.), *Methods for Testing and Evaluating Survey Questionnaires*, pp. 149–171. Hoboken, NJ: John Wiley and Sons.

Massey, Douglas S. 1987a. "The Ethnosurvey in Theory and Practice." *International Migration Review* 21(4): 1498–1522.

Massey, Douglas S. 1987b. "Understanding Mexican Migration to the United States." *American Journal of Sociology* 92(6): 1372–1403.

Massey, Douglas S. 1990. "The Social and Economic Origins of Immigration." *The Annals* 510: 60–72.

Massey, Douglas S., and Kristin E. Espinosa. 1997. "What's Driving Mexico–U.S. Migration? A Theoretical, Empirical, and Policy Analysis." *American Journal of Sociology* 102(4): 939–999.

Massey, Douglas S., Joaquin Arango, Graeme Hugo, Ali Kouaouci, Adela Pellegrino, and J. Edward Taylor (eds.). 1998. *Worlds in Motion: Understanding International Migration at the End of the Millenium*. New York: Oxford University Press.

Massey, Douglas S., Luin Goldring, and Jorge Durand. 1994. "Continuities in Transnational Migration: An Analysis of Nineteen Mexican Communities." *American Journal of Sociology* 99(6): 1492–1533.

Massey, Douglas S., Rafael Alarcón, Humberto González, and Jorge Durand. 1987. *Return to Aztlan: The Social Process of International Migration from Western Mexico*. Berkeley: University of California Press.

McKenzie, John. 1983. "The Accuracy of Telephone Call Data Collected by Diary Methods." *Journal of Marketing Research* 20: 417–427.

McLanahan, Sara. Forthcoming. *Fragile Families and the Marriage Agenda*. New York: Aldine de Gruyter.

Means, Barbara, Gary E. Swan, Jared B. Jobe, and James L. Esposito. 1991. "An Alternative Approach to Obtaining Personal History Data." In Paul Biemer, Gosta Forsman, Robert Groves, Lars Lyberg, Nancy Mathiowetz, and Seymour Sudman (eds.), *Measurement Errors in Surveys*. New York: Wiley.

Menken, Jane, and James F. Phillips. 1990. "Population Change in a Rural Area of Bangladesh, 1967–87." *Annals of the American Academy of Political and Social Science* 510: 87–101.

Mercer, Jane. 1973. *Labeling the Mentally Retarded*. Berkeley: University of California Press.

Merton, Robert K., Marjorie Fiske, and Patricia L. Kendall. 1990. *The Focused Interview: A Manual of Problems and Procedures*, 2nd ed. New York: Free Press.

Michalopoulos, Charles, Johannes M. Bos, Robert Lalonde, and Nandita Verma. 2000. *Assessing the Impact of Welfare Reform on Urban Communities: The Urban Change Project and Methodological Considerations*. New York: Manpower Demonstration Research Corp.

Miles, M., and A. Huberman. 1984. *Qualitative Data Analysis*. Beverly Hills, CA: Sage Publications.

Miller, Delbert C. 1983. *Handbook of Research Design and Social Measurement.* New York: Longman.

Mishler, Elliot G. 1986. *Research Interviewing: Context and Narrative.* Cambridge, MA: Harvard University Press.

Mitchell, J. Clyde. 1983. "Case and Situation Analysis." *Sociological Review* 31(2): 187–211.

Moffitt, Robert. 2000. "Perspectives on the Qualitative-Quantitative Divide." *Quarterly Newsletter of the Joint Center for Poverty Research* 4(1).

Moffitt, Robert. 2003. "Causal Analysis in Population Research: An Economist's Perspective." *Population and Development Review* 29(3): 448–458.

Moffitt, Robert. 2005. "Remarks on the Analysis of Causal Relationships in Population Research." *Demography* 42(1): 91–109.

Morgan, David L. 1997. *Focus Groups as Qualitative Research,* 2nd ed. Newbury Park, CA: Sage Publications.

Morgan, S. Philip, and Bhanu B. Niraula. 1995. "Gender Inequality and Fertility in Two Nepali Villages." *Population and Development Review* 21(3): 541–561.

Morgan, S. Philip, and Jay D. Teachman. 1988. "Logistic Regression: Descriptions, Examples, Comparisons." *Journal of Marriage and the Family* 50: 929–936.

Morgan, S. Philip, and Ronald R. Rindfuss. 1985. "Marital Disruption: Structural and Temporal Dimensions." *American Journal of Sociology* 90(5): 1055–1077.

Nassar-McMillan, Sylvia C., and L. DiAnne Borders. 2002. "Use of Focus Groups in Survey Item Development." *Qualitative Report* 7(1). Available online at www.nova.edu/ssss/QR/QR7=1/.

National Telecommunications and Information Administration (NTIA). 2000. "Falling Through the Net: Toward Digital Inclusion." Washington, DC: U.S. Department of Commerce.

National Telecommunications and Information Administration (NTIA). 2001. "A Nation Online: How Americans Are Expanding Their Use of the Internet." Washington, DC: U.S. Department of Commerce.

Niraula, Bhanu B., and S. Philip Morgan. 1996a. "Marriage Formation, Post-marital Contact with Natal Kin and Autonomy of Women: Evidence from Two Nepali Settings." *Population Studies* 50(1): 35–50.

Niraula, Bhanu B., and S. Philip Morgan. 1996b. "Son and Daughter Preferences in Benighat, Nepal: Implications for Fertility Transition." *Social Biology* 42(3/4): 256–273.

Neisser, Ulric 1988. "What Is Ordinary Memory the Memory Of." In Ulric Neisser and Eugene Winograd (eds.), *Remembering Reconsidered: Ecological and Traditional Approaches to the Study of Memory,* pp. 356–373. New York: Cambridge University Press.

O'Brien, Kerth. 1993. "Improving Survey Questionnaires Through Focus Groups." In David L. Morgan (ed.), *Successful Focus Groups: Advancing the State of the Art,* pp. 105–117. Thousand Oaks, CA: Sage Publications.

Oksenberg, Lois, Charles F. Cannell, and Graham Kalton. 1991. "New Strategies for Pretesting Survey Questions." *Journal of Official Statistics* 7(3): 349–365.

Pampel, Fred. 2002. "Cigarette Use and the Narrowing Sex Differential in Mortality." *Population and Development Review* 28(1): 77–104.

Pearce, Lisa D. 2002. "Integrating Survey and Ethnographic Methods for Systematic Anomalous Case Analysis." *Sociological Methodology* 32(1): 103–132.

Petersen, L. S., and J. Kerwin. 1992. "Testing a Life History Calendar as a Visual Aid in the National Survey of Family Growth." Paper presented at the annual meeting of the Population Association of America, April 30–May 2, Denver.

Petersen, Trond. 1991. "The Statistical Analysis of Event Histories." *Sociological Methods and Research* 19(3): 270–323.

Phelps, Erin, Frank F. Furstenberg, Jr., and Anne Colby. 2002. *Looking at Lives: American Longitudinal Studies of the Twentieth Century*. New York: Russell Sage Foundation.

Phillips, Derek L., and Kevin J. Clancy. 1972. "Some Effects of 'Social Desirability' in Survey Studies." *American Journal of Sociology* 77(5): 921–940.

Press, Julie E., and Eleanor Townsley. 1998. "Wives' and Husbands' Housework Reporting: Gender, Class, and Social Desirability." *Gender and Society* 12(2): 188–218.

Presser, Stanley. 1990. "Can Changes in Context Reduce Vote Overreporting in Surveys?" *Public Opinion Quarterly* 54(4): 586–593.

Presser, Stanley, and Jean M. Converse. 1986. *Survey Questions: Handcrafting the Standardized Questionnaire*. Beverly Hills, CA: Sage Publications.

Raftery, Adrian E. 1998. "Guest Editor's Introduction to the Special Issue on Causality in the Social Sciences, in Honor of Herbert L. Costner." *Sociological Methods and Research* 27: 140–147.

Rank, Mark. 1992. "The Blending of Qualitative and Quantitative Methods in Understanding Childbearing Among Welfare Recipients." In J. F. Gilgun, K. Daly, and G. Handel (eds.), *Qualitative Methods in Family Research*, pp. 281–300. Thousand Oaks, CA: Sage Publications.

Raudenbush, Stephen W. 1988. "Educational Applications of Hierarchical Linear Models: A Review." *Journal of Educational Statistics* 13: 85–116.

Raudenbush, Stephen W., and Robert J. Sampson. 1999. "'Ecometrics': Toward a Science of Assessing Ecological Settings, with Application to the Systematic Social Observation of Neighborhoods." *Sociological Methodology* 29: 1–41.

Richards, Thomas J., and Lyn Richards. 1998. "Using Computers in Qualitative Research." In Norman K. Denzin and Yvonna S. Lincoln (eds.), *Collecting and Interpreting Qualitative Materials*, pp. 211–245. Thousand Oaks, CA: Sage Publications.

Richardt, C. S., and S. F. Rallis. 1994. *The Qualitative-Quantitative Debate: New Perspectives*. San Francisco: Jossey-Bass.

Ringdal, Kristen. 1992. "Recent Developments in Methods for Multilevel Analysis." *Acta Sociologica* 35: 235–243.

Rook, Karen S. 2003. "Exposure and Reactivity to Negative Social Exchanges: A Preliminary Investigation Using Daily Diary Data." *Journal of Gerontology* 58B(2): 100–111.

Roseberry, William. 1989. *Anthropologies and Histories: Essays in Culture, History, and Political Economy*. New Brunswick, NJ: Rutgers University Press.

Rosenbaum, Paul R. 1999. "Choice as an Alternative to Control in Observational Studies." *Statistical Science* 14(3): 259–304.

Rosenbaum, Paul R. 2001. "Replicating Effects and Biases." *American Statistician* 55(3): 223–227.

Rosenzweig, Mark R., and Kenneth I. Wolpin. 2000. 'Natural 'Natural Experiments' in Economics." *Journal of Economic Literature* 38(4): 827–874.

Rossi, Alice, S., and Peter H. Rossi. 1990. *Of Human Bonding: Parent-Child Relations Across the Life Course*. New York: Aldine de Gruyter.

Rossi, Peter H., James, D. Wright and Andy B. Anderson (eds.) 1983. *Handbook of Survey Research*. New York: Academic Press.

Rossi, Peter H., Robert A. Berk, and K. J. Lenihan. 1980. *Money, Work and Crime: Some Experimental Results*. New York: Academic Press.

Rossiter, John R., and Thomas R. Robertson. 1975. "Children's Television Viewing: An Examination of Parent-Child Consensus." *Sociometry* 38(2): 308–326.

Rountree, Pamela Wilcox, Kenneth C. Land, and Terance D. Miethe. 1994. "Macro-micro Integration in the Study of Victimization: A Hierarchical Logistic Model Analysis Across Seattle Neighborhoods." *Criminology* 32(3): 387–413.

Rubin, Donald B. 1974. "Estimating Causal Effects of Treatments in Randomized and Non-randomized Studies." *Journal of Educational Psychology* 66(5): 688–701.

Rugg, D. 1941. "Experiments in Wording Questions II." *Public Opinion Quarterly* 5(1): 91–92.

Rutenberg, Naomi, and Susan Cotts Watkins. 1997. "The Buzz Outside the Clinics: Conversations and Contraception in Nyanza Province, Kenya." *Studies in Family Planning* 28(4): 290–307.

Salomon, Joshua, and Christopher Murray. 2002. "The Epidemiologic Transition Revisited: Causes of Death by Age and Sex." *Population and Development Review* 28(2): 205–227.

Sampson, Robert J., Jeffrey D. Morenoff, and Thomas Gannon-Rowley. 2002. "Assessing 'Neighborhood Effects': Social Processes and New Directions in Research." *Annual Review of Sociology* 28: 443–478.

Sanchez, Maria Elena. 1992. "The Effect of Questionnaire Design on the Quality of Survey Data." *Public Opinion Quarterly* 56(2): 206–217.

Saris, W. E. 1991. *Computer-Assisted Interviewing*. Newbury Park, CA: Sage Publications.

Sastry, Narayan. 1997. "A Multilevel Hazards Model for Hierarchically Clustered Data: Model Estimation and an Application to the Study of Child Survival in Northeast Brazil." *Journal of the American Statistical Association* 92: 426–435.

Sastry, Narayan. 1996. "Community Characteristics, Individual and Household Attributes, and Child Survival in Brazil." *Demography* 33(2): 211–229.

Schaeffer, Nora Cate. 1991. "Conversation with a Purpose – Or Conversation? Interaction in the Standardized Interview." In edited by Paul P. Biemer, Robert M. Groves, Lars E. Lyberg, Nancy A. Mathiowetz, and Seymour Sudman (eds.), *Measurement Errors in Surveys*, pp. 367–391. New York: Wiley.

Schaeffer, Nora Cate, and Stanley Presser. 2003. "The Science of Asking Questions." *Annual Review of Sociology* 29: 65–88.

Scheper-Hughes, Nancy. 1992. *Death Without Weeping: The Violence of Everyday Life in Brazil*. Berkeley: University of California Press.

Schofield, Roger, and David Reher. 1991. "The Decline of Mortality in Europe." In Roger Schofield, *The Decline of Mortality in Europe*, David Reher, and A. Bideau (eds.), pp. 1–17. Oxford: Oxford University Press.

Schuman, Howard, and Jacqueline Scott. 1989. "Generations and Collective Memories." *American Sociological Review* 54(3): 359–381.

Schuman, Howard, and Stanley Presser. 1981. *Questions and Answers in Attitude Surveys*. New York: Academic Press.

Schuman, Howard, and Stanley Presser. 1996. *Questions and Answers in Attitude Surveys: Experiments on Question Form, Wording, and Context.* Thousand Oaks, CA: Sage Publications.

Schwarz, Norbert. 1999. "Self-Reports: How the Questions Shape the Answers." *American Psychologist* 54(Feb.): 93–105.

Schwarz, Norbert. 2003. "Culture-Sensitive Context Effects: A Challenge for Cross-Cultural Surveys." In Janet Harkness, Fons J. R. Vande Vijver, and Peter Ph. Mohler (eds.), *Cross-Cultural Survey Methods*, pp. 93–100. Hoboken, NJ: John Wiley and Sons.

Schwarz, Norbert, and Seymour Sudman (eds.). 1992. *Context Effects in Social and Psychological Research.* New York: Springer-Verlag.

Schwarz, Norbert, and Seymour Sudman (eds.). 1996. *Answering Questions: Methodology for Determining Cognitive and Communicative Processes in Survey Research.* San Francisco: Jossey-Bass.

Sewell, William H., Jr. 1996. "Three Temporalities: Toward and Eventful Sociology." In Terence J. McDonald (ed.), *The Historic Turn in the Human Sciences*, pp. 245–280. Ann Arbor: University of Michigan Press.

Shrestha, Sundar S., Sujan Shrestha, and Ann E. Biddlecom. 2002. "The Household Registration System: Methods and Issues in Collecting Continuous Data on Demographic Events." Paper presented at the annual meetings of the Population Association of America, May 9–11, Atlanta.

Shryock, Henry S., and Jacob S. Siegel (eds.). 1976. *Studies in Population: The Methods and Materials of Demography.* New York: Academic Press.

Sieber, Sam D. 1973. "The Integration of Fieldwork and Survey Methods." *American Journal of Sociology* 78(6): 1335–1359.

Sills, Stephen J., and Chunyan Song. 2002. "Innovations in Survey Research: An Application of Web-Based Surveys." *Social Science Computer Review* 20(1): 22–30.

Smith, Christian. 2003. The Purpose and Goals of the NSYR. Paper presented at the Annual Meeting of the Society for the Scientific Study of Religion, October 23–24, Norfolk, VA.

Smith, Christian, and Melinda Lundquist Denton. 2005. *Soul Searching: The Religious and Spiritual Lives of American Teenagers.* Oxford: Oxford University Press.

Smith, Herbert L. 1989. "Integrating Theory and Research on the Institutional Determinants of Fertility." *Demography* 26(2): 171–184.

Smith, Herbert L., Tu Ping, M. Giovanna Merli, and Mark Hereward. 1997. "Implementation of a Demographic and Contraceptive Surveillance System in Four Counties in North China." *Population Research and Policy Review* 16(4): 289–314.

Snijders, Tom A. B., and Jacques A. Hagenaars. 2001. "Guest Editors' Introduction to the Special Issue on Causality at Work." *Sociological Methods and Research* 30(1): 3–10.

Spradley, James P. 1979. *The Ethnographic Interview.* New York: Harcort Brace Jovanovich.

Spradley, James P. 1997. *Participant Observation.* New York: Holt, Rinehart and Winston.

Stone, Linda, and Jeffrey G. Campbell. 1984. "The Use and Misuse of Surveys in International Development: An Experiment from Nepal." *Human Organization* 43(1): 27–37.

Strauss, Anselm, and Juliet Corbin. 1990. *Basics of Qualitative Research Grounded Theory Procedures and Techniques*. Newbury Park, CA: Sage Publications.

Stycos, J. Mayone. 1955. *Family and Fertility in Puerto Rico*. New York: Columbia University Press.

Suchman, Lucy, and Brigitte Jordan. 1990. "Interactional Troubles in Face-to-Face Survey Interviews." *Journal of the American Statistical Association* 85(409): 232–241.

Sudman, Seymour, and Norman M. Bradburn. 1974. *Response Effects in Surveys*. Chicago: Aldine.

Sudman, Seymour, and Norman M. Bradburn. 1982. "Measuring Attitudes: Formulating Questions." In Norbert Schwarz and Seymour Sudman (eds.), *Asking Questions*, pp. 119–147. San Francisco: Jossey-Bass.

Sudman, Seymour, Norman M. Bradburn, and Norbert Schwarz. 1996. *Thinking About Answers: The Application of Cognitive Processes to Survey Methodology*. San Francisco: Jossey-Bass.

Survey Research Center.1976. *Interviewers Manual*. Ann Arbor: University of Michigan Press.

Teachman, J., and M. Hayward. 1993. "Interpreting Hazard Rate Models," *Sociological Methods and Research* 21(3): 340–371.

Terry, William S. 1988. "Everyday Forgetting: Data from a Diary Study." *Psychological Reports* 62: 299–303.

Theriault, Stephen W., and Diane Holmberg. 1998. "The New Old-Fashioned Girl: Effects of Gender and Social Desirability on Reported Gender-Role Ideology." *Sex Roles* 39(1/2): 97–112.

Thomas, Duncan, Elizabeth Frankenberg, and James P. Smith. 2001. "Lost But Not Forgotten: Attrition and Follow-up in the Indonesia Family Life Survey." *Journal of Human Resources* 36(3): 556–592.

Thornton, Arland. 1991. "Influence of Parents' Marital History on the Marital and Cohabitational Experiences of Children." *American Journal of Sociology* 96(4): 868–894.

Thornton, Arland, Deborah Freedman, and Donald Camburn. 1982. "Obtaining Respondent Cooperation in Family Panel Studies." *Sociological Methods and Research* 11(1): 33–51.

Thornton, Arland, and Linda Young-DeMarco. 2001. "Four Decades of Trends in Attitudes Toward Family Issues in the United States: The 1960s through the 1990s." *Journal of Marriage and the Family* 63(4): 1009–1037.

Thornton, Arland, Ronald Freedman, and William G. Axinn. 2002. "Intergenerational Panel Study of Parents and Children." In E. Phelps, F. F. Furstenberg, Jr., and A. Colby (eds.), *Looking at Lives: American Longitudinal Studies of the Twentieth Century*, pp. 315–345. New York: Russell Sage Foundation.

Thornton, Arland, Terri L. Orbuch, and William G. Axinn. 1995. "Parent-Child Relationships During the Transition to Adulthood." *Journal of Family Issues* 16(5): 538–564.

Thornton, Arland, William G. Axinn, and Jay Teachman. 1995. "The Influence of Educational Experiences on Cohabitation and Marriage in Early Adulthood." *American Sociological Review* 60(5): 762–774.

Thornton, Arland, William G. Axinn, and Yu Xie. 2002. *Intergenerational Influences on Marriage and Cohabitation*. Manuscript in progress, Institute for Social Research, University of Michigan.

Tidwell, Marie-Cecile O., Harry T. Reis, and Phillip R. Shaver. 1996. "Attachment, Attractiveness, and Social Interaction: A Diary Study." *Journal of Personality and Social Psychology* 71(4): 729–745.

Tourangeau, Roger. 1984. "Cognitive Science and Survey Methods," In T. Jabine, E. Loftus, M. Straf, J. Tanur, and R. Tourangeau (eds.), *Cognitive Aspects of Survey Methodology: Building a Bridge Between Disciplines*, Washington, DC: National Academies Press.

Tourangeau, Roger. 1989. "Carryover Effects in Attitude Surveys." *Public Opinion Quarterly* 53: 495–524.

Tourangeau, Roger. 1999. "Context Effects on Answers to Attitude Questions." In M. G. Sirken, D. J. Herrmann, S. Schechter, N. Schwarz, J. Tanur, and R. Tourangeau (eds.), *Cognition and Survey Research*, pp. 111–131. New York: John Wiley and Sons.

Tourangeau, Roger. 2004. "Design Considerations for Questionnaire Development." In Stanley Presser, Jennifer Rothgeb, Mick. P Couper, Judith T. Lessler, Elizabeth Martin, Jean Martin, and Eleanor Singer (eds.), *Methods for Testing and Evaluating Survey Questionnaires*, pp. 209–224. Hoboken, NJ: John Wiley and Sons.

Tourangeau, Roger, and Kenneth A. Rasinski. 1988. "Cognitive Processes Underlying Context Effects in Attitude Measurement." *Psychological Bulletin* 103(3): 299–314.

Tourangeau, Roger, and Tom W. Smith. 1996. "Asking Sensitive Questions: The Impact of Data Collection Mode, Question Format, and Question Context." *Public Opinion Quarterly* 60(2): 275–304.

Tourangeau, Roger, Darby Miller Steiger, and David Wilson. 2002. "Self-Administered Questions by Telephone: Evaluating Interactive Voice Response." *Public Opinion Quarterly* 66: 265–278.

Tourangeau, Roger, Kenneth A. Rasinski, Norman Bradburn, and Roy D'Andrade. 1989. "Belief Accessibility and Context Effects in Attitude Measurement." *Journal of Experimental Social Psychology* 25(5): 401–421.

Tourangeau, Roger, Lance J. Rips, and Kenneth A. Rasinski. 2000. *The Psychology of Survey Response*. Cambridge: Cambridge University Press.

Tuchman, G. 1978. *Making News: A Study in the Construction of Reality*. New York: Free Press.

Vaughn, Sharon, Jeanne S. Schumm, and Jane Sinagub. 1996. *Focus Group Interviews in Education and Psychology*. Thousand Oaks, CA: Sage Publications.

Waite, L. J., and L. A. Lillard. 1991. "Children and Marital Disruption." *American Journal of Sociology* 96(4): 930–953.

Watkins, Susan Cotts. 2000. "Local and Foreign Models of Reproduction in Nyanza Province, Kenya." *Population and Development Review* 26(4): 725–759.

Weiss, Robert S. 1968. "Issues in Holistic Research." In Howard S. Becker, Blanche Geer, David Riesman, and Robert Weis (eds.), *Institutions and the Person*, pp. 342–350. Chicago: Aldine.

Weiss, Robert S. 1994. *Learning from Strangers: The Art and Method of Qualitative Interview Studies*. New York: Free Press.

Weitzman, Eben, and Matthew Miles. 1995. *Computer Programs for Qualitative Data Analysis: An Expanded Sourcebook*, 2nd ed. Thousand Oaks, CA: Sage Publications.

Winship, Christopher, and Stephen L. Morgan. 1999. "The Estimation of Causal Effects from Observational Data." *Annual Review of Sociology* 25: 659–706.

Winston, Pamela, Ronald J. Angel, Linda M. Burton, P. Lindsay Chase-Lansdale, Andrew J. Cherlin, Robert A. Moffitt, and William Julius Wilson. 1999. *Welfare, Children and Families: A Three City Study*. Baltimore: Johns Hopkins University Press.

Wong, George Y., and William M. Mason. 1985. "The Hierarchical Logistic Regression Model for Multilevel Analysis." *Journal of the American Statistical Association* 80: 513–524.

Wu, L. L. 1996. "Effects of Family Instability, Income, and Income Instability on the Risk of a Premarital Birth." *American Sociological Review* 61(3): 386–406.

Xie, Yu. 1994. "Log-Multiplicative Models for Discrete-Time, Discrete-Covariate Event-History Data." In Peter V. Marsden (ed.), *Sociological Methodology*, pp. 301–440. Cambridge, MA: Blackwell Publishers.

Yamaguchi, Kazuo. 1991. *Event History Analysis*. Newbury Park, CA: Sage Publications.

Zeller, Richard A. 1993. "Combining Qualitative and Quantitative Techniques to Develop Culturally Sensitive Measures." In David G. Ostrow and Ronald C. Kessler (eds.), *Methodological Issues in AIDS Behavioral Research*, pp. 95–116. New York: Plenum Press.

Index

DATE DUE
